THE ALL-BRITISH
MARENDAZ
SPECIAL

THE MAN, THE CARS and THE AEROPLANES

GRAHAM SKILLEN

FONTHILL

To Katharine

Fonthill Media Language Policy

Fonthill Media publishes in the international English language market. One language edition is published worldwide. As there are minor differences in spelling and presentation, especially with regard to American English and British English, a policy is necessary to define which form of English to use. The Fonthill Policy is to use the form of English native to the author. Graham Skillen was born and educated in Northern Ireland; therefore, British English has been adopted in this publication.

Fonthill Media Limited
Fonthill Media LLC
www.fonthillmedia.com
office@fonthillmedia.com

First published in the United Kingdom and the United States of America 2018

British Library Cataloguing in Publication Data:
A catalogue record for this book is available from the British Library

Copyright © Graham Skillen 2018

ISBN 978-1-78155-702-0

Typeset in Minion Pro 10pt on 13pt
Printed and bound in England

CONTENTS

Acknowledgements   4

Foreword   5

Introduction   7

  1   The Early Years   11

  2   The Great War   15

  3   After the Great War   23

  4   The Marseal   30

  5   The Marseal in Competition   39

  6   The Move to London   45

  7   London in the Twenties   48

  8   Marendaz Special in Competition in the 1920s   61

  9   The 1931 Marendaz Special: the 13/70 in London and Maidenhead   71

 10   The 1931 Marendaz Special: Production and the People   86

 11   The 1931 Marendaz Special: Cars, Customers, and Closure   99

 12   Technical Description   105

 13   Marendaz Special in Competition: 1931–1936   109

 14   The Moss and Don Connection   121

 15   The Move to Aircraft Building   127

 16   18B or not 18B?   143

 17   After the War   160

 18   Epilogue: Corresponding with the Captain   171

Appendix I: Sunday Express, 17 November 1940   179

Appendix II: Marseals Registered in Coventry   182

Appendix III: Marendaz Special: Known Cars   184

Appendix IV: Employees: Cars and Aircraft   188

Index   189

ACKNOWLEDGEMENTS

Three people above all others have made a major contribution to this book: John Shaw, owner and engineer; Stan Duddington, works apprentice and fitter; and Jim or Leslie Light, machinist. Their words and expertise made it all possible.

Then, there are the very many people and organisations who have helped me over a number of years to collect information, both in quantity and in snippets. It is difficult to set out here their individual contributions, but all are thanked equally: *Autocar*; *The Automobile*; The Brooklands Society; Brooklands Museum; Coventry Motor Museum; Haynes International Motor Museum; *Motor*; *Motor Sport*; The National Motor Museum; The National Archive; The Royal Air Force Museum; The Vintage Motorcycle Club; and The Vintage Sports Car Club.

Also thanks to Peter Arney; Fred Atkinson; Paul Barnes; Bill Boddy; Brem Bremner-Smith; Malcolm Clarke; Tom Clarke; Peter Cook; Tom Delaney; Peter H. T. Green; Guy Griffiths; Dick Hodge; Len Huff; Peter Hull; Tony Hutchings; David Jackson; Mary Jackson; Philip Jarrett; Jenna Leigh-Thompson; John Ling; Colin Mabberley; John Midford-Millership; Paul Mitchell; Robin Morris; Pat Moss; Peter Richley; Richard Riding; Dick Serjeantson; Keith Shaw; Nigel Smith; Peter Spiers; Don Summers; Simon Thomas; Rob Titherley; Terry Treadwell; John Warburton; Michael Ware; Jeremy Wood; Michael Worthington-Williams; and Greg Wrapson.

Should any copyright material have been used inadvertently, or if any contributor has been accidently omitted, please accept my apologies.

FOREWORD

I knew a little of the Marseal and Marendaz as they were included in Bill Boddy's *The Sports Car Pocket Book* (1961) and it was that photograph of Mrs Moss really pushing-on with that gorgeous white Marendaz that really sealed it.

Over the next thirty or so years, the Marendaz took on an almost mythical status for me. Like some rare bird, one would quietly appear in the apple orchard at Prescott only to disappear just as quietly and without any show or fuss. 'Marendaz? Think I saw one at Shelsley a couple of years ago but I can't be sure'. 'Marendaz? Haven't seen one in ages and can't remember when I last saw one for sale.' It was a car of myth and legend.

Imagine my surprise, then, when I saw one for sale in *Classic and Sports Car*—not discreetly hidden as a small ad but blatantly strutting its stuff as a featured car. It was still a joy to behold, with me wishing 'if only', and in an instant, I was back to July 1963.

Everyone knew I was the car nut, especially when it involved so-called old and vintage cars. 'Hey, Mike, there's an old car in Burton that might interest you'. Oh, how many times have I heard those words! What was then a garage and second hand (with a large pinch of salt) car dealership still exists, but it is now a QuickFit exhaust and tyre business adjacent to The Queens Hotel. Light years removed from today's LED-lit, chromium-plated, smoked-glass emporium, this garage was typical of its day; it was a scruffy shed with no signage—just stuffed with anything on four wheels.

Actually, no, because the car I went to look at was a Morgan Three-wheeler with a Matchless engine. 'Yours, squire, for 45 quid'. It might as well have been £4,000 as only two weeks earlier, I had blown all my savings, all £30 on buying a clapped out, fit only for the breakers yard, Swallow Doretti.

This dismal cavern intrigued me so I went into the garage. Light (if you can call it that) was provided by just two 60-watt bulbs shaded in the obligatory conical off-white shades. It was jam-packed with such an eclectic mix but right at the back, hidden in virtual darkness was something far removed from the Morrises and Austins that were hiding it.

'No, it can't be, can it?' First thoughts were of a Bentley but then the proportions suggested something else. Oh my God, a Marendaz! The asking price was something like £90 but it was patently obvious that Arthur Daley had no idea what a fabulous, if winged and injured, masterpiece he was purveying and quickly it became 'Look, give us fifty quid and it's yours.'

The same logic prevailed as with the Morgan, and so I left and until the ad in *Classic and Sports Car*, I have never seen another one for sale. The Marendaz had a similar body to the one advertised. Memory is dimmed as was the interior of the garage, so I couldn't now be certain of the colour, but dark grey? As for registration, I had no idea, ditto for the chassis plate.

What happened to it? Rumour had it that it ended-up as landfill at Castle Gresley. As soon as I heard about this, I went to have a look, but it was a hopeless task as in those pre-health and safety days, you could wander and firtle to your heart's content, but I found no trace and part of me was much relieved as I thought that some-one might, just might, have recognised the car for the masterpiece that it was and had purchased it.

Here endeth the lesson.

Mike Wheildon

Aileen Moss, with Alfred Moss beside her, really pushing on in her short-chassis Marendaz Special trials car. (*Pat Moss*)

INTRODUCTION

All this makes me wonder how anyone can be interested in this ghastly man and his awful cars.

Guy Griffiths

I had always known about Captain Marendaz—not because of his cars but because of his aircraft. I was a teenage aircraft enthusiast who bought the two volumes of *British Civil Aircraft*, by A. J. Jackson published in 1959 and 1960. These seminal volumes listed just about everything: from the everyday to the ex-military, to the one-offs and to the totally obscure, where even 'AJJ' had failed to find much information. The more obscure aircraft were a magnet for voyages of discovery around the United Kingdom and Ireland looking for the remnants of aircraft such as the Helmy Aerogypt (in a garden in White Waltham) and the Surrey AL.1 (in Arden's barn at Exeter with mantraps set outside). Yet the two Marendaz-built aircraft seemingly had gone forever and remain on my 'wanted' list to this day.

Fast forward to about 1976 when my interest was now more centred on old cars and there, parading round the ring at the Fairford Traction Engine rally, was a black Marendaz Special car with none other than Captain Marendaz in the passenger seat. An event noted and logged—so he made cars as well, did he?

Several old cars later and while attending the not-to-be-missed Beaulieu Autojumble in 1982, there sitting on a trailer in the Automart was what could only be described as a rather tired Marendaz Special, dark green four-seater, at what I considered to be a silly price. It went home unsold, but several months later, on one boring Thursday, I bought an *Exchange and Mart* and what was obviously the same car was advertised at a much more reasonable £4,500. I was hooked. By this time, I had done a bit of research and, unquestionably, the car was a bit strange and did not quite ring true, but where was there another one? Following a December visit to an archetypal South London wooden lockup and an inspection by torchlight of a car that would not start, with the mists of optimism hiding the realities of its history and provenance, it seemed to me to be a car I had to have, so paraphrasing Charlotte Brontë, it was a case of 'Reader, I bought it'.

Now started the research. The car was persuaded to run and drive without any great difficulty, but it was a mess mechanically with big cracks in the dynamo housing and the wonderful Anzani engine four-point mounting in a flexible chassis was cause for concern. Bodily, the bodged

The forlorn Anzani-powered Marendaz Special looking for a buyer in the Automart at Beaulieu Autojumble, September 1982. (*Author's collection*)

handbrake was at one's toes and nearly out of reach, indicating that perhaps it had been located elsewhere in a previous existence and the very tidy body did not match the bonnet very well. The car was rare as no one knew of another Anzani-powered Marendaz Special and eventually, Michael Sedgwick at the National Motor Museum let me down ever so gently by saying that the body looked very Swallow Wolseley Hornet-ish—a truth confirmed before long.

Of course, in 1984, Captain Marendaz was still alive and residing in Lincolnshire, so who better to ask? His first reply was fairly non-committal, but in my further response, to save disturbing this elderly man unduly, I suggested that I pay him a visit to learn at the knee of the 'Doyen of Automotive and Aeronautical Engineering' (his words). This was a big mistake as his curt reply indicated that invitations originate from Asterby Hall and none were planned for me then or later. Any exchange, however difficult, with Captain Marendaz always revealed some snippet and he had pointed out that all Marendaz Special cars had hydraulic brakes; mine of course were rod, so how was that to be reconciled?

So, with the Wolseley Hornet body removed, what was I looking at? It was pretty clear that not many 1920s Marendaz Specials had been built and most of them featured either in advertising material by Marendaz or press reports from Brooklands. Apart from one very strange four-seater Marendaz Special built in 1925, the first 1926 car and the first with the Bentley-style radiator could clearly be seen, courtesy of pin-sharp *Autocar* photographs, to have rod-actuated brakes and 10-inch brake drums, as my had car. All later cars had 12-inch drums and hydraulics, so a final review of all the myriad of holes drilled in the chassis of my car proved that what I had was the early 1926 car, which of course had Brooklands racing and record-breaking history. With this glad news, I elected to beard Captain Marendaz again, resulting in his damning response 'Furthermore UC3933 is not as I have already made clear to you, a Marendaz Special, and it has no claims whatsoever to such a pretentious title as being of "considerable historic importance". Such utter nonsense confirms your endeavour to get a free ride to fame and posterity by using my name ... in a manner contrary to law.' So, there I had it: it was not even a Marendaz Special according to the man who had made it. I can't say I was totally cut up about this as the evidence was pretty conclusive; in my opinion, it just had not been examined in an objective manner by the Captain. It did spur me to greater efforts, essentially to disprove my own conclusions, but in spite of many years research, I never have.

One of the people who had encouraged me in my researches was the late John Shaw of Cheltenham, owner of three 13/70 cars (it is worth noting that these cars were also referred to as 13-70s in some production paperwork). He had had a reasonable working relationship with Captain Marendaz but after a correspondence in *Motor Sport* in 1984, when he had mentioned the floppy gearbox problem, he was accused in the last letter he ever received from the Captain of '... a childish Sherlock Holmes kiddies' ploy,' while adding 'I do not find it entertaining ... to provide you with further opportunities to question my veracity'. Sadly, it did not end there. I suppose one could accuse John Shaw and me of bear baiting, but at all times we were both totally polite and respectful, the problems arising from, I think, a lack of objectivity on the part of the Captain. We were not setting out to knock his cars; we owned several, but no one, possibly barring the Captain, would say that they were perfect. So, a state of armed truce existed until the May 1985 edition of the *Automobile* was published, a copy of which was belatedly forwarded to Captain Marendaz by another owner, still on good terms with him, Paul Mitchell. The article appeared anonymously, but was in fact written by Michael Worthington-Williams, a highly respected author, whose bywords were insight and accuracy. He did say that the omission of his name was a mistake, but in his efforts to give credit where it was due, the names of John Shaw, Graham Skillen, and the late Michael Sedgwick did appear, thrusting us unwillingly into the firing line. Paul received a response dated 11 June 1985, not aimed at him of course, which bears repetition:

Not since 1923 when a charming young lady owner of a Marseal used to relate fairy stories to me of the conversations between her lonely little Marseal and the hundreds of Morris cars she parked it within the Morris factory at Cowley, when she visited her sister Isobel, married to Lanstadt, the Works Director which she often did, have I heard such Alice in Wonderland cum Old Time Music Hall Harry Tate's Comedy Act on motoring than that unfolded in the May edition of the *Automobile* 1985—by the clandestine undisclosed author and his named associates Skillen and Shaw but comprising, it has been suggested to me, three greedy purblind mice in this instance seeking fame and fortune by denigrating my name and professional reputation as well as Marendaz Special Cars—as other of their ilk have stooped so low to before them who burnt alive the World's greatest engineer, Gallileo [*sic*.], for also refusing to tell lies and would deprive William Shakespeare of his writings in favour of a corrupt Francis Bacon banished from court in his day and fined £40,000. But it is Gallileo and Shakespeare who live on all over the world, as I shall.

The restored Anzani-powered Marendaz Special in 1987. (*Peter Wallage*)

Notwithstanding the damning criticism directed at me here, I trust that this book will somehow make amends and that in it his memory will live on, his right and due, as he so obviously wished.

By 1987, I had sold the Wolseley Hornet body to Dick Sargeantson, anxious to return it to a Wolseley chassis, and had built a replica 1926 two-seater body. By great good fortune, the bonnet louvre panels from the 1926 car were with it, having survived the Hornet experience, so I had a good colour match, the car being 'mushroom'. A feature of all Marendaz cars was their strange colours. In 1987, I drove the car up to Brooklands from Kent to the Brooklands Society Reunion, probably its first return there since about 1930 and parked it up alongside some of its old friends from those days. Walking round, as one does, I idly noticed a vintage London taxi driving around with an old chap in the back, when the penny dropped: there was Captain Marendaz. I hotfooted it after the taxi but lost it and he was away, so I never ever did meet him or talk to him. After the event, I thought I would write him a nice letter saying I was glad he had seen the car and that on the run down the A21 towards Tonbridge, the car easily exceeded the legal speed limit—a tribute to his endeavours. Well, I received a charming reply.

The car had been seen by a number of people and Peter Wallage, then editor of *The Automobile* asked to write about it, but I gazumped him by writing the article myself, published under my name in the October 1987 issue. Obviously, I had not learned from the sagacity of Michael Worthington-Williams, as a multi-page rebuttal of practically everything I had said, verifiable or not as the case might be, arrived at speed from the Captain by way of Paul Mitchell. He asked for his 'corrections' to be published and I responded to the points he had made, but none of this was published, probably just as well as none of it really amounted to much.

In 1988, Eric Dymock of *The Sunday Times* wrote an article where he said that Enzo Ferrari, then just past his ninetieth birthday, was the 'only survivor of a select cadre of motoring pioneers who applied their names to classic cars'. He obviously did not know about Captain Marendaz, so assuming the mantle of the Captain, I wrote in response, pointing out that I was still receiving after sales advice from the manufacturer on a sixty-two-year-old car and that Marendaz Specials were on the road twenty-two years before any Ferrari. Publication followed and, inevitably, a letter from the Captain referring to the item 'coming as a pleasant surprise to me' was closely followed by a return to his earlier criticisms of my literary efforts. This letter was dated 27 February 1988 and was the last one I received from him as he died later that year.

So ended what one must consider a fractious correspondence, one that gave me sleepless nights and a lot of wrangling with the injustice of being accused of things that I was not responsible for and the intransigence of a man who was vastly defensive of his reputation to the point where calling black white was the opening bid. At least I had the consolation of not being alone in this respect. I have hopes that the story outlined in the following pages will, if not setting the record straight, will provide a basis for the reader to form an opinion, although one can be categorically certain that Captain Donald Marcus Kelway Marendaz would not agree.

1

THE EARLY YEARS

These notes on the early history of the Marendaz family are generally as set out and commented on by Marcus Marendaz in 1978 with various corrections and additions.

One Thomas Mansel Talbot from Margam, in South Wales, when on his Grand Tour in the mid-1700s, met David Emmanuel Marendaz in Lausanne, in the canton of Vaud in Switzerland, a young man and the youngest of seven sons. Emmanual Marendaz, as he was known, was well-educated and spoke seven languages, his passport to prosperity; his family position being unlikely to favour him financially. His family had been established in Switzerland since the 1200s, the family chateau at Mathod near Lausanne and Lake Neuchatel still being occupied by the Marendaz family. A coat of arms was granted in 1446 and many members of the family have distinguished themselves as presidents of the Canton Vaud. They were descended from the Marendaz of Douro family, from Douro in Portugal, so the name has a Portuguese root rather than a Spanish one, which might be an ill-informed first guess. Mansel Talbot invited his new friend Emmanuel Marendaz to return with him to Margam Castle, but they were shipwrecked in a storm in the Mediterranean, ending up together with the captain of the ship adrift in a small boat. With supplies running low, they cast lots as to who would be sacrificed for the benefit of the other two, thereby stretching the supplies. Mansel Talbot lost but Emmanuel insisted he take Thomas's place, as he was the youngest, but shortly before this dramatic preparedness for Emmanuel's death was enacted, all were successfully rescued. In gratitude, Mansel Talbot settled a portion of his vast property in Glamorgan on the young Marendaz, where he stayed to found a branch of the family in South Wales.

Not everyone agrees with this tale, it being put that Mansel Talbot, John Loveluck, and Emmanual Marendaz were set upon by Barbary pirates off the coast of North Africa, while visiting Italy in a search for Italian statues for the park at Margam Castle. In saving Thomas's life, both Loveluck and Marendaz were given a farm rent free for the rest of their lives. The references also state that Emmanuel Marendaz was a valet to Mansel Talbot.

Emmanuel Marendaz (1752–1823) married Anne Loveluck (1766–1834) in 1798, a daughter of John Loveluck, and so the succession continued. Their son, another David Emmanuel Marendaz (1799–1867) married Catherine Powell (1799–1836) in 1822 and, in turn, their son William Powell Marendaz (1828–1895) married Sarah Thomas (1826–1891) in 1851. Their son was Richard Emmanuel Marendaz (1859–1937). On 17 January 1897, Donald Marcus Kelway Marendaz was born at Court Farm, Port Talbot, Margam in the County of Glamorgan,

Monmouth School at the beginning of the twentieth century. (*Author's collection*)

his mother being Ada Frances Marendaz (formerly Kelway) and his father Richard Emmanuel Marendaz, farmer and hay and corn merchant. For the record, Donald Marcus Kelway was initially registered as Donald Richard Kelway, the name on the birth certificate being changed later. Also, his father's name was spelled 'Emanuel', one assumes a typographical error.

This made Marcus Marendaz a great-great-grandson of the original immigrant, David Emmanuel Marendaz, and at the time of Marcus's birth, the not inconsiderable clan of Marendaz descendants in South Wales had been there for over 100 years. Having a foreign-sounding name undoubtedly put Marcus Marendaz at a disadvantage and, not surprisingly, he was always very defensive and anxious to assert his long-standing British family history and nationality.

Another well-known member of this Marendaz clan was the world-famous poet Edward Thomas, his best-known work being the poem 'Addlestrop' about the deserted railway station in Oxfordshire. He was born in 1878 and died at Arras, 9 April 1917, and was a second cousin of Marcus Marendaz.

Marcus Marendaz was his parents' firstborn and he was followed by Greville (Richard Greville Frances) born later the same year, 1897, then by three sisters Veronica (Ada Veronica Aileen) (1899–1924), Mona Olga Lenore (1901–2005), and Ernestine Marjorie Hazel (1903–4). Finally, a further son, Stuart (Rupert Stuart St Pierre) (1907–1998) was born at Mathern near Chepstow. Marcus's nearest brother Richard, as well as being born just eleven months after his brother, died within a very few days of him in late 1988, a curious parallel. The 1911 census lists Richard Emmanuel Marendaz farming at Hayes Gate, Chepstow, with Marcus Marendaz at school, aged fourteen.

Marcus Marendaz attended Monmouth School where, it is reported he watched the Hon. C. S. Rolls on some of his ballooning flights. The late Peter Hull, in talking to the author, mentioned Marcus Marendaz's displeasure on revisiting his old school in later life and finding a lack of commemoration of his attendance there.

THE SIDDELEY-DEASY MOTOR COMPANY

After leaving school, Marcus Marendaz joined the Siddeley-Deasy Motor Company under John Davenport Siddeley at Parkside in Coventry as an apprentice, and although we have no evidence as to what caused this change of direction from a farming background to the new field of motor engineering, it may well have been the inspiration of the activities of the late C. S. Rolls. As well as his daytime apprenticeship work, he concurrently attended Coventry Technical College three nights a week to extend his knowledge of engineering. At Siddeley-Deasy, he found T. G. John as works manager and chief engineer. Indeed, as T. G. John, born in 1880, was also from South Wales where his father was a shipwright at Pembroke Dock, he may have helped in getting Marcus Marendaz an apprenticeship, or had even closer ties of some sort. Marcus Marendaz's mother was a Kelway from Pembroke and her father and brother had been at different times consul, vice-consul, and consular agents for a number of foreign countries such as France, Belgium, Brazil, and the United States as well as being shipping agents in Milford Haven. The date quoted in the Royal Flying Corps or Royal Air Force records for Marcus Marendaz joining Siddeley-Deasy is given as 1912, putting him at age fifteen, but this may well be incorrect, given that the date of birth he gave the RFC suggested that he was two years older than he really was. By the time he left Siddeley-Deasy in November 1916, the company's efforts were largely turned over to war work from the pre-war car production. During the war they built Siddeley Puma and Tiger aero-engines and ambulances, the latter no doubt based on the pre-war car designs. By 1916, they had a contract to build R.E.8 aircraft, familiarly known as the 'Harry Tate', 1,024 being built, although by the time Marcus Marendaz left, production would only just have started. Equally, production of Puma engines did not start until 1917, although design and development work on this new engine would have been in hand in late 1916.

In a letter to John Shaw dated 14 April 1984, Marcus Marendaz detailed the activities necessary to complete an apprenticeship, implying of course that this is what he had been subjected to or had had to learn:

T. G. John, founder of Alvis, seen in later life.

To serve your time to the Automotive Manufacturing Industry and making yourself proficient: Drawing Office; centre lathe turning; turret lathe operating and setting up; automatic machines operating and setting up; plain milling operating and setting up; vertical milling operating and setting up; universal milling operating and setting up, including the mathematics involved in dividing heads; gear cutting machine operating, setting up and working out the necessary gearing; spline machine setting up and operating; grinding in all its aspects; drilling small, medium and large; inspection; jig and tool design; tool room general experience; heat treatment operating and scheduling; machine tool maintenance; stores experience; vertical and horizontal boring, operating and setting up; engine fitting; engine testing; gear-box fitting and testing; front and rear axle fitting; general assembly; chassis testing; foundry work, press and forging. Bodywork in all its aspects from design to finish test. Theoretical and technical educational proficiency in the above at College or University level.

In writing this comprehensive list, one detects a mind soaked for many years in the minutiae of engineering, as nothing seems to have been missed. In conclusion, Marcus Marendaz added that also needed was 'A similar number of years experience as acquired by me in the application of the above from apprentice to Chief Executive'.

As Marcus Marendaz left Siddeley-Deasy in November 1916 to join the armed forces, one could argue that he might not have completed his apprenticeship by that time; one would normally assume that to complete the above long list of training tasks around four years would be needed, only possible if Marcus Marendaz had indeed joined the company in 1912, aged fifteen. This would in turn suggest that he had no time to achieve any further position or responsibility within Siddeley-Deasy before he left, yet in a letter to the Alvis Register *Bulletin* in 1982 he claims that he was assistant works manager at Siddeley-Deasy before his departure to join the RFC. It seems most unlikely that a company would make a formal appointment of this nature to someone just out of an apprenticeship, as his ability to function in the real world would at the time have been unverified. It seems much more likely that Marcus Marendaz worked as an assistant, with a small 'a', to the works manager, sitting just outside his office and doing the menial donkey work, an appropriate position for a bright apprentice, anxious to learn and get on. Whatever the situation was, there is no doubt that he was thoroughly grounded in the absolute detail of car engineering and manufacture. It is very interesting to have the information of what was required of a young apprentice before the Great War, although one wonders how many corners were cut to speed the war work. His RAF record does itemise his work as a 'Motor Engineer—7 years experience, 5 with Siddeley-Deasy on construction of Cars, Aero Engines & Planes; being employed in Machine Shop, Engine & Car testing Departments'. The five years with Siddeley-Deasy seems about right, but seven years experience seems merely to fill in the gap with the fictitious date of birth given to the military. Marcus Marendaz returned to Siddeley-Deasy after the war, as we shall see.

2

THE GREAT WAR

Marcus Marendaz left Siddeley-Deasy in November 1916 at an age of just under twenty. One has to assume that he volunteered for military service, rather than having been called up. In 1916, the attrition of volunteers for the military due to the carnage on the Western Front meant that the likelihood of being called up was increasing. Yet as Marcus Marendaz was already almost certainly working on war work in Siddeley-Deasy, he probably was in a protected position, so this alone suggests that the move was deliberate. Also, if you were called up, there was little choice as to the direction your service might take and if you elected to join the Army, your unit was determined by military need, not by your choice. Generally speaking, one did not join the Royal Flying Corps straight away, with men selected for flying duties being seconded or recommended by their superiors from other units—in other words, after a period of service in the trenches or wherever. Again, as the war wore on, the arrangements were changing and with expansion needed everywhere, it became possible to join the RFC directly. As Marcus Marendaz's entry was direct to the RFC, this again suggests that he volunteered. Curiously, his record of service states his date of birth as being 17 January 1895, two years before his true birth date, so undoubtedly, he was anxious to be certain of being accepted, with too young volunteers generally being dissuaded from joining.

Having been commissioned into the RFC at Oxford as a temporary second lieutenant, his initial flying training from April 1917 was with 39 Reserve Squadron at Montrose, Forfarshire, on Maurice Farman Shorthorns. There is a photograph of Marcus Marendaz in one bearing the Swiss Marendaz family crest (a heart), but it seems likely that the crest is a later photographic addition, given that a student under training would almost certainly not be allowed to personalise a unit aircraft in such a way. He records that his first flight lesson ended in disaster with the over-confident instructor stunting, the result being both men and the aircraft going through the roof of a hangar. Apparently, the instructor was sent to the trenches and young Marendaz was eventually persuaded to continue with his chosen career. Initial flying training at that time had moved on from the pre-war pattern where a putative pilot would be placed in a very low powered single-seater and allowed to dart and hop up and down the airfield until he had got the hang of it. The Maurice Farman MF.11 Shorthorn (named as such as it no longer had the forward mounted elevator of its predecessor, the Longhorn) was not a very pleasant aircraft by all accounts, being marginal in most aspects, but it did have dual control, so the student could

Marcus Marendaz in the cockpit of a Maurice Farman MF.11 Shorthorn at Montrose, Scotland, 1917. The family crest appears to be a later addition to the photograph. (*John Shaw*)

follow the instructor as he handled the aircraft. Its stalling speed and cruising speed were not very far apart, so the potential for upsets was high and crashes amongst *ab initio* pilots were frequent. As it was a pusher configuration, the crew were nearer the accident and in front of a 200-kg Renault air-cooled V-8 of some 70-hp (7-litre) or 80-hp (9-litre) models WB or WS respectively. Cooling a pusher in-line engine seems tricky and the engine was appropriately baffled using a fan driven off the crankshaft, the propeller being driven off the camshaft and hence running at half engine speed. The engines were run over-fuelled so that the excess fuel also gave an element of cooling. Machine tolerances are greater for air-cooled engines to allow for differential expansion, so the Renault V-8 when first started rattled. Nevertheless, this arcane arrangement all round did produce an engine that was more reliable than some of the others of the day. Both the Shorthorns and Renault V-8s were licence-built in England.

He was posted to 69 Training Squadron on 21 June 1917, an Australian Flying Corps unit involved in training for the RFC at South Carlton, close to Scampton, Lincolnshire, but two weeks later on 2 July 1917 he moved to 37 Training Squadron at Brattleby, also very near Scampton, where he remained until 26 September 1917. Aircraft listed for 37 Training Squadron include Avro 504, Armstrong-Whitworth F.K.3 and R.E.8, although Marcus Marendaz is recorded to have flown the D.H.4 and Bristol F.2b Fighter as well, probably at this location. Having completed initial flying on the Shorthorn, a trainee pilot would be presented with a variety of service types to broaden his abilities before completing his training. He gained his wings as a flying officer on 28 July 1917, a mere three months after signing up and on 26 September 1917 was posted to the Wireless and Observers' School, late of Brooklands, but at Hursley Park, Winchester, no doubt to learn the idiosyncrasies of aerial observation and communication. Types in use included the B.E.2c and the R.E.8. Marcus Marendaz noted in 1930, 'Brooklands was in 1914–1918 an RFC. artillery observation and reconnaissance school at which I, amongst others, did my share of writing off the death traps with which our good Government provided us for our aerial activities'.

35 SQUADRON, ROYAL FLYING CORPS

On 4 October 1917, he went to France to join the war to end all wars, being sent to No. 1 Aircraft Depot, Pilot's Pool, at St Omer. His service record merely records 'E.F.' (Expeditionary Force, in other words France), so it rather looks as if the squadron allocation was actually done in France and was dependant on the tactical situation or local need. On 7 October, he joined 35 Squadron at La Lovie, recently arrived there from La Gorgue, under 2Lt Rees as commanding officer, possibly only a temporary assignment, Major A. V. Holt being absent. The daily weather appears in the squadron records as was the habit: the day he joined being recorded as fine early becoming stormy with heavy rain later. No. 35 Sqn at the time was part of 12th Wing RFC and an army co-operation squadron flying Armstrong-Whitworth F.K.8 biplanes supplied from No. 2 Aircraft Depot at Candas (north of Amiens) and was attached to the Cavalry Corps. Their duties could be summarised as offensive and defensive formation patrols and reconnaissance. It was important that airmen, both pilots and observers, 'learnt the line'—in other words familiarised themselves with the local topography over which they were likely to be flying so that reports and reconnaissance were meaningful. A squadron had to do this on arrival at a new base before they could become properly operational and for someone joining a squadron already familiar with an area, this learning was their first task. Each squadron so involved had their own operating area and were in contact with the other army units on the ground.

The Armstrong-Whitworth F.K.8 was a substantial general-purpose biplane, powered by a Beardmore 160-hp inline engine, and carried two crew: a pilot and an observer. Armament was a Lewis gun for the observer and a fixed forward-firing Vickers gun for the pilot, mounted on the fuselage side, with provision for carrying up to 260 lb as a bomb-load. The 'F.K.' in the designation refers to Frederick Koolhoven, a Dutch national employed at the time by Armstrong-Whitworth. He became very well known in later years as a prolific aircraft designer in both the United Kingdom and his native Netherlands.

Armstrong-Whitworth F.K.8, B312. This was not a 35 Squadron aircraft. (*Philip Jarrett*)

Of the estimated production of 1539 F.K.8s built, Sir W. G. Armstrong Whitworth and Company built 701 at their factory in Gosforth, Newcastle-upon-Tyne, the remainder, some 838, being built nearby by Sir William Angus, Sanderson and Company. The aircraft, it is believed, were delivered from both companies to No. 9 Aircraft Acceptance Park (AAP) at the nearby Town Moor, before onward movement to the front.

Like all the designs of the early part of the Great War, it was assumed that a stable gun platform was preferable to a manoeuvrable single-seater, leading to rather unexciting types, the F.K.8 with a maximum level speed of 95 mph undoubtedly falling into this category. Nevertheless, the 'Big Ack' was well liked, 35 Squadron being the first to use the F.K.8, until they moved onto the Bristol F.2b Fighter in February 1918. Sadly, no F.K.8s survive today, although examples of the Beardmore engine are to be found.

Army co-operation at that time was done using a trained pilot flying an experienced cavalry officer observer, it being assumed that the pilot was too busy controlling the aeroplane to engage in other activities. Presumably, the trained observer was more in touch with the general goings on on the ground and possibly had a need to make notes or signals. The officers assigned to Marcus Marendaz were Lt Chapman RGA (SR) (Royal Garrison Artillery, Special Reserve) from Mortlake, London and 2Lt Adamson, RFA (Royal Field Artillery), from Manchester, who had been with the squadron since the previous June. These officers were both 'gunners', so undoubtedly their work mostly involved observing fall of British shot or noting German gun positions.

During what appeared to have been a dull and wet October, Marcus Marendaz flew regularly, although his hours flown were few in number. It started with a practice flight in A2717, then practice landings in A2703, and then moving on to learning the line in B2721. On 17 October 1917, the entire squadron moved from La Lovie to Bruay, one hour away, Lt Marendaz in A2721 having Air Mechanic Second Class (2AM) Jones in the other cockpit. On the 21st, his longest flight yet of seventy minutes was bombing from 7,000 feet under conditions of fair visibility at Annay. This activity was continued with further bombing in A2721 at Billy Montigny, Douvrin and Pont à Vendin. These were squadron raids, seven aircraft for example going to Douvrin. Sadly A2721's undercarriage was smashed as a result of a forced landing at Aix Noulette following the raid on Pont-à-Vendin.

On 7 and 8 November 1917, 35 Sqn moved from Bruay to Estrées-en-Chaussée in preparation for the impending offensive that became the Battle of Cambrai, but probably due to the damage to A2721, Marendaz remained at Bruay. The squadron records that Marendaz made the move with A2721 on 18–19 October taking three hours flying and a night stop at Amiens, when the rest of the squadron only took one hour. Due to the intensity of the operational flying activity on the squadron at the time, it is unlikely that this detour was either social or deliberate, and one has to assume that the young Marendaz with Lt Chapman got lost while attempting to navigate their own way. The main activity here was photographic reconnaissance and counter battery work with the 76th Brigade RGA (Royal Garrison Artillery) and with the French 144th Regiment of Artillerie Lourd.

On the dull Tuesday 20 November, Lt Marendaz flew a forty-minute machine gun test, now with Lt Adamson. Then, on 22 November, also dull, Marendaz made his last flight with the squadron, again with Lt Adamson, and recorded as seventy-five minutes of reconnaissance, with an away landing at 'I,27.d.central, Sheet 57C', resulting in a crashed undercarriage. The map referencing system was capable of giving a location to within a small number of yards,

An Armstrong-Whitworth F.K.8. This is not Marendaz in the cockpit. (*RAF Museum*)

which was essential for the determination of gun fall of shot or German positions; consequently, we know that Lt Marendaz ended up about halfway between the villages of Lebucquière and Fremic, 3 miles to the east of Bapaume. It is entirely possible to walk to the exact spot today.

The squadron records do little to flesh out the surrounding circumstances of what must have been a traumatic and eventful period in a young man's life. The clinical record of about fourteen hours flying on the Squadron seems trivial but given a likely life expectancy of ten hours operational flying, his record is not abnormally short. Fortunately for us all, Marcus Marendaz's words on the subject were set down in print.

The Battle of Cambrai began on 20 November. It is famous as the first use of massed tanks in battle and the British intent was to use the tanks to penetrate the German lines, thereby allowing the cavalry through to outflank the enemy. It can be seen that being a cavalry observer was a critical task. Marcus Marendaz relates, having climbed to 5,000 feet.

Couldn't see a thing from up high, so came down to 150 ft. Bit close with all that rifle fire, but only way to get under the fog. Then I saw a British tank trying to creep over the bridge across the canal at Masnières which the cavalry were to use. The bridge simply bent beneath its weight. Useless. I wound down my signal wire, and sent a message in Morse to tell them to stop ... go back. Just after that, my plane had all the air taken from its wings by a salvo of shells from the huge twelve-inch guns they had brought up for the assault. Felt it go past. Plane started to side-slip down into the canal—about 70 ft wide and just about as deep, as I recall. No water – just a sort of huge concrete

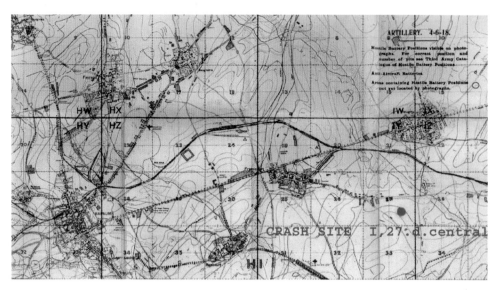

ARTILLERY. 4-6-18.

Hostile Battery Positions visible on photographs. For correct position and number of pits see Third Army Catalogue of Hostile Battery Positions.

Anti-Aircraft Batteries.

Areas containing Hostile Battery Positions not yet located by photographs.

CRASH SITE I,27.d.central

The Trench Map showing the site where Marendaz crashed with his F.K.8, A2721, 22 November 1917. (*War Department*)

trench. We had practically stopped dead and were just falling out of the air. Didn't fight the slip ... instead I increased it into a vertical bank. Then, using the rudder as an elevator and the elevators as the rudder I climbed straight up out of the canal.

Wasn't sure the cavalry had got the message, so I found a bit of a flat patch near a field station, put the plane down and went to find a telegraph. Odd thing- my observer was unconscious. Poor chap had fainted dead away when we started to slip. Thought he was dead, I suppose.

Got back to the mess that night and heard that church bells were sounding all over Britain for the "victory". We knew better. The rains had started. The tanks were bogged down. In a week the Germans had taken back our gains, about 600 yards wide on a six mile front. But at least we hadn't lost the cavalry. They were dying to go ... but if I hadn't seen that bridge go, they would have been slaughtered. So it's quite wrong what some historians have suggested, that the cavalry failed to carry out their assignment. Simply, they couldn't.

Marcus Marendaz's account was first published in *The Times* on 6 December 1986 in response to an item that stated that the impetus of the attack by 300 tanks was lost due to heavy rain and a strong German counterattack. As he claimed to be the only RFC flier to penetrate the mist that obscured Masnières bridge on the first day of the battle, his was a unique view and his assertion that the cavalry were unable to proceed may be correct.

Although 35 Squadron were very active throughout the remainder of the Battle of Cambrai, Lt Marendaz is not mentioned in their records. F.K.8 A2721 was struck off charge, presumably being damaged beyond economical repair on 22 November 1917.

Although he was away in France, he returned home for his wedding to Dorothy Robinette Evans (1896–1973) on 20 February 1918, a month after his twenty-first birthday, in the parish church at Pembroke Dock, having been given leave to return home. How he met her has not been recorded, although the families, both from Pembroke Dock, would have been known to each other. Soon afterwards, on 18 March 1918 and in deteriorating health, he was posted back to England and the Home Establishment, his operational career ended, being tasked as a delivery pilot at No. 1 Aircraft Acceptance Park (1 AAP) at Coventry, Radford, from 28 March. This AAP was started as a private venture by Daimler with Siddeley-Deasey and Humber joining in later, aircraft being towed by road from the factories to the site for testing. Aircraft acceptance parks everywhere were the collecting points for new aircraft arriving from the myriad factories around the country. The aircraft were not all delivered from factories as flying specimens, but they were frequently roaded to the AAP, should the factory, such as a car manufacturer, not be adjacent to a suitable flying ground. They were then either inspected and accepted in a broken-down state for onward shipment to France or elsewhere, or else assembled by a small factory team at the airfield before being handed over to the RFC or RAF. Service pilots, such as Second Lieutenant Marcus Marendaz, would then have to deliver them to their planned service unit and destination, which might even be the British Expeditionary Force (BEF) in France, where there was a further collection point, the aircraft then being allocated to a unit, as losses or military needs dictated on the day. It must be said that it is unlikely that a pilot at Coventry would have been in the habit of flying regularly to France, as No. 8 AAP at Lympne was generally used as the collecting point for aircraft heading over the Channel and hence pilots from this unit would have been much more likely to be responsible for these duties.

The posting undoubtedly suited Marcus Marendaz, having been at Coventry before joining up and at the AAP, he would have been dealing with R.E.8s coming from his old employer, the Siddeley-Deasy factory at Parkside.

Marendaz's medical record through 1918 records him at various times as only being fit for light duties or ground duties only. He was posted from 1 AAP to 14 AAP at Castle Bromwich on 17 August 1918 but the posting was rescinded the same day, possibly because at the time he was medically unfit and off flying for a period of four weeks from 16 July 1918. This medical categorisation was later extended in August for a further eight weeks and, by 22 October, he was classified medically as Category C.2, meaning able to hear and see for ordinary purposes, but only suitable for home garrisons, hence unlikely to be sent back to France. On 26 October, presumably because he was off flying and of no use as a delivery pilot, he was posted to the Observers' School of Reconnaissance and Aerial Photography at Monkmoor, Shrewsbury, no doubt on instructional duties. At the time, the training fleet was varied and comprised B.E.2c, R.E.8, Handley Page O/400, and D.H.9. With the Armistice being declared in November 1918 and not being a complete German surrender, there was in theory a continuing need for aircraft

R.E.8s awaiting dispatch from the Siddeley-Deasy factory. (*Chaz Bowyer via Terry Treadwell*)

and trained airmen, but as the threat of the war restarting diminished, military activity wound down rapidly.

Marcus Marendaz was demobilised in the rank of lieutenant on 12 April 1919 and put on the unemployment list the day afterwards, having being passed permanently unfit and receiving a disability allowance of 80 per cent. Jumping ahead, he relinquished this at the time of the great depression, saying 'I thought my country needed the money more than I'. His military record states that he had flown the following service types: Armstrong Whitworth, no doubt the Armstrong Whitworth F.K.8 of 35 Squadron, R.E.8, D.H.4, and Bristol Fighter.

So ended his military career, there being no question that Marcus Marendaz was enormously influenced by his service in the Great War. He was immensely proud of his time with the Royal Flying Corps and wore their tie in later years; he was, as we know, in later life always addressed as Captain Marendaz, a status to which we will return later in this story. His record in the Royal Flying Corps and the Royal Air Force was not extensive and his role was one of observation rather than as a fighter pilot. Nevertheless, he did his bit and he survived and this is to his credit.

3

AFTER THE GREAT WAR

At the War's end, Marcus and Dorothy Marendaz were almost certainly living in Coventry and with his demobilisation he returned to Siddeley-Deasy. Manufacturers who had been on war work were subject to an enormous change at this time, which proved the end of some of them, particularly those who were building aircraft, for which there was absolutely no demand. Many aircraft manufacturers turned to vehicle manufacture as a desperate move to survive, but of course met the already established car manufacturers 'reverting to type' as fast as they could. This meant that, in 1919 and 1920, there was an immense jockeying for commercial success that caused a large number of closures, mergers, and re-emergences in changed guise and name all, fortunately, driven by a large demand for cars, essentially at any price. Not surprisingly, this state could not survive; prices falling through the early twenties as engineering lessons learned during the war were acted on to produce better and more keenly priced vehicles. This meant that the euphoria of selling anything with wheels, including marginal lightweight cyclecars, turned into a slow death for many manufacturers as the decade progressed.

In Coventry for the period 1919 to 1924, there were twenty-six manufacturers of all sizes listed, not to mention engine manufacturers, coachbuilders, and manufacturers of every accessory imaginable; it was after all the centre of motor manufacturing in England, with everyone cheek by jowl in the same town. To someone involved in this activity at the time, it must have been exhilarating, although the technical, commercial, and personal pressures must have been immense. This was the world re-entered by Marcus Marendaz.

Marcus Marendaz rejoined Siddeley-Deasy, one assumes immediately on demobilisation, his old job no doubt having been retained for him. Peter Hull in conversation with the author said that Marcus Marendaz returned to Siddeley-Deasy under a Government scheme for employing ex-officers. This implication that he needed help to get back into manufacturing was protested vigorously by Marcus Marendaz who said 'I needed no Government Schemes ... to get me a position after the War, having two waiting for me'. Obviously, one was Siddeley-Deasy, the other presumably with T. G. John, whose plans were shortly to involve Marcus Marendaz.

The detail of Marcus Marendaz's activities after the Great War has been discussed at length by various historians and writers, spiced with frequent outbursts from the man himself defending his status, a passion he maintained until his death. In many ways, the opposing statements made by either side are not in fact opposing, but merely based on a view of events or facts looked at from opposite directions. Maybe this sounds convoluted or irrational, but as opinion is heavily involved, the truth of the matter is never likely to emerge. One overarching point that has to be said is that we cannot apply today's standards to events of the 1920s. When someone talks of a car manufacturer today, you think of multi-national concerns employing thousands, most of whom never see a car, less even lay a hand on one. In the 1920s, a car manufacturer could be a handful of people in loose alliance working in a tin shed on a £50 bank overdraft. There was not a regulated hierarchy with appointed positions as we would expect today, but rather a group of people with a common objective, where roles were flexible, depending on the demands of the moment. While not exactly like that, Marcus Marendaz's activities in the early 1920s were at the lower end of this scale but not very different to many others, some of whom went on to create empires. So on to the facts, the near-facts, the misleading statements, and the opinion.

Marcus Marendaz restarted at Siddeley-Deasy in the spring of 1919, a married man with a child on the way. At this point, he would have met Thomas George John again and also Harold Irving, a name that later on was synonymous with Alvis cars, who had joined Siddeley-Deasy in 1917, working on the Puma engine. The company was obviously not in a very good state at this time, the bulk of their order book collapsing with the end of the war and before long they were bought out by the Armstrong-Whitworth Development Company and reformed as a wholly-owned subsidiary Armstrong-Siddeley Motors manufacturing aircraft engines and motor cars. About March 1919, Marcus Marendaz rejoined his old company, his boss T. G. John still in position as works manager, left, having bought the company of Holley Brothers, of 17 Hertford Street, in the centre of Coventry, a British branch run by two English engineers of the American carburettor concern. He renamed it T. G. John and Company Limited and continued in the carburettor business but also branched out into scooters and stationary engines. According to Peter Hull, in conversation with the author, one of the investors in the newly formed company was George S. Kelway, an important figure in Pembrokeshire, Consul and shipping agent and uncle to Marcus Marendaz; one suspects that the investment was due to the Welsh connection rather than the influence of a twenty-two-year-old nephew, but undoubtedly it assured Marcus a position within the newly formed company.

T. G. JOHN AND ALVIS

So Marcus Marendaz's stay at Siddeley-Deasey was short indeed, following as he did T. G. John to his new company along with Harold Irving. By later in 1919, design work was afoot at T. G. John Ltd for the first Alvis car, based on a chassis design by Geoffrey de Freville of D.F.P. (Doriot, Flandrin and Parant), the marque favoured by W. O. Bentley before he built his own cars. The first 10/30 Alvis cars quickly established a reputation for good engineering and 120 were sold in 1920, their first year of production. The fortunes of T. G. John and his Alvis cars prospered, such that he expanded and moved to Holyhead Road in April 1921 and changed the name of the company to the Alvis Car and Engineering Company Limited in December 1921. The later history of Alvis has been told elsewhere; suffice to say that the name Alvis survived as an independent entity at Holyhead Road, Coventry, until 1965, when taken over by British Leyland.

Turning to Marcus Marendaz's role at T. G. John Ltd we find a number of contradictions in his words and the comments of others. Writing in 1973 to the editor of the Alvis Register

The 1923 Alvis Racing Car No. 1, built after Marendaz left Alvis, but which he would probably have seen on the track. (*Author's collection*)

Bulletin, he says 'At that time I was works manager of T. G. John Ltd and of course responsible for its translation into the Alvis Car and Engineering Company'. And again in 1982 'I was the Works Manager of T. G. John Ltd and initiated as well as concluded the Alvis Contract'. Going back a little further, we have a possibly more realistic comment in a letter to *Motor Sport* in January 1962: 'As you may know, I brought Alvis cars into existence, which was in 1919'. This assertion was very rapidly refuted by G. H. Wiltsher, publicity manager of Alvis the following month, saying 'the statement in the first paragraph is not correct,' going on to add that 'after T. G. John was founded in 1919, John employed Marendaz as one of his staff. They disagreed, and Marendaz left Alvis and had nothing to do with the Company from that date onwards'. In mitigation, one has to admit that he could probably claim that he had helped found Alvis on the basis that his uncle had funded T. G. John, without which money Alvis might not have happened, Marcus Marendaz pointing out 'I was also a shareholder, holding with my friends more shares bought with money than T. G. John ever had to put up when he promoted the company'.

It appears that Marcus Marendaz stayed at T. G. John for less than a year, leaving to form his own engineering works probably very early in 1920. In his time at T. G. John, through from March 1919, the first Alvis car had been produced, so his later statement about bringing Alvis cars into existence in 1919 is not far off the truth, as he was undoubtedly close to T. G. John and the whole creative process. The Kelway incentive, if I can call it that, of having an influential backer undoubtedly helped Marcus, the ties only loosening when T. G. John achieved his initial success, such that the concerns of any backer would have been assuaged. Marcus Marendaz's

The chassis-less Emscote car fitted with the gearbox built by Marseel Engineering. (*Michael Worthington-Williams*)

later claims from 1973 and 1982 are undoubtedly incorrect as the formation of the Alvis Car and Engineering Company at the end of 1921 was nearly two years after he had left T. G. John, at a time when all events were moving very rapidly, and it is unreasonable to assume that any efforts on his part in 1919 would have carried over, other than the financial backing of his uncle. A final comment on G. H. Wiltsher's letter is that there was no further response from the normally litigious Marcus Marendaz, which rather confirms the point. In mitigation, I would emphasise again that Marcus undoubtedly played a significant role in the production of the first Alvis cars. The falling out with T. G. John may possibly have been over technical disagreements, as Marcus Marendaz undoubtedly had ideas of his own that were fairly un-Alvis like when we look at his own later designs, particularly the gearbox and torque-tube back axle arrangement of his cars. The Alvis produced by T. G. John was to a design that lasted nominally unchanged for many years and hence was proven to have been based on sound principles.

The disagreement between T. G. John and Marcus Marendaz cited above may possibly have been for other reasons if we refer to a letter written in 1974 by A. W. Cummings who stated that he had worked on the first two Alvis cars. He added that 'Marendous [*sic.*] had proved to be hopeless, producing hundreds of pounds of scrap and then stayed away from the works'. As a consequence, John said he would not be allowed back.

Whether Marcus Marendaz had been planning to leave we do not know, but frequently when an underling 'knows better', a parting of the ways happens. The position at the end of 1919 was that T. G. John had demonstrated that he could build a successful car from scratch, so the temptation for Marcus to leave and repeat the process as a competitor must have been strong. By the end of 1919, he was a father, his daughter Mifanwy having been born in the late summer of 1919.

MARSEEL ENGINEERING AND THE GEARBOX STORY

Marseel Engineering Co. Ltd of Victoria Park, Coventry was formed in 1920. Note that the name is 'Engineering' not 'Cars'; maybe the intent was to walk before running, although events precipitated this change of emphasis before long. The names behind the name were, obviously, Marendaz (taking the first three letters) and Seelhoff (taking the first four), one Charles B.

Seelhoff, another ex-Siddeley-Deasy apprentice. Joining them was Harold Irving as Works Manager who commented that this title was rather grand for a somewhat small organisation with a couple of tin sheds at the bottom of Northumberland Road. Harold had been born in Ilkston, Derbyshire in 1892, and was son of a cyclemaker who had moved to Coventry. Writing in 1982, Marcus Marendaz denied that Harold Irving was ever works manager, having applied to Marendaz for the position of fitter but being taken on as a chassis erector. A search today for Victoria Park reveals nothing, but it seems likely that this name may in fact have referred to the aforementioned tin sheds. The name Northumberland Road crops up later on in the Marendaz story, 46 Northumberland Road being the address cited for Marseal cars initially registered to D. M. K. Marendaz in 1922, so one assumes that this is where the family were living during this period, as the building is a house in a terrace with no industrial connections. Northumberland Road is off the Holyhead Road and a very short distance from the site where Alvis moved to in 1921 and, coincidentally, No. 46 was the residential address before the war for one of the two Holley engineers that sold out to T. G. John in 1919. One gets the impression that at that time, the whole mix of people and places was much closer than one would ever imagine.

On starting his business, Marcus Marendaz quickly made progress with a contract for gearboxes for the Emscote light car. This car was the idea of Edwin S. Marlow, a prototype being developed during 1919, the Emscote Motor Company Limited, being formed in December 1919 at Emscote in Warwickshire. Following favourable reports in the *Light Car and Cyclecar,* who tested a prototype, sales seemed assured and production began, with deliveries promised in May 1920. To this end, Marlow ordered 500 gearboxes from Marseel Engineering—a considerable quantity by any standards. The Emscote car was curious insomuch as it did not have a proper

A Marseal seen with Dorothy Summers and handwritten caption by Marcus Marendaz. (*Paul Barnes*)

chassis, other than having the engine mounted in a cradle, with the gearbox being located behind this cradle using eight long bolts. Bolted behind the gearbox was a conventional torque-tube system, differential and back axle all 'in-unit'. In describing the Marseel-built gearbox, the *Light Car and Cyclecar* commended its accessibility, with an easily removed cover plate and, unusually, a removable bottom plate. Purchasers seemed pleased with this moderately priced light car, but after the initial euphoria had died down, it started to become clear that there were not enough of them—not cars but purchasers. Some 260 gearboxes had been delivered before Marcus Marendaz got the feeling that all was not well, having found himself in the position that he was owed money plus had a lot of gearboxes on his hands for which he had no foreseeable use. Force of circumstance or an acceleration of already laid plans provided a solution to the over-abundant supply of gearboxes and the Marseel car was born.

Notwithstanding the gearbox setback, Marseel Engineering undoubtedly survived substantially unharmed as the company moved to 17 Hertford Street, Coventry, at some date between September and December 1921, at the same location and following the T. G. John exodus to the Holyhead Road the preceding April. T. G. John's Alvis was selling well and he needed bigger premises, so presumably Marcus Marendaz was moving up as well from his tin sheds. At the time of writing there are no recorded details of what Marseel Engineering were up to during the latter part of 1920 and into 1921, but it seems logical to assume that Marcus Marendaz was busy building prototype Marseel cars and sourcing the myriad components necessary to put a car into production. Cars were registered to customers in July 1921 and the *Light Car and Cyclecar* wrote a piece describing the 1922 model in September 1921.

On a personal level, early 1921 also saw the arrival of Marcus Marendaz's second daughter, Brenda Cynthia.

To finish the Emscote story, Edwin Marlow left the board in July, 1920, who agreed in the following October that they could no longer meet their liabilities and the company should be wound up. Interestingly in May 1921 creditors were asked to lodge claims with a Mr E. F. Pearson at 17 Hertford Street, Coventry. This address was that of T. G. John until April 1921 and Marseel Engineering at the end of the year, but in spite of this coincidence, it seems unlikely that Marendaz was associated with the Emscote winding up. Emscote spares were still being

An Alvis engine similar to the one allegedly spirited from the company stores and fitted to a Marseal. (*Roger McDonald*)

advertised by a Mr Holland of Hearsall Lane Corner in Coventry in April 1922, including brand new Marseel-built gearboxes at £10, he having undoubtedly bought up the factory stock. One wonders if Marcus Marendaz bought any of them.

There is one curious story dating to December 1921: the case of the disappearing engine. A Marseel registered at that time was fitted with an Alvis engine, No. 6461; something that might not be remarkable as many manufacturers sold engines to other assemblers, either to try out for future adoption or for development purposes. However, this particular engine number in the Alvis production records has nothing entered against it, seemingly not being fitted to an Alvis car, but equally not being marked 'sold to Marseel Engineering'. This seems to give some truth to the story that Marcus Marendaz, an old T. G. John employee and therefore recognisable by the workforce, spirited one away from the company without their knowledge. It has also been said that the poor storeman involved lost his job over it.

The Marseel car turned into the Marseal car as the result of Marcus Marendaz and Charles Seelhoff parting company, Marcus Marendaz revising the name accordingly. It has been widely stated that Charles Seelhoff left Marseel Engineering in 1923, returning to T. G. John or the Alvis Car and Engineering Company as a chargehand in their toolroom. However, the split came much earlier as cars were being registered as Marseals, with an 'a', in April 1922, just about the time that production for the 1922 model really got going. This was associated with a further move by Marendaz, cars being assembled at the Atlantic Works, Harefield Road, Coventry, and registered at that address from that date. Photographs taken inside the Atlantic Works were used in Marseal advertising, but regrettably are unfit for reproduction. C. B. Seelhoff writing in *Motor Sport* in 1970 said that his father, C. H. Seelhoff, had no connection with the gearbox saga, having broken away from the company before their production, but was involved in the 'Lambretta-style' advanced scooter, a registered example appearing in June 1922. On leaving, he went into general engineering.

Turning again to the works manager, Harold Irving, it rather looks as if he stuck it out with Marendaz until he joined Alvis in early 1924.

A feature of any biographical notes on Marcus Marendaz are his brushes with the law. It would appear that his earliest recorded offence was on the A5 at Stony Stratford when he failed to display his road fund licence. Irritatingly, it was in his pocket, having fallen off earlier, but he still got 'done' for £10. His future record before the law was not so trivial. Having outlined the changes inside the company, we can now look at the Marseal car, both technically and as Marcus Marendaz promoted it competitively.

4

THE MARSEAL

A TECHNICAL DESCRIPTION

In writing about a car marque, the usual starting point is a review of surviving cars, as that gives you a clue regarding what the company actually built as opposed to what they indicated they were going to build by way of various magazine plugs and sales brochures. For the Marseel and later Marseal, this is a bit of a problem as none have survived. What we do have is a single Coventry Simplex engine with a provable Marseal provenance, another Marseal timing cover plate, and a solitary radiator badge in a museum. After nearly thirty years of looking, that is not a lot to go on, considering the production numbers claimed for the marque, which would suggest that at least a handful should have survived. However, there is another car that qualifies. The earliest surviving Marendaz Special, dating to 1926, is also the only surviving Anzani-powered car from the late 1920s production run and, frankly, is not typical of this model for various reasons. In fact, it appears to be more Marseal than Marendaz Special, with possible Emscote overtones, so we will include reference to it in our review.

Considering a car of conventional layout (such as a Marseal or an Alvis), one of the arguments that raged in the early days concerned the advantages or not of having un-sprung weight in a vehicle. If one considers the springs on a car they are between the wheels and running gear, which are unsprung and the chassis, engine and body which are sprung. Depending on the installation, the ratio between the two can vary and a torque-tube system in unit with the back axle gives you more unsprung weight than a system where the prop-shaft is in the open with universal joints and the back axle is located by other means. Equally, a beam front axle, hubs, and wheels will give you a car that has more unsprung weight when compared with an installation such as the front-wheel-drive Alvis where there is no front axle, the hubs and wheels being hung directly on the springs. Opinions varied as to which was the best way to go, invoking arguments about stability, road-holding, and manoeuvrability. Generally, more unsprung weight gave you a smoother ride and Marcus Marendaz in his time at Siddeley-Deasy would have been aware of high-quality cars, such as the Rolls-Royce with a torque tube system. Mainly for weight saving reasons, essential on a low-powered smaller car, other manufacturers did not generally favour torque tubes. The Emscote, discussed earlier, with its semi-chassis engine pan almost by necessity needed a torque-tube system to compensate for the lack of chassis at

Above left: A Marseal chassis and running gear, complete with an ex-Emscote gearbox. (*Light Car and Cyclecar*)

Above right: The gearbox that started it all: a Marseal relic belonging to the surviving 1926 Marendaz Special. (*Author's collection*)

the rear in spite of its low price-tag. So, when Marcus Marendaz set to designing his Marseel, it is no surprise that he adopted this system as his objective seemed to be to build a quality car at low price. In fact, as it turned out this arrangement was fundamental to his philosophy for every car he ever built, all the way through to his last car in 1936.

In the *Light Car and Cyclecar* review of the Marseel in September 1922, they described the transmission installation thus, 'The most interesting feature in the design is the combination of gearbox, torque tube and axle in a single unit. This is attained by allowing the gearbox to pivot about a ball joint arranged centrally in the fore and aft line of the drive, and accommodated in a cross-bracing member of the frame'.

In these words, we are introduced to the Marendaz gimbal-mounted gearbox, torque tube, and rear axle, as shown in the adjacent photograph. The actual swivelling joint seen in the picture above is not particularly clear, but it follows that the ball-joint forward of the gear-box must also provide fore and aft location of the entire gearbox, torque tube, and back axle, given that the cantilevered rear springs had to slide in the axle mountings. We are also looking at a Marseel-designed Emscote gearbox, redirected but modified by the removal of the eight long attachment bolts that were needed for the Emscote engine tray. Turning to the aforementioned Anzani-engined Marendaz Special, this car's gearbox is shown in a further photograph and the similarities are very obvious. In this car, the forward gimbal ball-joint is not present, movement being permitted by a plate mounted on the front of the gearbox that allows it plus the torque tube and back axle to rotate about a longitudinal axis (that is left wheel up, right wheel down) on a large trunnion and about a lateral axis (both rear wheels up or down together) on two smaller plain bearings. As mentioned in the Emscote description, the top cover is removable, as is the bottom. In fact, with the need for fore and aft mountings for the gearbox shafts, the whole box is essentially a cast aluminium frame, a position exacerbated by the bolted-on patch on one side to accommodate

The Marseel oil-cooled engine. (*Light Car and Cyclecar*)

an enlarged gear, the whole assembly being a mass of difficult to seal joints and oil leaks.

The other technical innovation that the young Marseal Motors tried was an oil-cooled engine. Boiling water-filled radiators had been an obvious irritant to motorists right from the earliest days, so the idea of having an oil-filled radiator that could run at a higher temperature with the added advantage that it would not freeze very readily either seemed a good one. Belsize is the marque best remembered for oil cooling, successfully building an engine around the same time with a mixture of oil and air cooling. The development Marseal engine was written up in *Light Car and Cyclecar* in March 1922 being designated 7–11 hp with a capacity of 1,018 cc (60-mm bore × 90-mm stroke); in fact, a car using such an engine was entered in the Edinburgh and District Motor Club six-day trial in May 1922, to be driven by a Mr W. C. Brookes. Sadly, he non-started, so we have idea how the engine might have fared alongside the Belsize also entered. The four-in-line cylinder barrel was immersed in the oil filled crankcase, with an air-cooled head complete with over-head valves operated by single push-rods. As the article noted that the sole manufacturing and selling rights had been secured by Marseal, it can probably be assumed that the engine was not a Marcus Marendaz design.

Hiding among all the known Marseel/Marseal registrations is one, HP4137, for a Cycle Scooter of 1.25 hp, registered as a Marseel in June 1922. As in other documentation the name change to Marseal appears to have taken place around April, the continued use of Marseel here is for unknown reasons but may be because of the continued involvement of C. H. Seelhoff. There is very little recorded information relating to the cycle scooter other than what appears in *Motor Cycling* for 8 September 1920. The 'step-through' frame was made in two pressed steel parts, sandwiching other components, including the engine, between them. The two-stroke engine was reported to be of 216 cc, 2 hp, which does not accord with the registration information quoted above. Aluminium cooling fins for the engine were shrunk on to the steel cylinder. One has to conclude that the Marseal cycle scooter was not a success and its demise seems to be a result of the break up between Marendaz and Seelhoff.

The 1922 Marseel Cycle Scooter. (*Marseel Engineering*)

HOW MANY MARSEALS WERE BUILT?

Moving on to the burning question of how many Marseel/Marseal cars were built, two figures have been quoted—1,400 and 800—with no particular justification for either, both probably originating from Marcus Marendaz. As noted above, no cars survive, or are likely to turn up, so no verification of numbers based on survivors is possible. The most reliable source of information is, in fact, registration documentation and very far-sightedly the City of Coventry have kept theirs, a massive source of facts surrounding the motoring heritage of the City. A trawl of all registrations issued in Coventry between January 1921 and March 1925 for Marseal related vehicles is reproduced in Appendix II. This of course will not cover all vehicles produced in the various Marseel/Marseal factories, but it is likely to produce a representative sample, sufficient to determine with reasonable confidence production numbers, models actually built and so on.

Using the information contained in Appendix II, some broad conclusions can be drawn. The first Marseel registered in Coventry appears to date to July 1921, a date when Marseel Engineering were still at Victoria Park, although the second one listed, in December 1921 was produced at 17 Hertford Street. Assuming that the percentage of cars registered in Coventry remained roughly constant at a figure between 5 and 10 per cent of the total produced, then perhaps fifty cars, probably all called Marseels, were built in that year. All the cars listed for 1922 through 1924 were produced at the Atlantic Works, Harefield Road, although as dates for the 1922 cars only start in April, the starting delay was presumably due to moving the production line. Normally, within the car industry, production for any model year started the preceding October, around motor show time, and ran through until the works holiday the following August. It rather looks as if around 100 cars were built in 1922, 160 in 1923, and 240 in 1924, giving a grand total of 550. If one compares Marseel/Marseal production with that of Alvis cars then initially Alvis were producing seven times as many cars as Marseel in 1921, but later on from 1922 to 1924, Marseal did better and got up to a point where they were producing about a quarter as many cars as Alvis. The production rate for Marseals over this period seems linear with no noticeable drop off, so the reasons for terminating production seems to have been economic rather than a lack of orders. It seems strange that no Marseals have survived; given the survival rate for Alvis cars at about 1 to 2 per cent, one would have expected to find a handful of Marseals. Of the cars listed in Appendix II, all were defunct by the mid-1930s; a life of ten to fifteen years was considered good for the period.

If we turn to the engines fitted to the Marseels and Marseals, the registration information tells a number of stories. Marcus Marendaz always averred that his cars were fitted with his engines, the implication being that he made the engines as well. The truth is that this was not always the case and for the Marseel/Marseals, the engines were nearly all bought in. There is quite a lot of what appear to be recording errors in the Coventry registration information regarding engines but reading through this as best we can, some conclusions emerge that paint the overall picture. As taxation was based on horsepower, the records for this should be more exact, but in fact, the bores quoted seem to be the more accurate based on the known engines fitted, with the associated horsepowers being somewhat approximate.

Generally speaking, the bulk of Marseal chassis and engine numbers appearing in the Coventry records are straightforward and are explained in more detail below. The early engine numbers mostly carry an 'A' prefix, but the earliest are anomalous. The two 1921 Coventry registrations both have engine numbers that are unusual. One, 6461, is an Alvis number with an Alvis engine horsepower, so almost certainly is an engine supplied from Alvis, possibly without their consent, as recorded earlier. The other number looks also to be an Alvis engine capacity and number, but there is no corresponding evidence from Alvis records. Alvis did not supply a batch of engines to Marcus Marendaz, so this engine's provenance is not clear. The earliest quoted 1922 engine number is for a 1,040-cc (60 mm × 92 mm), 9-hp engine and

Robert Jones with his 1924 Marseal. The engine of this car survives with the author. (*Vivienne Mason*)

11/27 h.p. Marseal 2-Seater All-Weather

A brochure illustration of a 11/27 Marseal. (*Marseal Motors Ltd*)

it seems very likely that this was the oil-cooled prototype engine, although the dimensions do not agree with the press information stated above. Following this period of experimentation, the decision to give up on the oil-cooled engine and a speedy move to Coventry Simplex as engine supplier seems to have happened.

The 1922 to 1924 engines with 'A' prefix to the numbers were supplied by Coventry Simplex and are 1,247 cc and 9.8 hp. Some are missing the 'A' prefix in the records. One has an 'S' prefix, maybe denoting a sports variant. Cars with 11.8-hp and four-figure engine numbers are 1,496-cc British Anzani engines. This leaves one or two anomalous cars in the list. Chassis numbers 7001 and 8001 seemingly denote a new production sequence with engine numbers to match, possibly one Anzani engine and one Coventry Simplex engine, yet date-wise, they fall among the other 1924 cars.

Model definitions for all cars in the 1920s and 1930s are rather variable. They are usually quoted in the style 9-26, where '9' refers to 9-hp RAC rating and '26' to 26-bhp engine rating. This convention was used by most manufacturers, although the actual numbers any manufacturer chose to use were not constrained by a need to be accurate or bound by some standard, merely numbers that looked right or suggested a power that may or may not have been there. Road Tax was charged at £1 per horsepower or part of a horsepower such that a Marseal owner at 9.8 hp would have been charged £10 yearly. So, manufacturers tended to sell on the fact that a car advertised as a 9-26, looked to a potential owner as being a cheap to tax 9 hp, when in fact it was actually taxed at 10 hp. Conversely, a car could be sold as a 12-27 model, when the salesman could point out that it was actually only taxed at 10 hp, the new owner could then proudly boast to friends that they were wealthy enough to have a 12-hp model. Marcus Marendaz placed his various Marseal cars in both these marketing camps, to the confusion of the reader and the world at large. The only number that actually mattered was the one inscribed in the log-book at the time of registration. Consequently, it is a little strange to see the variety of numbers recorded by the registration authorities and the errors they contain, although in every case a bore is recorded, apparently accurately, so perhaps they always used that as their sole reference. Given that the calculated RAC horsepower is a function only of the bore and the number of cylinders, this makes sense.

THE MARSEEL AND MARSEAL MODELS

The 10.5 Marseel model was introduced in early 1921 and received the usual appreciative and non-critical review by the *Light Car and Cyclecar* for 12 February 1921. The feature noted by the reviewer that drew his attention was the very wide centrally mounted door each side, which allowed access to both front and rear seats of the four-seater. These doors were rear hinged and to assist access to the front seats the front cushions hinged centrally. The intention was to create a stronger body with fewer cut-outs, thereby reducing weight and making manufacture easier and cheaper. From the Coventry registration records, it rather looks as if these cars were Alvis powered and it is anyone's guess how many were built—perhaps only prototypes. In June 1921, the same model was said to have semi-elliptic rear springs replacing the quarter-elliptics, plus other mechanical improvements including electric starting. In August 1921, a Marseal two-seater was announced at the same price as the four-seater (£393) and in September, *Light Car and Cyclecar* carried an article on the forthcoming 1922 Marseel. It rather looks as if Messrs Marendaz and Seelhaft were struggling with logistics at this point as it seems pretty certain that cars were not produced in any quantity. The reason for this may have been difficulty with finding suitable premises, or perhaps even premises that were affordable, as they moved, first to 17 Hertford Street and then in quick succession to the Atlantic Works, Harefield Road, neither move obviously being conducive to smooth running. Although the car was destined at this stage to have the 10-hp Coventry Simplex engine, none were registered as such, so the delay may also have been due to late delivery of engines. Early 1922 also was the date when they were experimenting with the oil-cooled engine and the Cycle Scooter. As the first mention of Marseal was associated with the oil-cooled engine, these few months must have been when Marcus Marendaz and Charles Seelhaft parted company. *Light Car and Cyclecar* carried an article on the new 7–11 hp Marseal in April 1922 and while it is not identified by name, this must have been fitted with the 1,248-cc Coventry Simplex four-cylinder engine, the engine change one assumes necessitated by the lack of success of the oil-cooled engine and whatever difficulties were being experienced with the earlier conventional engine supply. Cars were being built and registered from July 1922 onwards; this date must qualify as the start of proper production with around 100 being built before the end of the year, nearly all with the Coventry Simplex engine, but some with a 11.9-hp Anzani of 1,496 cc. In July 1922, and for the first time, Marcus Marendaz had enough confidence and presumably cash to put a full-page advertisement for his product in the *Light Car and Cyclecar*, offering the 2-seater at a price of £215 and citing an impressive list of country-wide agents.

Model years ran from motor show to motor show, with many factories stopping major production in the summer with the works break, production from September onwards being for the upcoming year's model, ready for the October rush of orders. That Marcus Marendaz got going in July 1922 rather cuts across this way of working; he must have been trying very hard to catch up. The 1922 Motor Show was held in the October and Marcus Marendaz had a

How access is gained by a single door to both front and rear seats.

The curious door arrangement of the earliest Marseal, as planned in 1921. (*Light Car and Cyclecar*)

stand in prime position: very close to the entrance. The Show Guide listed four 1923 models, three of which were called the '7/11 hp', the two-seater at £215, four-seater £255, and a coupé at £275. Additionally, there was the '11.9 hp Sports Car' at £400, fitted with the Anzani engine. Production was modest during the model year with about 160 cars being built.

A sales brochure dated March 1923 elaborates on the 1923 models, not helped by a change in model titles, not necessarily indicating a change in specification. It noted that there were two engines fitted; the Coventry Simplex (1,247 cc; 63 mm × 100 mm; 9.8 hp) and the Anzani (1,496 cc; 69 mm × 100 mm; 11.8 hp). Of the five models advertised, there was a 9-26 two- or four-seater in Marseal blue and a 9-26 Coupé two-seater in parma violet or Marseal blue. The distinguishing feature of this model was the frameless disappearing windows. Finally, there was a Sports model, either 9-26 or 11-55 in polished aluminium or painted to order, but both with semi-elliptic front springs instead of semi-cantilever. The brochure quotes March 1923 prices but, interestingly and a reflection of the increasingly difficult times, these were hand amended downwards in October 1923. The two-seater goes from £215 down to £195, the four-seater from £255 to £235, and the Coupé from £275 to £255, the Sports models remaining unchanged at £250 and £400. This price reduction reflects the increasingly competitive market of the early 1920s and the need to sell and succeed.

Curiously, looking at the Coventry registration information (Appendix II), the highest recorded 1923 Model registration is dated May 1923, some months before the end of the model year production. There is no reason for this and it does not mean production stopped due to stockpiling; in that event, one would expect a flood of late registrations with the disposal of excess stock. It is possible that Marcus Marendaz found it more convenient to apply for 'factory' registrations elsewhere.

For the 1924 model year, Marcus Marendaz completely revised his model designations; although the cars themselves were not very different, the main technical change was the introduction of semi-elliptic springs at the front on all models. The brochures contained details of a six-cylinder model, his first; the *Autocar* noted in February 1924 'that the 14-48 hp 6-cylinder has nearly reached the end of its experimental stages'. It seems unlikely that any reached the public and details of the engine used have never been stated. *Light Car and Cyclecar* reported in November 1923 that experiments were being conducted into a clutched supercharger, mounted in front of the radiator in a large circular aluminium case, but again no further details are available.

There is a healthy list of models for 1924; this did not mean all were produced and, as was the case in many factories, it is likely that many cars did not reflect the specification on offer. As for the preceding year, the models were based on the Coventry Simplex engine (1,247 cc; 63 mm × 100 mm; 9.8 hp) and the Anzani (1,496 cc; 69 mm × 100 mm; 11.8 hp), but now dressed up as the 11/27 Model and the 12/40 Model respectively. This change was very much a retitling only, with nothing substantive involved. For some reason, the 'economy' model (or cheapest one in the list) remained there as a 9 hp, called the 9/26 hp Universal two-seater at £175. One has to suspect that these were cars from earlier production years, possibly with the 'old' cantilevered front suspension being sold off cheaply. All the other models were much as before, but with the new titles: namely the 11/27 hp Two- and Four-Seater at £197 and £227 respectively, the 11/27 Coupé at £275, and the Sports guaranteed 60 mph at £250. The Anzani models listed were the 12/40 Two-Seater and Dickey at £255, 12/40 Four-Seater at £275, and the 12/55 Sports guaranteed 75 mph. 6-cylinder cars, stated to be 1,754 cc and overhead valve, were listed as the 14/48 Two-Seater and Dickey and 14/48 Four-Seater at £325 and £350 respectively.

It is difficult to work out the names of other associates or employees at Marseal, although some are listed against cars registered to the company. One is H. Thompson, listed against what is believed to be the car fitted with the oil-cooled engine, but the entry for this car in the 1922 Six Day Trial stated the driver to be W. C. Brookes, who probably was not an employee as he is listed elsewhere as an owner. Dorothy Summers was employed in a secretarial capacity and her role in the story is covered later in Chapter 6.

The RFC Pilot's Wings as altered by Marendaz as a badge for all his cars. (*Author's collection*)

5

THE MARSEAL IN COMPETITION

I t is undoubtedly true that competition improves the breed and Marcus Marendaz, aged twenty-five, a young man with proven flying skills, must have seen this in 1922. The drawback is, of course, that one has to produce a level of success that causes improvements and sells cars. The Marseel was not an out-and-out sporting model, but it had, like many other cars of the era, sporting pretentions. There were a number of avenues, various hill-climbs, sporting trials such as the Exeter and Land's End, sprints, and, of course, Brooklands to go about this.

The first recorded sporting entry anywhere for a Marseal car was not auspicious and possibly a case of trying to run before being able to walk. The car in question was called a 7-11 hp, but unlike the other 7-11s, it had an oil-cooled engine and was entered in the Edinburgh and District Motor Club's Scottish Six Days Trial, but non-started. The engine is discussed in Chapter 4 and one can assume that development of it had not reached a point where Marendaz was confident that it would survive 1,000 miles of running. Undaunted, and again with objectives set well above projected capability, Marcus Marendaz turned to the big race at Brooklands for his next competitive sally.

At the time, Brooklands was the only proper circuit in the United Kingdom where speeds were unlimited and, as most events were run as handicaps, a Marseal nominally assessed as a less capable car could beat the handicappers and win. Based at Coventry as he was, Brooklands was not close by, but the pull of potential success in a field of serious players was sufficient to get Marcus there.

The Marseal was first seen at Brooklands in August 1922, entered in the Junior Car Club 200-mile race. This was the 'big' race of the year at Brooklands, equivalent today to the British Grand Prix, and a large field of cars with engines limited to 1,500 cc raced against each other in a handicap system. The Marseal had not previously been seen by Mr A. V. Ebblewhite, the handicapper, so was an unknown quantity—likely to be handicapped out of the money or given an easy ride, we just do not know. Once again it ended in failure, though of a more obvious kind, in that the car non-started, having been crashed by Cyril Maurice Harvey, Marcus Marendaz's chosen driver, the night before while practising. Possibly subscribing to the tenet that there is no such thing as bad publicity, and according to the Marseal advertisements, published a month later in *Light Car and Cyclecar*, the Marseal crashed at 90 mph, not a bad speed for 1,247 cc, and was unable to continue, being too badly damaged in the crash having turned over and round twice. The advertisement made a point of stressing the quality of the material used in the construction of the car and the resultant safety factor, but we are left to speculate

The brave advertisement telling of a Marseal crash. (*Marseal Motors Ltd*)

on the words used by Marcus Marendaz at the time and admire his nerve at making capital out of what anyone else would have regarded as a disaster. C. M. Harvey, writing in *Autocar* in January 1928, recalled his accidents at Brooklands:

> I have had three, the most remarkable being the occasion when practising the day before a big race I was amazed to see the flags at the pits several times within a few seconds. What actually had occurred was that the car had suddenly performed two 'flat spins' before turning completely over.

Harold Irving said that he was riding mechanic to Marcus Marendaz in the 1923 J.C.C. 200-mile race, but as Marendaz did not run in this event, as he was quick to point out, it may be that Harold was actually referring to riding with Harvey the previous year. Photographs of the cars on the track were frequently taken during events but rarely during practice, so without photographic evidence we are unlikely to find the exact truth.

Undoubtedly frustrated by earlier events at the hands of nominated drivers and two weeks after this inauspicious start, on 2 September 1922, Marcus Marendaz himself for the first time took the wheel of a car at Brooklands. The car is recorded as being in an aluminium finish but may well have been an unpainted 'Blancmange', which was Marcus Marendaz's mount for a serious season's racing the following year, 1923. 'Blancmange' was pink with cream wheels,

The Marseal 'Blancmange' in a fetching pink and cream after Marendaz won the 75 Long at the 1923 Whitsun Brooklands Meeting. He is wearing *pince-nez*, which explains the curious look of his eyes. (*Autocar*)

initially with a 1,496-cc Anzani, but later with the standard Coventry Simplex engine of 1,247 cc, each essentially representing one of the two models of Marseal available to the public.

Moving swiftly on to possibly less demanding fields of endeavour, Marendaz entered the Bath and West of England hill climb at Devizes in August 1922 where the Marseal recorded first on formula, first on time, and fastest time of the day; and a month later, on the sands of Southport two firsts and a second in the Trade and Experts Class—all very good results for someone new to the game and an undoubted fillip to his ambitions. His competitive year ended in December with an entry in the Gloucester Trial when he broke a stub axle and retired through being out of time, his disappointment no doubt being slightly mollified by a Silver Cup and First Class award to S. J. Carswell in another Marseal.

The first success for a Marseal at Brooklands came, not with Marcus Marendaz, but with his cousin Altair Kelway who gained a second place in the 1923 Easter meeting Novices' Handicap. Senior members of the Kelway family had invested in the Marseal concern and Altair, born in 1901, was close to Marcus in his various activities. 'Blancmange', driven by Marcus Marendaz, was doubly successful at the 1923 Whit Monday meeting gaining a first and a second, the first win for the marque on the track. Wins for Marcus Marendaz were not prolific, suggesting that while the cars may have been tuned they were not subjected to intense effort to improve performance and probably were entered as much to promote sales as to win silverware.

As noted, 1923 was a busy year for Marcus Marendaz on the Brooklands track, starting with the Junior Car Club Efficiency Trial in March, followed by entries for most of the main meetings, choosing to enter a number of races on each occasion. It is of interest that Dorothy Summers also ran in one race in April 1923, this being her first appearance on the track at Brooklands. Another Marseal entrant was Captain Frederick Charles Hipolyte Katon in an

Ralph Don with his brother Kaye Don in a Marseal on the 1923 Essex Winter Trial. (*Autocar*)

aluminium finished car with purple wheels—whether this was a works drive or if he was a private entrant is not clear, although we do know that, like Marendaz, he had been aircrew in the Royal Flying Corps. Although entered in the big event in October 1923, the J.C.C. 200-mile race, Marendaz non-started.

In 1923, Marseals were also seen in other competitive fields, such as the Land's End Trial, the Essex Motor Club Winter Trial (where a car was entered by Ralph Don with the rather better-known Kaye Don, his brother, as passenger), the Essex Motor Club hill climb a month later, and, once again, Southport on the sand, three firsts being gained there, two driven by Marcus Marendaz and the third by E. R. Hall (another well-known name of later years). A Farrer-Hockley gained a Gold Award in the London–Manchester trial, S. J. Carswell ran in the Manville Trophy Trial, and R. Don in the Coventry Club Goblet Cup trial. The Aston Hill Climb in May 1923 included an entry by E. R. Hall; September saw Marcus Marendaz and Dorothy Summers both running in that most famous of hill climbs, Shelsley Walsh, for the first time. We have his words, recorded in *Motor Sport* for December 1930:

In 1923 at Shelsley Walsh when after weeks of hard work and contriving a single-seater chassis, weighing hundredweights less than standard, graced with a body weighing but a few pounds, was ready for the great day. As the flag dropped the car shot forward and it was evident during the first 100 yards that she liked the hill well. In my endeavour to get full throttle after changing down at the first bend by the well-accepted method of getting your back hard against the rear squab and your foot hard down on the accelerator, the fairy-like wisp of plywood serving as a rear squab decided to divide in twain. I think it will generally be conceded that this is likely to put one off one's stroke, and although the result was considerable loss of speed there was fortunately no loss of control and the car clocked 55 1/5th seconds in spite of this grave handicap.

A Marseal in the 1923 Coventry Club Goblet Cup Trial. This is not Marendaz driving. (*Autocar*)

Marcus Marendaz driving in the 1924 Small Car Trial. (*Autocar*)

The year 1924 saw a tempering in the competitive activities of Marcus Marendaz, with no obvious reason other than the presumption that his skills would be better served making and selling cars rather than running around Brooklands and elsewhere. The previous year had seen reasonable success, such that his racing pedigree was now established, but 1924 saw no appearances by him. However, Captain Katon with his grey and royal purple Anzani-powered Marseal did his bit entering the Easter Monday meeting in April and the important J.C.C. 200-mile race in September. On that occasion, his Marseal got off the start line but was soon back in the pits with an elusive carburation problem, running many laps to the bad.

An entry in the RAC Small Car Trial in April 1924 produced no rewards for Marendaz, having retired at Brecon on the second day, but the draw of the sands at Southport, scene of previous success, meant that he competed there at least twice in 1924, picking up two first and two thirds in August and a third in September. Other triallists were J. A. Wathes who ran his Marseal in the Victory Cup Trial in March in the Midlands and the Surbiton and District Motor Club's Mellano Cup Trial featured a Marseal Coupé, probably driven by Marcus Marendaz.

So, 1924 was not a startlingly competitive year for Marcus Marendaz but it would appear that greater things were afoot—a removal to London and the birth of a new marque, the Marendaz Special.

6

THE MOVE TO LONDON

On a personal level, the story of Marcus Marendaz was left in Chapter 3 at a point where he was married with a family living in Coventry, developing his Marseal cars, and competing in them when the opportunity arose and achieving some success.

Putting a bit more flesh on these facts, his address in 1921 was a small Victorian terrace house—46 Northumberland Road, not far from the Alvis works and a short drive from his later works in Harefield Road. His wife Dorothy bore him three daughters all in Coventry: Mifanwy D. in the summer of 1919, Brenda Cynthia early in 1921, and Diana M. K. late in 1922. Yet in spite of this, it would appear that all was not well with his marriage.

At this point, Dorothy Olive Summers should be introduced to the story. Born in 1900, she was taken on as a secretary to Marcus Marendaz at his works in Harefield Road and before long was contributing to the business. A number of cars were registered in her name, the first dating to December 1922, presumably as works vehicles or pending sale to a customer and she also featured in publicity photographs of the Marseal cars. Yet it was more than that and she was the cause of the break-up of Marcus Marendaz's marriage. With the attraction of the sporting scene at Brooklands and the dropping off of Marseal sales, Marendaz undoubtedly decided that a move to London would open up new doors for him. His racing in 1924 was curtailed as business pressures to sell the cars he had produced and develop new models that had better prospects took precedence with his time. There may also have been domestic pressures to spend more time in Coventry rather than gallivanting at Brooklands. However, like for so many other companies, the writing was on the wall and the end of Marseal cars was nigh, the last cars being registered in Coventry in September 1924 with demise not far behind. A move to London followed with employment in the Stock Exchange, but this was not to last, as undoubtedly engineering was in his blood and 1925 saw Marcus Marendaz back racing at Brooklands again but this time in a car bearing his own name.

Dorothy Summers also made the move and she remained with him until the war years. It seems unlikely that his wife and family moved to London as well and certainly Dorothy Marendaz (*née* Evans) had an address in 1940 in South Wales, so she and the daughters probably returned to their roots there in the mid-1920s. There was no question of a divorce as Dorothy Marendaz was a practising Roman Catholic and divorce was not to be countenanced.

Apart from his time at Brooklands, both with the Royal Flying Corps and motor racing exploits with Marseal cars, Marcus Marendaz does not seem to have had any previous strong

Brixton Garage in 1925, with the Marendaz works at the rear on the right, the white sign declaring D. M. K. Marendaz Ltd Engineers. (*Pistonheads*)

connection with the capital. Putting a little more detail on the setting up of the new business, *Lost Causes of Motoring*, largely compiled by Michael Sedgwick, states that Marendaz 'after a brief period on the Stock Exchange, took premises in 1926 in the London General Cab Company's garage at the Camberwell end of the Brixton Road'. Whereas previously he had manufactured cars, he was now involved in selling new and second-hand cars as well as repairs and tuning, trading under the title D. M. K. Marendaz Ltd at 1 and 3 Brixton Road. Advertising material says that the company were proprietors of the Brixton Garage, South London's largest garage, and, of course, manufacturers of Marendaz Special cars. In fact, his premises were established by July 1925, so it is not entirely clear where the first Marendaz Special car might have been built, given that it appeared at Brooklands on Easter Monday, April 1925.

The London premises were, or rather are as they still exist, interesting in their own right. The whole site was owned by Brixton Estate Limited, with the three-storey buildings erected in 1909 giving accommodation for 1,500 vehicles on all floors by way of outside ramps and was an early example of reinforced concrete construction. Its principal use was as the home of the London black taxis with the General Motor Cab Company but additionally it was used to house other motoring related activities. A grand opening of Brixton Garage took place in July 1925, it being claimed to be the largest and most up-to-date petrol service station in the country and, typical of the times, sold a range of different fuel brands.

Marcus Marendaz was on the first floor, one level up from the ground. Curiously, although they were present, Bugatti on the ground floor are not listed in *Kelly's Directory*, so possibly they were sub-leasees, in a business run by Captain W. L. Sorel, DSO, where chassis delivered from Molsheim were built up. Bob Bass, who worked there from 1926 until the war was interviewed by Bill Boddy (*Motor Sport*, January 1986). He had a few comments on the Marendaz cars noting that they were attractive but not very saleable. The garage at road level was effectively inset in a U-shaped set of tall brick buildings, with, on the right as you faced it, ramps running down to a lower ground level and upwards to the first-floor level. At the top of the first-floor level ramp was a bridge structure in steel over the lower roadways and the Marendaz works was located at the right-hand end of the building facing you. A further car-bearing ramp continued up the side of the building to a second-floor level. The layout seems slightly bizarre at first glance but given that the building was built to accommodate cars on all levels, it worked perfectly well, it would appear. It was a big site with numerous small businesses, motor engineers, insurance, a wireless manufacturer, two electric lamp manufacturers, a business dealing in hydraulic hoists, and a coffee blending firm. A name that springs out to the motoring enthusiast is Atalanta Ltd, Engineers, but this is unlikely have any connection with the later Atalanta Motors of Staines. However, they were interesting as a company run and staffed completely by women, with about twenty employees, no doubt a hangover from the Great War, but providing a high-quality service supplying the aircraft industry.

In an interview by Wesley Tee for *Motor Sport* in 1930, it was noted that the premises of D. M. K. Marendaz Ltd contained an Avery connecting rod specific-gravity balancer, crankshaft dynamic balancer, Heenan and Froude dynamometer, and an Avery tensile testing machine, while the manufacturing of camshafts, gear cutting was considered possible. One has to wonder how a dynamometer fared on an upper floor given that a large throughput of water was necessary for this sort of machine. If this was the same dynamometer that Marcus Marendaz later moved to Maidenhead, it certainly used lots of water, as noted in Chapter 9. We can now turn to the emergence of a new marque, the Marendaz Special.

The Marendaz works in Brixton Road, seen in more recent times. The door on the right used to be a window. (*Author's collection*)

7

LONDON IN THE TWENTIES

At the time of writing (2017), it is ninety years since the events described took place. Some thirty years ago, I met a few of the people involved in them, but today we have to rely on the written word or second-hand information. When you combine that with D. M. K. Marendaz's reluctance to share information, unless it was under his control, the parlous state of the motor manufacturing industry in the late 1920s, and the paucity of factual information, the task was not easy.

THE FIRST MARENDAZ SPECIAL CAR

When he moved to London, it was undoubtedly Marcus Marendaz's intent to build cars from the off, but the very first car to bear the name and as it appeared at Brooklands at the Easter Monday Meeting on 13 April 1925 is an enigma. In all senses, this car has to be regarded as a transition vehicle. Records regarding its use on the road have not surfaced so far, the only photographs of it are on the track at Brooklands and none are close enough to provide any useful detail. Having said that, the car is an open four-seater, powered almost certainly by a 1,496-cc Anzani four-cylinder engine, with a flat fronted radiator which is probably Marseal. The seats are reached by two doors on the left-hand side, the rear one positioned in a way that would appear to make reaching the generous rear seats difficult. Marcus Marendaz used this car on the track at Brooklands throughout 1925, but it would appear that the design was not sporting enough and a return to the drawing boards produced a very dissimilar second car. Where this first car was built is not known as it probably predates Marcus Marendaz's acquisition of the Brixton Road premises.

One wonders slightly about titling the marque Marendaz Special as more usually the marque might have been called Marendaz and then the racing versions or track cars 'Specials'. There may be a reason as in 1925 the Junior Car Club insisted that every entrant at Brooklands be referred to as a 'Xxxxxx Special' to avoid manufacturers claiming that cars they sold, only called 'Xxxxxxx' were the same as those seen on the track. One has to conclude that Marcus Marendaz's riposte to this was to say that 'every car I sell is a Special', by so naming his marque. Anyway, although he was not selling his own cars at this point, a Marendaz Special, named as such, took to the Brooklands track in 1925, winning its first race with Marcus Marendaz driving.

The very first Marendaz Special. Unlike every other, it was a big four-seater. (*Autocar*)

THE SECOND MARENDAZ SPECIAL CAR (UC3933)

This car is equally unique in the panoply of the marque and has to be regarded as another development prototype. Unlike the mysterious first car, the second car is now the sole vintage survivor of the marque, but at least it exists and allows us to examine it forensically regarding its provenance. One would normally expect its pedigree to show, in that many Marseal components might be found, but as no Marseal survivors exist, this aspect also has to be guesswork to some extent.

Starting with the engine, this is a completely standard 1,496-cc 4-cylinder Anzani, bearing their engine number MC4166 and two other numbers 5A and 6A, 5A being both the recorded chassis number and engine number for the car, plus a 1924 casting date. For a car first run in 1926, this date seems early and probably confirms the fact that Marendaz bought up the engines intended to be sold by Anzani to A. C. who later cancelled. The Marendaz installation uses a four-point pickup which was not regarded as being satisfactory by other manufacturers as chassis twist loads could be transferred to the crankcase; the surviving Marendaz engine shows signs of this problem.

The gearbox (three and reverse) is almost certainly Marseal, and as described in the chapter on Marseal, probably also Emscote, being part of the cancelled order that got Marcus Marendaz started as a car manufacturer. It seems very likely that the torque tube and back axle are also Marseal units.

The radiator on this car was the very first of the Bentley-style items and also almost certainly this and later cars were the source of the rumours that Bentley were about to produce a baby-Bentley. The car is small and when parked next to a Bentley 3-litre looks tiny.

With regard to the radiator, built by Delaney, therein lies a tale. When the author discussed this radiator with Tom Delaney, a youngster in the works in the 1920s, he said Marendaz asked his father, Terry Delaney, to build a small Bentley radiator. Well, Delaney senior realised that this might not please Bentleys, but went ahead, business being business. W. O. Bentley, unsurprisingly, did object and threatened to take Marendaz to court, but in the end, he took no action as, in the almost certain event of winning his case, he regarded it as unlikely that Marendaz would be able to pay damages and anyway the cars were only being produced in very small numbers.

The running gear with fifty-two Rudge-Whitworth hubs and racing-style (outer-laced) wire wheels are dissimilar to Marseal but were standard for all production Marendaz Specials through until 1936. The brakes are rod-operated with an arrangement dissimilar to both Marseal and all later Marendaz Specials that use Lockheed hydraulics. The design of the arrangement is extremely poor with geometry leading to brake application on one side with front wheel deflection. The car has 10-inch brake drums, all later cars having 12-inch drums. The rear drums contain a single pair of shoes but are broad, such that a secondary brake system could have been fitted; this probably means that the axle and drums can be dated to a period when double shoes and rear-wheel-only brakes were the norm. The front axle is cast with forked ends—an old-fashioned arrangement common to all the 1920s Marendaz Specials.

The doorless body was undoubtedly a special design, but interestingly was built in accordance with the provisions of the 1926 Automobile World Championship and Grand Prix regulations that stipulated a minimum body width of 80 cm (31.5 inches). The chassis is also narrow to accommodate this dimension. Although riding mechanics were banned for racing, the cars had to have a second seat, but for this Marendaz Special the two seats are not staggered as in an Amilcar but probably should have been.

Marcus Marendaz in the second Marendaz Special, the 9/20 record-breaking car, outside the works, probably around February 1928 before going to Montlhéry. (*Autocar*)

The bonnet louvres are dissimilar left to right and the rear Hartford shock absorbers are not symmetrically mounted, both these attributes being indicative of hasty preparation for track use. The car was raced at Brooklands between the spring of 1926 and 1929 and used for record breaking at both Brooklands and Montlhéry as described in the chapter on competition.

In summary, the car does not display many forward-looking or innovative features but seems to have been produced in a hurry using available or proprietary parts specifically for track work.

PRODUCTION ANZANI-ENGINED CARS

A small number of Anzani-powered Marendaz Special cars were produced between 1927 and 1930. As one might expect, a range of models were offered but the cars actually built seem to have all been 1,496-cc Anzani four-cylinder powered, two, three, or four seaters with minor body style differences. In keeping with Marendaz's style, all were pretty looking.

Running through the formally published sales information, the impression given was of a progressive company building sporting cars in some numbers, but this was not actually so and one concludes that the variations in models offered were mainly to test the water or to cast the net wider in an effort to collect business. Undoubtedly, the overhaul and tuning work kept the business functioning and car manufacturing was probably secondary. The mechanical specification of the cars actually built seems not to have varied much.

Particulars published in *Light Car and Cyclecar* for the 1926 Models (2 October 1925), in other words before the first appearance of the second 'prototype' Marendaz Special, specify a 12-40 Model, this not being a model title used thereafter, although like all the others it was almost certainly fitted with the Anzani engine. For the 1927 cars, we are probably on slightly firmer ground (*Light Car and Cyclecar*, 15 October 1926 and *Motor*, 1 March 1927) as two main models are offered: the 11-55 and the 9-90, the former being essentially the model name for

Marcus Marendaz, scowling for the camera, in an Anzani-powered Marendaz Special on the banking at Brooklands, around 1927. (*Author's collection*)

all the cars actually built. The published specifications vary slightly, but the cars had a cone clutch and either three- or four-speed gearboxes. The three-speed box was almost certainly a Marseal box, similar to that fitted to the second car, but probably not used for any of the later cars. The four-speed box was of Marendaz design and construction and was used right through to the mid-1930s Maidenhead cars. Curiously, no mention is made of the Lockheed hydraulic-braking system, which was standard for these cars and had dual master cylinders.

The Model 9-90 used a 1,093-cc engine, the 1,496-cc Anzani being linered down to a bore of 59 mm. It was on offer for 1927 and 1928, but no production cars to this specification are known. The second car, UC3933, while being very non-standard in other respects, did run at various times with this engine, both normally aspirated and supercharged by Cozette, vertically mounted in place of the dynamo and driven off the crankshaft. One has to say that a 9-hp Marendaz Special was unlikely to appeal to a sporting public unless supercharged.

Additionally, to the 11-55 and 9-90, and featured in almost all of the publicity material, an ephemeral 11-120 Model was offered with overhead valve and overhead camshaft, dry sump lubrication and a supercharger, but again there are no cars known to have been built to this specification, neither is it clear how the overhead valve arrangements or supercharging were to be achieved. Marcus Marendaz may have had a design of his own on the drawing board, but it is more likely he was planning to buy a proprietary item.

By 1929, the 9-90 had been dropped, leaving the 11-55 essentially alone, but with the 11-120 still listed, plus a new development: the 14-55, having a 1,495-cc, eight-cylinder supercharged engine of Marendaz design. In all of Marcus Marendaz's activities, he advertised his car engines as being of his own design, although they were invariably modified versions of proprietary products, with one exception, this straight eight. The sole photograph of this engine appears in the 1930 catalogue, where a bare, sumpless block can be seen. It has been stated by various authors that the arrival in a company of an eight-cylinder model presaged the company's demise, but in Marendaz's case, this was not so as no car is believed to have been built or sold with this engine and it is not known if it even ran. Nevertheless, it was advertised in the listings until 1931 and did not cause the downfall of the company. *Motor Sport* for August 1930 gives further insight into it:

> The straight eight Marendaz Special, some of which were just being assembled, have some very interesting features. The cylinder head for instance, has the valves arranged on the inlet-over-exhaust principle, but in place of the usual method they are not directly superimposed, but at opposite ends of the head, thus giving a gas flow right across the head, with improved scavenging.

I leave the reader to interpret this statement. One straight eight in the Marendaz works that did run was the record-breaking Miller once used by E. A. D. Eldridge and this car is discussed in more detail shortly.

Passing over the publicity material, what can one divine from the information on the ground, namely the cars that were built that we know about? In very bald terms, at the time of writing, there are six recorded registrations for Anzani-powered Marendaz Specials, for which only two chassis numbers are known. The sales leaflets and advertising show photographs of various car that can be identified, either by registration or by physical characteristics, such that there is a fair degree of certainty that there are not any photographs of an 'unknown' car. Then there are a very few photographs or records of cars with owners, remote from the Marendaz organisation. Running through their early history, we have:

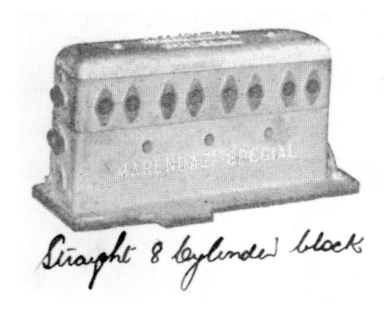

Straight 8 cylinder block

UC3933: Chassis number FS5A. The second Marendaz Special built to a racing specification and used at Brooklands 1926–1928 before being road registered for a visit to Montlhéry for record breaking. Returned and used at Brooklands until 1929.

YH6538: Reported by *Autocar* 11 February 1927 as having been supplied to Mr Frank Allen, of Duke Street, London, who intends using it for racing at Brooklands. The elegant low-tailed body was built by H. G. Davis of 6 Worcester Yard, Charles Street, Barnsbury, London N7. Marcus Marendaz handwrote a comment on a copy of this *Autocar* note saying, 'One of the very few bodies not built by me—nevertheless designed by me'. Whatever transpired with Mr Allen is not known, but the car was first registered in May 1927 and used by Marendaz as a works car at Brooklands, Shelsley Walsh and undoubtedly elsewhere between September 1927 and 1930.

YT1378: First registered June 1927 and used at Brooklands from around September 1927 and for the 1928 publicity material.

EC9183: First registered 14 April 1928. A dark painted two seater sold to W. B. Wakefield in Cumbria. Later owned by H. G. Webb in 1930 when painted white and probably the car photographed at Brough in 1931.

YW6480: First registered 13 June 1928 to L. L. Hanks. Chassis number FS19. Used for record breaking at Montlhéry in November 1928 and also featured in the 1930 Sales Catalogue.

GC5800: First Registered February 1930. Probably the car used in chassis form for advertising, see *Autocar,* 20 June 1930.

There has never been any comment by Marcus Marendaz about the number of cars he actually built in London. The information above seems very thin indeed to support an argument that around one car a month was being achieved, the production rate later on at Maidenhead. February 1927 to February 1930 is thirty-six months, but there is no sign of thirty-six cars. So, were there lots of other ones out there that we do not know about? The answer has to be 'some', but what happened to them?

TAX £12.

The 11/55 H.P. MARENDAZ SPECIAL.   Standard 2 seater.   Fully stream lined, under trays enclosing and protecting from mud all parts.   Tank may be in rear or dash to choice.   Trimmed antique leather.   Any other type wings fitted, no extra. Painted any colour to choice.   Top speed performance, 7 to 100 m.p.h. stripped.   7 to 90-95m.p.h. in full trim.   Any type of 2/3 seater bodywork supplied to customers design: usually no extra.   Concealed Dickey in above model £10 extra.

A stylish Marendaz Special two-seater with oyster wings. (*Author's collection*)

A Marendaz Special rolling chassis outside the works before bodying. Note the white steering wheel and duplicated Lockheed master cylinders. (*W. Boddy*)

Interviewing Fred Atkinson in 1985 has provided the only 'background colour' of the life at Marendaz Limited in the 1920s. Fred said that the cars were generally assembled from stock parts, rather than built from scratch—in fact not very different from many other manufacturers of the day. Marcus Marendaz did not have a stand at the motor shows as he had fallen out with the Motor Agents Association but did have a display elsewhere in motor show week usually at the Olympia Motor Company, 3 Hammersmith Road. Some cars were sold in Spain and one wonders if the Iberian name, albeit Portuguese, helped. An agent took the cars there and sold them, with the brief to collect the money to be remitted to Marendaz less expenses, but of course, needless to say, this resulted in rows. As ever, money was short and on one occasion Fred said there were no wages for two or three weeks. As we know, Dorothy Summers, Miss Summers to the staff, was also in evidence and as Fred put it 'God's gift to man'. She was part of the Brooklands scene where anyone who was anyone was to be seen, all in their best finery, but whether at this stage as was the case later on, she passed as Mrs Marendaz we do not know. She was entered in various races at Brooklands in a works car, but always as D. O. Summers. Marcus Marendaz was a ladies' man and very popular with them. Fred was there at the time of the outings to Montlhéry for record breaking but stayed in London. The Marendaz Special engines used for racing were assembled to about 1,000 miles wear, so that seizure would be averted and they did not require running in after overhaul. Marendaz did obtain a Bentley engine, presumably a 3-litre, at this time bought cheaply after the fire at the Bentley works and tried it in a Marendaz chassis, but it would not fit without moving the bulkhead. All the mechanical parts on the racing cars, such as drop arms and stub axles, were emeried until bright and then varnished, so that if a crack appeared it would show up having picked up oil. Underpans at this time were nearly banned at Brooklands as they kept falling off—the second car, UC3933, ran there with an underpan—but today, it is impossible to decide how it might have been attached, which may well make the point. Fred never worked on a supercharged engine with Marendaz, although there was a lot of talk about it. The Miller car, regarded as 'that old thing', was in the works at the time Fred was there. Kaye Don, who drove it, had no mercy on machinery. The cars went down to Brooklands on trade plates.

So, some cars went to Spain, but it still leaves a bit of a gap between cars known about and suggested production. The late Michael Sedgwick agreed that around thirty cars were built, so whatever way you look at it, there is a shortage of information. One other clue is that the 13/70 cars built from 1931 onwards started with chassis numbers around thirty, so that might have

been a continuation from the earlier cars. An alternative solution to this quandary might be that during the 1920s car production was not in line with publicity and the impression created outside and that actually only a handful were ever built, with convenient gaps in the chassis numbers. While we have not enough knowledge of the chassis numbers to make a judgement on this, we do know that in the 1930s Marcus Marendaz did use every fourth number for the 15/90 chassis.

As stated earlier, there is no absolute evidence for the mechanical specification for the Anzani cars, but in 1930, a set of photographs were taken of a rolling chassis outside the works entrance. This shows a car that looks remarkably like the later 13/70s. The Marendaz gearbox with the ball mounting is well in evidence, as is the tubular chassis member towards the rear. Two Lockheed master cylinders can be seen for the split braking system—the later 13/70s used a single system. The trademark white steering wheel is in evidence as is the instrument panel Castrol badge proclaiming 'D. M. K. Marendaz, 1 & 3 Brixton Road'.

THE WORKS MILLER

During the late 1920s, there was a Miller racing car to be seen inside the Marendaz works. Exactly where it came from, who owned it, and what its role in life might have been is unclear, but it stayed with Marcus Marendaz, essentially gathering dust in his works, right through until 1936. It was a supercharged Miller 122 (2-litre) brought over to Europe by E. A. D. Eldridge, the American race formula having changed from 122- to 91-cubic inches (1.5-litre) capacity. Eldridge used it at Montlhéry for record breaking in both 2-litre and 1.5-litre (destroked) form, but was badly injured in a crash in 1927, losing the sight of one eye, the crash being caused by a joint in the fabricated front axle giving way. He brought the car back to England, but by April 1928, the engine of the car was in a Vulcan-made Lea Francis 14/40 in the hands of Kaye Don and later Harold Purdy. By July 1928, the engine had been restored to the Miller chassis, Eldridge still being the owner of the car and with Harold Purdy driving, further record attempts were planned. By 1930, the car was in the D. M. K. Marendaz works, possibly owned by Kaye Don, who was a friend of Marendaz, in a stripped condition. Around this time, as well as hints regarding the Marendaz straight eight engine, there were rumours of a Marendaz-Miller car or possibly a Miller-Marendaz. What combination of either element was planned is not known but it seems unlikely that the magnificent supercharged Miller engine would be replaced by the development Marendaz eight cylinder and the photographs taken in the works show essentially the Miller fitted with a new sloping radiator and a Marendaz front axle. Now while the Miller front axle had been shown to be weak, the old-fashioned cast Marendaz axle with forked ends was no substitute. The car in this form was never completed and taken on the road but it was removed with Marcus Marendaz to Maidenhead in 1932, where it continued to gather dust, un-run, a monument to the magnificent works of Harry Miller.

MARCUS MARENDAZ IN THE 1920S

He was twenty-eight years old when he moved to London and with his works at the Camberwell end of the Brixton Road but living at 12 Westmoreland Road near Camberwell in what is now SE17 and a few minutes' walk from the business.

Inside the Brixton Road works with the Miller foreground. It did not appear on the track with this very sloping radiator. (*W. Boddy*)

Fred Atkinson who worked for Marcus Marendaz at this time, as noted above, first met him at the Grove Garage, Westbourne Grove, and was employed to keep the various car running, rather than on the work of building cars. He considered his boss as being quite a linguist, but that he was also 'an awkward sod and a bit of a devil'. He reckoned that he got on with him quite well with a good working partnership. There are several other names of employees known from this period, P. F. L. Lawson, an engine builder, who came down from Coventry with Marendaz, J. Vennings, and Mr Bailey in the London showroom at Westminster Bridge Garage Ltd, 5 Lambeth Palace Road as noted by *Autocar* 30 October 1931.

MARENDAZ AND THE GRAHAM-PAIGE

In 1929, as well as running Marendaz Special cars at Brooklands, Marcus Marendaz formed an alliance with the American Graham-Paige company, whose London premises were in the same building as Marendaz at 1–3 Brixton Road; they may have seen the opportunity to use the experience of an organisation well versed in turning and racing to obtain some publicity. Graham-Paige was the manufacturer of large engine capacity cars, many thousands having been sold in the United States. An expansion of their activities into the United Kingdom seems strange given the restrictive horsepower-based taxation system, but one supposes that in view of the quantities of up-market Rolls-Royces around, they must have decided there was a market for their products. It is not known how many cars they sold, or whether the cars arrived complete from the US or were bodied by English bodybuilders. Marcus Marendaz's involvement with Graham-Paige was centred on racing and record breaking and is covered in the next chapter.

BACK TO FLYING

Marcus Marendaz, along with everyone else, was struggling to make a living during the depression of the late 1920s and, having diversified with American Graham-Paige cars, turned once again to his flying experience and background. He had, of course, flown during the Great War and obtained his Royal Flying Corps wings, probably not something that would stand him in great stead in 1929 but enough to show that he was competent and knowledgeable about the art. Having forsaken it at the end of the Great War and having turned to motoring both as a manufacturer and a competitor, he must at a later date have felt some yearnings to be involved in flying again. His advertising from around 1929 onwards in both the aeronautical and motoring press refers to aircraft as well as cars, for example in *Motor Sport* for October 1930, Marendaz uses the phrase 'Aeroplanes and Engines Bought, Sold, Repaired and Tuned'. Editorial material a month earlier refers to D. M. K. Marendaz Ltd as being the first motor agents in the country to supply a D.H. Moth and that they were now using a D.H. Cirrus Moth for business purposes. On offer was the arrangement whereby a customer in any part of the country requiring to exchange his old car or aeroplane or wishing his car or aeroplane repaired or tuned could be visited by aeroplane at his nearest aerodrome. With the advent of the economical two-seater Moth in the late twenties, private flying by owner pilots 'took off' and this announcement by Marcus Marendaz illustrates very neatly typical entrepreneurship of the period.

The aircraft that Marcus Marendaz obtained at this time was a D.H. Moth, G-EBOT, powered by a Cirrus 1 engine, first registered in July 1926, and painted silver and brown. It was sold by the

G-EBOT, the DH.60 Moth used by D. M. K. Marendaz, seen here before the name was written in large letters on the fuselage. (*A. J. Jackson collection*)

then owner Lionel Hill (whose adventures in this Moth are told in *Flypast* magazine for February 1988) at the end of 1929 to Marcus Marendaz, the aircraft being based at Woodley and probably used on loan by the Reading Aero Club. This is where later on Charles Powis and the Miles brothers were to build the Miles family of aircraft and it is quite possible that this association with Berkshire by Marcus Marendaz was to influence his decision to move to Maidenhead some years later. The Moth G-EBOT was entered in the King's Cup air race, scheduled for 5 July 1930, possibly to be flown by Marcus Marendaz, although the demands of a 753-mile flight going as far north as Newcastle may well have been beyond his capabilities at that date. In the event, W. H. Sutcliffe, an instructor at the Midland Aero Club flew the aircraft which, due to its limited performance, was first off in this handicap race. Fog and tappet trouble slowed him on the leg to Bristol overflying Hamble, but he was still in the lead at the second stop at Manchester. *Flight* notes that he failed to round a turning point, so either retired or was disqualified before reaching Newcastle. One cannot help but believe that Marcus Marendaz made much of his aircraft leading at Manchester, although with a handicap system this was more than likely.

Around the same time, in August 1930, *Flight* magazine announced that D. M. K. Marendaz Ltd had been experimenting with a car exhaust silencer for his Moth, as entered in the King's Cup Air Race. Aircraft noise was a public concern as far back as the mid-1920s with stringent controls in place at airfields such as Brooklands. The unit he was using was a Vortex Silencer, where the inertia of the gases was being used to create vortices and better mixing, which reduced the noise, noting that Major F. B. Halford, designer of the Cirrus and Gipsy engines was on the board of Vortex Silencers Ltd.

As noted above, W. H. Sutcliffe flew the Marendaz Moth in the King's Cup Air Race, possibly as a substitute for the owner. This may well have been because Marcus Marendaz was unable to fly as a cryptic note in *Light Car and Cyclecar* notes. 'Readers will learn with regret that Mr D. M. K. Marendaz, the designer of the 1½ litre cars of that name and holder of many records, met with a bad accident on May 1 (1930). We hear that he is progressing favourably'. Also, *Motor Sport* for August 1930 noted:

> D. M. K. Marendaz, who, as many of our readers will remember, had a nasty accident some time ago with a flywheel coming adrift, is now well on the way to becoming fit again, I am glad to say, and we shall probably see him out for some more records soon.

This serious accident put an immediate end to his season's racing at Brooklands. It happened on 1 May, which being a Thursday meant it was not a race accident. As his medical record stated in October 1940 that he had received a compound fracture of tibia and fibula around this time, we can almost certainly assume that this was the result of a flywheel coming adrift. Further details of this unfortunate accident have still to be revealed, but undoubtedly the inevitable period of convalescence will have provided Marcus Marendaz with time to ponder. The Moth was sold in May 1931 and did not survive the year as it was written off in a fatal crash in Essex, near Broxbourne, on 13 December 1931. Lionel Hill, the owner before Marcus Marendaz, wrote that Marendaz was flying G-EBOT at the time of the accident, but this is not correct.

Marcus Marendaz was in the wars in 1930, but it was not the first time. Somewhat earlier in his Brixton Road career, he was involved in an industrial accident in the works, probably involving a lathe, causing the loss of his right forefinger. The photograph taken somewhat later of him sitting in the second Marendaz Special outside the works clearly shows this. Then again, just before he started his reenergised flying career, he was involved in a fatal road accident on the Kingston Bypass on the 30 November 1929, involving a car being driven by a Mr Brown, whose car was apparently hit while crossing the Kingston Bypass at Woodstock Lane, Thames Ditton. Mr Brown's wife was awarded damages of £1,850 the following year against Marendaz and D. M. K. Marendaz Ltd due to negligent driving, an amount worth around £100,000 today.

By late 1931, Marcus Marendaz had other plans afoot. During the depression in the late 1920s, he had obviously tried every avenue to expand his business, by racing success, alliance with the Graham-Paige concern, and aviation, but it was to his original success—car manufacturing—that he returned.

Inside the Brixton Road works with the Miller in the centre flanked by Marendaz Specials. (*W. Boddy*)

8

MARENDAZ SPECIAL IN COMPETITION IN THE 1920s

The debut of a Marendaz Special at Brooklands with its creator driving was at the Easter 1925 meeting in the 32nd 75 Short Handicap, and it turned out to be a winning combination. It is always a moot point whether the handicapper was being kind or got it wrong, but it must have pleased Marendaz. He ran at a number of meetings as the year progressed, but his best placing over the remainder of the year was a third in June. For the entire season his mount was believed to be this first Marendaz Special of uncertain provenance with its large four-seater body, the opposition generally being more sporting. While a first at Brooklands was not to be sneezed at, his endeavours in 1925 centred on sand racing at Southport and Skegness, plus winning the Braid Challenge Cup at the Colwyn Bay speed trials. At the Littlehampton Speed Trials, he recorded two second places. On the sand at Skegness, he had two firsts but was disqualified for both as not being eligible for the class but did pick up a second and three thirds. At Southport, over two meetings, he recorded five firsts, two seconds, and six thirds. *Autocar* recorded at the 12 September 1925 meeting that Marendaz 'pulled up with nasty engine noises and eventually had to be towed away'.

When the 1926 Brooklands season started early in April, Marcus Marendaz non-started probably because his 'new' car was not ready, but it is believed that it did appear at the Surbiton Motor Club meeting later in the month and in subsequent meetings through until the J.C.C. 200-mile event in September. He seemed at this stage in his sporting career to run a single car during a season and for 1926, it appears to have been the car later registered as UC3933, the first car with the Bentley style radiator. Looking at the car today and as noted in Chapter 7, there are a number of features that suggest the car was put together in a hurry, such as the asymmetric rear shock absorbers and dissimilar bonnet louvers, and the front rod brake arrangement is badly designed, but that was the way the car remained throughout its racing career over several years. Total success was not Marendaz's reward during the year, but he did come home with two seconds and a third. As recorded by Bill Boddy, Marendaz at the autumn meeting came to the start line, stopping very close to E. A. A. Stone in his A.C. who warned him that his car was likely to skip sideways slightly on getting away. He was ignored by Marendaz and, of course, the inevitable happened the A.C. rear hub hitting the Marendaz Special's front hub, the A.C. going on and a furious Marendaz returning to the paddock, scratching further entries for the day. Stone received a bill, which remained unpaid, for damage to his rival's axle and for wasted entry fees.

"GREAT BRITAIN'S OWN SPORTS CAR"

A GROUP OF MARENDAZ SPECIAL CARS WITH SOME OF THE TROPHIES WON BY THESE FAMOUS CARS AND THEIR DESIGNER.

A very respectable array of silverware won by Marendaz Specials cars at Brooklands and elsewhere. (*Author's collection*)

The big race of the 1926 season was the British Grand Prix, but there was no Marendaz Special entry. However, he did enter the J.C.C. 200-mile race which attracted as usual a large number of cars. The *Autocar* of 24 September 1926 noted:

The Marendaz, which by the way, has a very neat looking radiator and has been running at Brooklands a good deal this season, has a four-cylinder Anzani engine and should be fast, but it is not, of course, a machine specially designed and built for racing purposes, as are some of its rivals.

On this occasion, a broken oil pipe put him out.

A Marendaz Special ran at Shelsley Walsh in September 1926, but it is not known which car was involved. It seems likely that sand racing at Southport and speed trials at Colwyn Bay were also on Marendaz's agenda for 1926, and Fred Atkinson had the stories which refer to either 1925 or 1926, he could not quite remember which:

There was a lot of sand racing and promenade speed trials at that time. I remember one where the car had a two-gallon petrol tin under the front scuttle which was fine for racing but not for the long journey getting there. We caught up this old Sentinel steam lorry going real slow and Marendaz couldn't get past, but eventually did with a lot of arm waving and swearing in his foghorn voice. Just after that we ran out of fuel and the big gorilla of a lorry driver caught us up and stopped and got out and gave Marendaz an earful in return. At Colwyn Bay the car lost fourth gear and he ran the race in third which melted the piston ring lands. Before we could drive home I had to strip the engine and refile the grooves by hand, such that by the time I'd finished my knuckles were all bloody. That night in the hotel I bled all over the sheets and had to turn them round and make a discreet departure in

Pat Densham driving in the 1928 J. C. C. 200-mile race. He was unplaced. This is the car registered as UC3933. (*Brooklands Society*)

the morning. Marendaz always stayed in the best hotels. Another time the car kept oiling and I was sent off to buy trouser buttons to put in the ignition leads to give a hotter spark.

The year 1927 for Marcus Marendaz was a case of more of the same, although his attendances at Brooklands were more spasmodic, possibly due to actually having to build some cars, several being registered in the year. The best he could manage was a fourth and first in the 1,500-cc class in the 150-mile fuel consumption race in September when he was driving a new car YH6538, distinguishable by its low-set tail and larger drum brakes. This car was entered in the J.C.C. 200, *Autocar* noting that his engine had failed him. It was also entered at Shelsley Walsh where *Light Car and Cyclecar* reported him 'coming round the corner in a wide skid'. Curiously, Marendaz was entered in the French Grand Prix at Boulogne, but non-started, his pit board with the name being the only evidence on the day.

Brooklands in the autumn was the season for record breaking, after the last race event and before the track closed for winter repairs, so as recorded in a letter to the author, 'at the suggestion of Mr A. V. Ebblewhite, Brooklands starter and handicapper', Marcus Marendaz tried his hand. On Thursday, 10 November 1927, he set two Class G British and International records for 500 kilometres and three hours, at speeds of 71.13 mph and 70.53 mph. The car used was the second car, but for Class 'G' (up to 1,100 cc), it was fitted with a linered down Anzani engine; it had run earlier at Brooklands at this engine capacity, representative of the Model advertised

Marcus Marendaz seated in the oil-stained 9/20 Marendaz Special that later became UC3933, probably seen after setting Class 'G' records at Brooklands, November 1927. (*Author's collection*)

as a 9-90. No doubt encouraged by this success, Marcus Marendaz started the next year with a sally to France with the same car to try his luck at Montlhéry, where running was permitted day and night, unlike at Brooklands where night running was not permitted. Until this time, the car had been run unregistered on trade plates, but to take it abroad, it had to be properly licensed and was duly registered as UC3933 several days before travelling. Marendaz, writing to Paul Mitchell on 16 December 1987, said:

> The decision to break the 24 hour Class G 1,100 cc Worlds International 24-hour record was taken at the dinner I gave to A. V. Ebblewhite at his favourite restaurant in Soho and I lost no time in breaking new ground for England at the French track 18 miles from Paris – Montlhéry, a track that I came to know so well with all its dangers.

The Times, no less, reported:

> Linas, Montlhéry, February 15 1928—Marendaz, Kaye Don, and Hawkes and Mrs. Stewart started out as a team yesterday afternoon in a special Marendaz car with the intention of breaking the 24 hour record and achieved their object. They also broke the records for the 100 mile, 2000 kilometre and the 12 hour record. The run was officially controlled and timed and the official figures will be published later.

Hawkes was Douglas Hawkes, who later married Mrs Gwenda Stewart; they ran an establishment at Montlhéry that built cars and helped with record breaking activities. Bill Boddy, writing in *Veteran and Vintage Magazine* for December 1959, added to the story:

D. M. K. Marendaz, aided by Montlhéry resident Douglas Hawkes, took the Class G 24-hour record
... in a very shapely 2-seater Marendaz Special. This was apparently a stripped Anzani-engined sports
Marendaz with the bore of the engine reduced to bring it within the 1,100 cc class limit. The car
averaged 58.1 mph for the two rounds of the clock, collecting various other class records on the way,
such as the 12 hour record at 54.67 mph. Kaye Don was to have helped throughout but a clumsy
mechanic drove the car into a petrol pump (can you imagine what Marendaz said!) and so damaged
the back axle that a new half shaft had to be machined from an old lorry propeller shaft. So Don only
had two hours left in which to drive, after which Douglas Hawkes and Gwenda Stewart helped out.
Then the night was rendered horrible by gusty winds and rain squalls, a gearbox defect left only the
highest ratio available, and 1½ hours were lost replacing a broken timing chain.

Marcus Marendaz gave his word on this event in a letter to the author dated 11 February 1988,
which you may take or leave as you wish:

Driver's team included Mrs. Stewart and Kaye Don: such an assertion is fantastic nonsense; Kaye
Don was of Jewish persuasion holding himself and speaking in a manner close to aggression to many
people whilst Gwenda Stewart was a wild and rabid anti-Jewish person well able to stand up to him
as a driver as well as physically and verbally. They fought literally like the proverbial cat and dog. I
have seen them having to be physically restrained.

Whatever the background, this was a good result for the Marendaz Special car, and although
the twenty-four-hour period was eaten into, a bit of mathematics suggests that the running
speeds were in excess of 70 mph for a recorded average of 58.18 mph.

Marcus Marendaz in UC3933, entered for the 1928 Whitsun 25-mile Gold Star handicap. He was unplaced. (*John Shaw*)

The 1928 German Grand Prix: somewhere at the back of this grid is a Marendaz Special. Marcus Marendaz crashed on the first corner. (*Mercedes-Benz*)

With this excellent start to the season, Marcus Marendaz returned to the track at Brooklands with the Montlhéry car now restored to 1,496 cc, but occasionally running with the 1,093-cc engine, but with no placings. A further car, the low tailed YH 6538, also a works entry, ran from time to time and both cars were entered in the by now familiar J.C.C. 200-mile race, one driven by P. L. Pat Densham (UC3933) and the other by J. N. Forrest. Curiously, the well-known Dr J. D. Benjafield entered a Marendaz Special in two races in the Essex Motor Club meeting in September, to be driven by Marendaz and Forrest, but both non-started.

Possibly buoyed by his Montlhéry success, Marcus Marendaz made an entry for Le Mans in June, with Marendaz and Densham the drivers, but again non-started. There is no record if he even travelled. July 1928 did see him turning up for the German Grand Prix, a non-championship event run on the Nürburgring, but it was not his day as a front tyre burst while cornering caused a skid that put him into the bank and retirement on the first lap.

At the end of 1928 Marcus Marendaz made a further trip to Montlhéry for record breaking, this time with a new customer's car, YW6480, owned by L. L. Hanks. Curiously, the BARC Yearbooks do not list the records but *Light Car and Cyclecar* gave the details. The car had a standard 1,496-cc Anzani, in other words in Class 'F', and ran over 5 and 6 November to establish a twenty-four-hour record at 59.4 mph, based on only twenty-two hours of running. Drivers were Marendaz, Forrest and Hanks and the report states that the figures were subject to official confirmation.

As covered in the preceding chapter, Marcus Marendaz's activities broadened at this time and competitively in 1929 and 1930, he ran his own cars regularly, collecting two seconds

Seen close to the works, the Marendaz Special YW6480 used for record-breaking at Montlhéry in November 1928. The single headlight is unusual. The driver may well be the purchaser, L. L. Hanks. (*Author's collection*)

and two thirds in 1929 but nothing in the first four months of 1930. During this time, the old 1,093-cc car was run by Dorothy Summers and F. B. Roura to no effect. Marendaz non-started in his entries for the Saorstat Cup in Dublin in July and the Ards TT (Tourist Trophy) near Belfast in August, but did run at Shelsley Walsh in September, recording a very poor time. In writing to the *Light Car and Cyclecar* of 3 August 1928, he may have given a reason for his non-appearance in Ulster.

> The almost impossible task before the 1,500-cc unsupercharged cars. This ... means that the 1,500-cc car for a 26% increase in capacity over the 1,100 cc cars has to carry a 71 per cent increase in weight and, in addition, has to concede one complete lap of 13¾ miles.

COMPETITION AND RECORD BREAKING WITH A GRAHAM-PAIGE

The Graham-Paige marque was not well known for racing success even in the States. Marendaz seems to have been given or lent two cars, a six-cylinder dark blue open four-seat tourer of 4,634-cc engine capacity, based on the Model 621 Royal Sportsman's Saloon and a Model 835 Sedan (closed saloon) straight eight-cylinder of 5,297 cc. His starting point was an attack on the Class B (5,000–8,000-cc) 200-km and 200-mile records in the eight-cylinder saloon, which he gained at 76.97 and 77.77 mph respectively on 26 March 1929. *Motor* recorded that the car ran with full equipment including two spare wheels. Captain A. G. Miller in Delage I (5,954 cc) retook both records in April 1929 at 93.06 mph for the 200-km and 88.87 mph for the 200-mile race, spurring Marendaz and Graham-Paige on to greater efforts. These involved a major rethink and it was not just the two spare tyres that were ditched, but the entire body, a new very smooth 2-seater body being specially built. With these changes and a replacement engine, success was achieved on 18 July 1929 at 93.87 mph for the 200-km race and 92.52 mph for the 200-mile run, but only just beating Alastair Miller's speeds. Next up was an outing to Montlhéry with the smaller six-cylinder car for more record breaking, it having run in a couple of races at the Whitsun meeting on 20 May 1929, achieving a third. At Montlhéry, driven by Marcus Marendaz, J. N. Forrest, and A. F. Ashby records for Class 'C' (3,000–5,000 cc) were gained for 3,000, 4,000, and 5,000 miles and 4,000 and 5,000 km with a fastest lap at 87.5 mph, a prodigious effort over two days, although they did not stand for very long. On its return to England, the six-cylinder car was once again on the track at Brooklands, with no placings, but the eight-cylinder car with the lightweight body achieved a first and a second with Marendaz driving. Record-breaking for the year was not yet over and immediately before Christmas Marendaz, Tulloch and E. L. B. Veendam set off for Montlhéry again with the eight-cylinder two-seater, returning successfully with the 2,000 and 3,000 km, 2,000 mile, and twenty-four-hour Class 'B' records, the last gained at 86.36 mph. Dutchman Veendam had a limited Brooklands career of his own appearing in the 1929 Double Twelve with H. J. Aldingham in a Frazer Nash.

We have Marcus Marendaz's words on record breaking at Montlhéry, firstly in an interview with *The Modern Boy* for 20 September 1930:

> People imagine that driving a car at high speed is a perpetual thrill, but you can tell the readers of Modern Boy from me that long-distance records work at Montlhéry is the most monotonous task under the sun—or moon! Montlhéry is more monotonous than Brooklands on these occasions. In

Marcus Marendaz in the rebodied eight-cylinder Graham-Paige, probably while breaking records at Brooklands in July 1929. (*Author's collection*)

the first place, it is a much shorter circuit. One completes a lap in about one minute, whereas one lap of Brooklands takes at least twice as long, which means the same scenery twice as often at Montlhéry! Again the surface of the French track is much better and there is no blind corner such as exists at the fork on Brooklands. This means that there is less need to concentrate on what one is doing – to the exclusion of boredom. One great adventure which I shall never forget was my hectic backwards plunge down the Montlhéry banking with a stalled engine during my record attempt. It was raining and rather foggy and I had lost a lot of time owing to bad weather and slight mechanical defects. The result was I was running a good deal behind schedule time, the weather was so much against me that it was impossible to increase speed much to pick up what I'd lost. However I calculated that if I kept going at about 105 mph I might just scrape through and get the record. In order to save as much time as possible I was cutting the inside of the track. Owing to the bad visibility on one occasion I overdid it and my near-side rear wheel dropped into the soft earth. In a flash the car shot up to the top of the parapet, then down again nose first. Then she slithered back and turned round in the centre of the wet track, finally getting into an uncontrollable backwards slide. It is amazing how even in a breathless moment such as this one may be aware of details. It was while I was skidding backwards down the track towards the soft earth in the centre at about 80 mph that I realised that my engine had stopped. In a moment I visualised what this meant—failure in the record attempt, for to start the engine of a racing car which is embedded in soil is practically an impossible feat. No self-starter is carried, you see, and to start the car needs a bunch of fellows pushing it along with the engine in gear. I suppose I shall never know what happened next. In some miraculous manner, although my engine had stalled and I was sliding tail first for the bottom of the banking, I managed to engage reverse and let in the clutch. With a roar the engine re-awoke. By means of going backwards and forwards in the soft earth which I struck a moment later I managed to regain the track, so I carried straight on, just capturing the record by the skin of my teeth!

In more recent times, writing to Paul Mitchell on 16 December 1987, Marcus Marendaz said:

I took the Worlds Class B International 24-hour record and other records on Christmas Eve 1929 and arrived back in London on Christmas Day after crossing in a howling gale sharing the ship standing on its end with the only other passenger—a Frenchman of about my own age—whose command of the filthiest words in the English language were an inescapable education the like of which I have never heard before or since. We both remained on our feet the whole voyage. My haste to return to England was entirely due to one of my mother's rare journeys to spend Christmas with me.

This was the third successful 24-hour record that Marcus Marendaz had driven. In the 1970s, his strap line on his headed notepaper read 'THE ONLY CARS ON EARTH THAT HAVE EVER OBTAINED THREE WORLDS INTERNATIONAL 24 HOUR RECORDS—AMONG HUNDREDS OF OTHER SUCCESSES'—a claim that was nearly true, only two of them having been gained on a Marendaz Special car, the third being on a Graham-Paige. Other quibbles could be made, but in general, his successes should be rightly applauded.

Marendaz ran the big eight-cylinder car at two meetings early in 1930, his best placing being a third, before he broke his leg in May as recorded in Chapter 7. This put an end to his track efforts for the rest of the year, but in December 1930, he returned to Montlhéry with the eight-cylinder car to attack some shorter records, accompanied by Mr E. L. B. Veendam. Marendaz set the 200-mile Class 'B' record at 101.85 mph, but the car crashed in fog with

Veendam driving in an attempt on the 200-km record. A photograph of Marendaz, Veendam, and the car at Brixton Road shows it to be greatly changed from the immaculately streamlined two-seater of earlier runs, the body having been lowered by cutting 6 inches off the bottom and dropping it, with the bonnet correspondingly chopped to fit, all set off by a horrible front cowl over a heavily sloping radiator. The radiator is possibly the one given a trial fit to the Miller car as seen in the works around the same time, but with the filler cap moved to the scuttle.

Long after Marcus Marendaz had ceased racing the Graham-Paiges at Brooklands one was raced there by G. L. Baker in 1935, 1936, 1938, and 1939, winning the very last race on the complete Brooklands track in August 1939. It was almost certainly Marcus Marendaz's old straight eight rebodied yet again by Harrington of Hove. A neighbour of G. L. Baker, G. P., George Harvey-Noble, ran a Graham-Paige in the 1935 RAC rally, probably using the same car.

So ended the 'Roaring Twenties' with Donald Marcus Kelway Marendaz having done his fair share of the roaring.

The eight-cylinder Graham-Paige outside the Marendaz works in 1929, with the brutally cut down body and sloping radiator. On the right is D. M. K. Marendaz with E. L. B. Veendam beside him. (*National Motor Museum*)

9

THE 1931 MARENDAZ SPECIAL:
THE 13/70 IN LONDON AND MAIDENHEAD

By 1930, Marcus Marendaz was selling a four-year old Model, with engines probably bought in the early 1920s. While it was undoubtedly pretty and had achieved success on the track at Brooklands, it probably did not have a great future sales potential. His essays into other lines of business such as selling aircraft or promoting the Graham-Paige car, while undoubtedly helping to keep the wolf from the door were not likely to have been great money-spinners. The overhaul and tuning of customer's cars, again was bread and butter work, and not the image of a successful businessman. The answer was a major revamp of his product, allied to a new engine, leading to a move away from London to Maidenhead, which happened early in 1932, and the re-establishment of his business. This rearrangement and success is remarkable in that it took place in the dog days of the depression, when business survival in any form was everything.

For the historian, this period of the Marendaz history is graced by the survival of many of the cars, unlike the Marseals and Anzani Marendaz Specials. Furthermore, many of the people involved were able to have their say, so a more rounded picture is possible. Then Marcus Marendaz was an inveterate letter writer and defended himself and his product with remarkable vehemence against any criticism implied or otherwise until his death in 1988, thereby providing any historian with boundless copy.

The Model 13/70 was conceived at the Brixton Road works in London. It is invariably associated with the Maidenhead works but did have a life in London of around eighteen months before the move in May 1932, having been formally announced in late 1931 (see *Autocar*, 30 October 1931). Right from the early days, there was a photograph of five 13/70s lined up annotated in Marcus Marendaz's hand '1931: A group of famous Marendaz Specials', the photograph being generally assumed to be of an early Maidenhead production, notwithstanding the discrepancy with the date. Research revealed that the photograph was actually taken in Cranmer Road, a few hundred yards from the Marendaz London works, thereby proving that at least five cars were produced before the move.

There appears to be no surviving information relating to the gestation of the 13/70 prior to the launch, it arriving on the scene fully formed. This obviously cannot be the case and in fact the car surviving today as BGW770, while registered in September 1934 appears to be the development prototype, either being used in 1931 with trade plates or being previously registered. A comparison between the arrangements on this car and every other 13/70 reveals

Five Marendaz Specials in Cranmer Road beside the Brixton Road works. The yellow car at centre was the development prototype that later became BGW770. (*Marendaz Special Cars*)

a number of curious differences. The chassis carries many more drilling holes than one would expect revealing that the brake master cylinder was tried in several locations and that the tubular chassis cross-member likewise moved around. The bodywork timber is of 1-inch section, every other car is 1.25 inches. The bodywork clearance at the front of the rear wheel arch is unrealistically small, around 1 inch, indicating that it was either constructed off the car or that the chassis to body alignment was changed at some point. The clincher is the windscreen, which, unlike every other post 1931 Marendaz Special, has more pronounced and pointed lower corners. These can be seen in the middle car of the five-car photograph.

The changes between the 13/70 and the earlier cars were not enormous really, apart from the engine. The chassis was a new design, but still the conventional ladder layout, a plate clutch was used, a single brake master cylinder was used operating on all wheels, both the brake and clutch pedals having a 2:1 gearing to reduce foot-loads. The body was a new sporting design by Max Miller, the *Autocar* artist, the floorless body being attached to the outside of the L-section chassis with the floor itself sitting inside the chassis, thereby dropping the seats by several inches.

Turning to the engine, therein lays a tale. Taken at face value it is a six-cylinder Continental Model 8F (nominal capacity 2,394 cc) and later Model 9F (nominal capacity 2,630 cc), modified by Marcus Marendaz to suit his purposes. Rumours circulated right from when the car was announced that they were fitted with second-hand American Continental engines, a point never admitted by him. For example: 'No engine ever fitted into Marendaz Special cars by me was ever made by Erskine or any subsidiary of the Studebaker Corporation' (*Autocar*, 2 November

A Continental engine manufacturer's plate of the type removed from Marendaz Special engines. The rivet holes were the giveaway. (*Author's collection*)

1945). He went on to outline his production of engines inside the Maidenhead works. Well, the fact is that he started producing the cars with second-hand Erskine engines but later on, presumably after the supply of relatively rare Erskines had dried up, he did build complete engines. His own production articles are identifiable by the revised internal oil pick up from the sump, the Erskine-built engines having a priming hole externally on the block. The clincher giveaway is that Erskine engines left their factory with a Continental brass manufacturer's plate on the left-hand side of the block affixed by four rivets. Of course, Marendaz removed these, but the four rivet holes remain—it is an easy check. If further proof is needed, here are the words of Stan Duddington:

> He did all the engineering for the engines in the works, but the stories were that he was using secondhand engines from Erskines when he started, but that was before my time. The early engines were second-hand and he had some rough old stuff come in sometimes. Apparently the engines were at his house in the garage or a shed and an apprentice was sent over to clean them up and make them look like new, before they were brought over to the works for rebuilding. Do you remember Reeves? I heard he had some in his shed at his house at Bray and Reeves used to have to go over and clean them and put some aluminium paint on and Marendaz would say 'Put it on nice and thick and make it look like new'.

The engines, including the Erskine ones, were reworked by Marendaz, the bores being linered down to give a capacity of 1,869 cc, the cylinder head was changed to a high-compression one giving around 7.5:1 as opposed to the Erskine 4.5:1. It was complete with curiously angled plugs for which no plausible technical explanation was ever given. The manifolding was changed to give the car the sporting triple exhaust look only equalled by Mercedes-Benz, although this image was slightly tempered by the running together of the exhausts under the after bodywork. The distributor, starter, and dynamo were changed for Lucas items. Capping it all, literally, was a long dummy rocker-box cover over the plug leads but suggesting that this side-valve motor was packing an overhead cam.

The development prototype, BGW770, today. (*Author's collection*)

THE FIRST ANGLO-AMERICAN SPORTS CAR

Standing back and looking at this 1931 car today, we can see the very first Anglo-American hybrid or muscle car, a British Sports Car with a big American engine, albeit one not recognised as such by its constructor. It showed remarkable foresight on the part of Marcus Marendaz to see that a lightly loaded American flathead engine, linered down to 13 hp to ease the taxation problems, was a good way to go, predating Railton, Brough Superior, Batten, Allard, Lammas-Graham (with a Graham, formerly Graham-Paige engine), and Atalanta. Of course, there were British cars fitted with American engines before 1931—for example the one-off Bond and Morris fitted Continental engines during the First War—but this was the first time that a production sports car was being fitted with a big lazy American engine. The fact that the first car so fitted marking this seminal departure in British motoring history survives is something to be noted.

THE WORKS AT MAIDENHEAD

Having built at least five 13/70s in London, Marcus Marendaz, along with Dorothy Summers and some of the other employees, decamped to Maidenhead and the Cordwallis works. An area close by the Marendaz works was occupied by G.W.K. (Grice, Wood, Keiller), who had been on this site since before the war, but the cavernous building taken over by Marendaz in a semi-finished state was part of wartime building, construction of which had been abandoned with the armistice. When Marendaz took over, there remained various problems with it due to

The christening of the first car to be made at the new Marendaz Works in Maidenhead, which took place on Saturday, 13 August 1932. The Mayoress of the town is here seen performing the ceremony and reading from right to left: The Mayor (Councillor E. B. Norris), Mr Marendaz, The Mayoress (Mrs E. B. Norris), Mr Murray of Marendaz Cars, Ltd, Col. Johns, Councillors Archer, Chamberlain, and Thomas, Mr Heaton, Councillor Baker, and extreme left Mr Wadwha of the Empire Building and Trading Co. Ltd. (*John Shaw*)

its unfinished state; he spent time in the courts in London off and on over two or three years arguing about the money he owed.

The works themselves were brick built with a zig-zag north light roof. Inside were two offices, one for Marcus Marendaz and Miss Summers and the other a drawing office, unoccupied. These led onto the shop floor, a very large space occupied at the end nearest the offices by the machine tools necessary for the work with the adjacent space used for building up the engines and cars. Beyond the lathes and machine tools was the stores, a caged space in the centre of the shop floor. The working area was served by large sliding doors, which allowed cars to be moved in and out easily.

THE 13/70 MODELS

As with everything that Marendaz did, there are variations on what models were actually available or on offer; it was all rather fluid. The 13/70 as built was generally what was referred to as an open two-four-seater, but a few closed Coupés, rather straight backed, were also built, all with the closely fitting wings that gave them their style. For 1933, a 17-hp model was introduced, variously referred to as a 17/80, 17/90, and 17/97. This was of 2,450 cc and was identified by the thermostatically controlled radiator shutters and the long open-sided front wings. It was available as a Tourer, Saloon, Convertible Coupé, and Drop-head Coupé. The Convertible Coupé, now also available in 13/70 form, was identifiable by doors that extended to the bottom of the bodywork, so arranged to permit the window to be lowered. All models were considered available in supercharged form, a Zoller instrument being used, but again the model range and model designation defies accurate interpretation and any car produced or illustrated was seemingly given an almost arbitrary designation. Suffice it to say, the cars were referred to inside the works as 13 hp or 17 hp with a further qualification regarding the body style or other modification.

All coachbuilding was done in the works, with the exception of the Saloons which, it is believed, were completed by Abbots of Farnham.

To complete the model line up for the cars, a 15-90 model was introduced in November 1935, the Continental/Marendaz engine being abandoned and a 1,991 cc Coventry-Climax six-cylinder inlet over exhaust being offered. This engine was clearly identified by the Marendaz three-part cylinder head, unique to these cars. Bodily, styling was improved with a more fashionable high door line in keeping with the mid-1930s trends, set off by long wings with closed sides at the front.

LIFE AT THE WORKS

So that was the framework of the cars, the models, and the factory, but it only tells a very small part of the story and misses the personalities and the tales from the works. In this respect we are very lucky as two ex-employees at Maidenhead had very vivid memories of the cars, the people and the events that transpired. The first is Stan Duddington, who was an apprentice and general factotum between about 1933 and early 1936, and the other is Jim Light, who was a machinist in the works. There were others who played lesser roles.

The Maidenhead works seen in the 1990s with Stan Duddington (left) and John Shaw. This shows the side of the works with alterations to the brickwork and, on the right, a later facade. By 2017, the building was completely gone. (*Author's collection*)

Stan Duddington was born in 1916 and was cousin to driver Duddington who took the speed record on LNER's *Mallard* in 1938. After Marendaz Cars he worked on bikes at HRD and Vincents, was off Sword beach with the Royal Navy in 1944 and went on to work for BRMs at Bourne on the famous or infamous V-16 engine and later Rolls-Royce in London. Despite this impressive *curriculum vitae* he was immensely modest and with it very knowledgeable. Jim Light (as he was known at Marendaz Cars) was really called Leslie Light and worked for Marendaz for seven years, first with the cars and later with International Aircraft and was still living in Maidenhead in the 1980s. These gentlemen provided the author with many hours of taped information that brought to life the times of the 1930s, with a very clear insight into the personality of Marcus Marendaz.

Jim Light started with Marendaz not long after the move to Maidenhead:

He [Marendaz] hadn't been down there long, but I can't remember whether it was six months or seven months later that I got sent there by the labour exchange. Well, I thought, I'll go round, shan't be there long, 'cos he was renowned around Maidenhead for sacking people. They were in and out of there like flies. Every day you'd start in the morning, sacked in the afternoon. Hell of a reputation, he had. So I went round in the morning and the first job he gave me was on the old Superior lathe, the first one on the left just as you come out of his office. Not long after I'd been there I was boring the bores through the rear hubs on it, to be sent away for the splines to be put in, you see. And it was tapering like hell, about 10 thou taper on a distance about so much and you couldn't hold the end or nothing to get the taper out. I was scraping them to get them parallel. And Marendaz came out of the office about 4 o'clock and I was just about fed up and I turned on him and told him what I thought of him, what I thought of his lathe and what he could do with his lathe. Well, that's it, he stamped off I thought to get my cards. Well, he never spoke to me for six months.

[Stan Duddington:] Just as well, probably!

[Jim Light:] If he wanted to complain to me he got Eddie Long and Eddie had to come and tell me. The very next time he spoke to me, he had me in the office and he asked me if I could start turning these hubs out complete and I said yes. I was knocking out one of those hubs complete in about 2½ hours, ready to go for the reversible screwing and splining. You could tell the money he was saving on those, Eddie had been taking about 8 hours on a lathe to finish one off. Anyway, I was standing there looking around and he's standing watching me and he starts going on 'Can't you turn them out any quicker' and I turned round to have a go at him and he stepped back saying, 'All right, all right, only joking.'

Continuing the tale of the second-hand engines, there is absolutely no doubt that Marcus Marendaz did make his own engines, copied of course directly from the Continental Model 8F or 9F and fitted with his own modifications. One can be certain that no royalties were ever paid to Continental. Stan Duddington remembered the blocks arriving:

All the time I was there Carter Paterson would come with the cylinder block un-machined castings and they'd be bumped down outside the door and be dragged in. Then they'd be machined and we'd use the big Hermes vertical miller to do the bores. It had a big cut out on it to face up the head joint and then we'd turn it endways for the timing cover joint and the one at the back.

[Jim Light:] Along the back there was a massive plunger. We had a plate along that with six holes in it and when you'd finished one you moved along till the plunger dropped down into the next

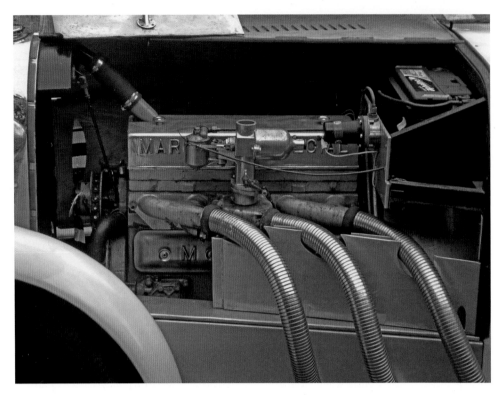

An Erskine Continental 9F engine converted to a Marendaz Standard. (*Author's collection*)

hole, all to keep the centres right. Then there was the horizontal miller that was used to cut the caps off the con-rods, before being bored out on the big Ward lathe. That was also used for the hubs and the brakedrums—huge thing it was. All the machining was done there. We'd start the hubs on the Ward and then they went up to Whitworths for splining and screw cutting, but later in the end we were doing the lot including the splining on the hobbing machine. The actual flywheel didn't have a starter ring on it and the teeth were cut onto the flywheel with a hobbing machine, each individual tooth one at a time and it took forever. It took about a week to cut them all. There were a lot of things like that in those days, not very cost effective. The funny thing was that the teeth didn't seem to wear much and we never had much trouble with them, so not having a shrunk-on starter ring wasn't a problem. There was a Warner and Swasey big capstan lathe which was a handy old machine, very superior, with a fairly long bed to put the propshafts on it. They were high tensile, used to take them along with a steady behind them and the last two or three cuts were a hell of a job, which is why in the end a needle race was fitted half way up the torque tube. It was drawn tube, you see, and was pretty accurate. I was impressed with it. Then there was an Archdale drill for drilling the oilways for the camshaft feed from the mains.

[Jim Light:] One funny thing that happened there—you know the big ten-inch aluminium ball that goes on the front of the gearbox that then fits in the housing mounted across the chassis, the bit the whole back end is hung on. Well, Eddie Long used to do those. He had a big forming tool and it was a hell of a job to get the ball to fit the sockets. He'd just got one nearly done, just finishing—well, you can guess what happened when it started sliding on the tools. Old Eddie nearly went mad.

The beautiful lines of John Shaw's 13/70, seen near Cheltenham in the 1980s. (*Author's collection*)

[Stan Duddington:] Do you remember putting the liners in, with that great big screw, walking round, you put Baker's Fluid on it and then walked round it?

[Jim Light:] In the end he had liquid oxygen. But I tell you, one of the worst jobs, a job I used to hate doing, was cutting the oil channel in the sides of the block. It was about 3/16 inch, but we only ever broke one drill and we managed to get that one out.

Working on the shop floor in the 1930s was very different to factory work today. There were absolutely no facilities for washing or getting yourself clean at the end of the day, there was virtually no lighting when you had to work late, and then there was the overhead belting, standard for any engineering works of the day. Stan Duddington recalls:

Sometimes when I had a big drill, drilling a cylinder head or something and you'd be hanging on it and you'd hear the old motor driving all the belting slowing up and you'd know the belt might just come off and Eddie'd come round saying 'Ease up, ease up, ease up', because he'd have to get the ladder out to put the belt back on again. Some days it would come off twice, with someone on the big lathe and someone else on the drill, pulling well on it. You could tell what colour car was being sprayed by looking at the belt—blue belt, red belt, multi-coloured, as the belt would pick up the colour. There was no extractor, you all got choked when the painter was spraying.

[There was absolutely no heating in the cavernous works. Stan:] I remember we used to wear gloves and overcoats, didn't we? I worked in my overcoat many times with my scarf tucked in. Put your overalls on and find you've got to put your overcoat on top. You'd stick to the machinery it was that cold and the water all froze up to ice such that it really burned you some times. Marendaz reckoned you could work and keep warm, but he was walking about with his hands in his teddy-bear coat and then he'd go into the office and stand over one of those little Aladdin stoves. He was too mean to pay for the electricity!

A long-chassis 17-hp Marendaz Special Saloon on delivery by Stan Duddington. (*Stan Duddington*)

… If you were there at night you could hear all this flapping and clattering going on with the wind blowing through the corrugated iron. There was always a lot of overtime and if you were working late into the evening, fiddling about with something, the problem was that there'd be only one or two light bulbs, just ordinary little light bulbs, one over the lathe and one over the bench and that would be it. We also did repairs to the cars, so often you might be working on a new car in the morning, but taking an axle out of a customer's car in the afternoon and you'd have a wandering lead light with you. When you worked overtime and it got dark in wintertime you probably had to go and get a bulb and put it into some lamp nearby, but quite often you were working completely in the dark. You'd hear a creaking and a groaning noise and you'd look and there'd be a chap working taking something out and he'd be in the dark as well, doing it all by feel. I remember once we worked all night on something and we wanted a cup of tea and you know we had no tea things and there was never a tea break, was there? So someone went into the office and found a teapot that the office girl used to have, and we set about making a cup of tea. We found the tea, but we'd nothing to heat it with, until someone found a blowlamp from somewhere and put it on the side of the metal teapot and boiled the water and then put a handful of tea in.

[Stan:] We never got any meals or anything and there were no washing facilities either. To wash your hands at the end of the day there was a big tray where we used to do the honing of the cylinder blocks and it had dirty paraffin in it and you just had to go and put your hands in there to clean them and then go to one of the lathes and get some of that soluble lathe oil and wash 'em in that and then find a bag of sawdust, if there was any, and rub your hands in that and then wave them about. There were no towels or sink or anything, nor any toilets. There was a little old toilet on the estate, but it was a terrible place to go; it was a shocker if you wanted to go to the toilet. Well, if you wanted a wee, you used to have to go round the back, where there was an open space about 50 feet by 100 yards. This space was normally dry, but when an engine was on test the water from the Heenan and Froude dynamometer discharged onto it with no drain. It just had to soak into the ground and after it had been running for a day, when you nipped out for a wee the whole ground was waterlogged. The engines on test could be running full bore all day exhausting into the inside of the works from the three little exhaust stubs. The noise … !

The baby Bentley. A 15/90 Marendaz Special is alongside a 4.5-litre Bentley, giving a measure of the difference in size. (*Author's collection*)

… One night I was working there in the big open factory space with the caged stores in the middle and various chassis in the course of construction round about sitting on carpenter's trestles waiting for the various brackets and axles and all that to be fitted. Well Marendaz and Alfred Moss were in the office talking loudly and arguing and laughing and so on, when suddenly they came out and Marendaz said to me 'Pull that bench over there will you', like that, 'and put that other bit out of the way'. Then Moss got in his car and Marendaz in his—don't forget it was pitch black inside the works except for one bulb—and they belted around the stores one after the other, chasing each other with their headlights on. I don't know why they did it but the things I had to move were to make it a bit more of a track. If you'd have stepped out you'd have been killed and it went on for about 20 minutes. I suppose if you are the boss and you own the place this is the sort of thing you can do; it seemed so daft!

LIFE WITH MARCUS MARENDAZ

The reader so far will have detected an underlying comment on the personality of Marcus Marendaz. He was charming to the ladies, hard on his employees, perhaps underlings would be a better word, very difficult to work with particularly if you represented authority. No doubt many of these traits had to be bottled up, should he be dealing with a customer from whom money was to be made. In spite of this he had a number of allies that seemingly weathered his personality as they stuck with him, three famous names among them being Kaye Don, racing driver, and Alfred and Aileen Moss, racing and trials drivers, owners of three Marendaz Special cars, and, of course, parents of Stirling Moss.

Perhaps we should start with him coming to work in the morning. Stan stated:

He used to blow his horn when he came in in the morning to open the door, wearing his big teddy bear coat. I wonder if he still has that—I wouldn't be a bit surprised? I thought it was the only one

The 17-hp car that belonged to Alfred Moss. Note the radiator slats and longer wings. (*John Shaw*)

he had. He used to arrive about a quarter to ten outside and put his hand on his horn and blow until someone opened the doors. He was ever so impatient and you had to let him in. He would never get out and open them himself, would he?

Marcus Marendaz was of a rather sallow appearance, his origins Portuguese, not Spanish but with many generations in South Wales. While undisputed, his background was subject to some discussion in the works. Stan commented: 'He used to always tell us he was a Welshman. I used to think he was a funny coloured Welshman'.

Unsurprisingly given it was the depression, money was always a problem for Marcus Marendaz and while it obviously caused upheavals from time to time, it does not look as if Marendaz was worse than any other employer at the time. Jim Light stated:

I know what I was going to tell you, you might not believe it, he paid threepence an hour over the rate. The going rate for a skilled man was 1 and 3*d* an hour, and he gave me 1 and 6*d*. Mind you, 'e didn't have enough money and you had to wait to get your wages in the end.

[Stan:] If he'd lost you the works would have come to a standstill. Eddie couldn't have managed on his own. If that had happened then he'd have had to teach somebody new his way of working all over again. But he wasn't a very good business man as people found him such a rotten person to deal with, although the cars were pretty good. If he'd had somebody to market the cars he'd have been all right.

[It is pretty clear that Marcus Marendaz appreciated the efforts of Jim Light, such that one Christmas ... Jim Light:] When I told people I'd had a Christmas Box from Marendaz they wouldn't believe me, that was when we were on International Aircraft, he had us all over at his house in Bray there with a Christmas tree with presents on it. My present was a box of 50 cigarettes and a cheque for a pound. They cashed it too—surprised it didn't bounce, although I wondered if it would. He also paid me half wages for a week's holiday. When I told people that knew him they called me a liar. You're not

A 15/90 with Coventry Climax engine. Note the closed sides to the front wings and higher door line. (*Author's collection*)

going to believe this—but when I went back to the job again, he stopped that, he took it back, he stopped that money. How I stayed with him seven years and how he kept me seven years, I don't know.

Marcus Marendaz's personality obviously interfered with his relationships with his fellow man. However, his driving style, while a thorough nuisance to some was not to be faulted regarding ability.

[Jim Light:] I never felt nervous with him. He was real mad with a car, all racing changes, although that's why he was always in trouble with the law. D'you know King Street in Maidenhead and Castle Hill? I saw him do this one night when I was walking along there in the dark. There were two of those Thames Valley buses and they turned out a bit wide to get round the corner and he went past them on the inside. He did, and up the hill!

Somebody told me once he was coming back from Brooklands and having a do with a chap in an Aston Martin or a Frazer Nash and he did these racing changes and pulled the top off the gearbox. Came off in his hand and he had it in second gear and belted it all the way and still saw the chap off. I don't know who went down with him, that night one broke down at Reading, this bridge at Reading on the A4 road, it's at an angle, he went round there with on-coming traffic headlights on, knocking on seventy. I suppose it was all good for his reputation when selling high performance motor cars—the more times you got your name in the papers for speeding the better. He came in one Saturday morning, this was when we were International Aircraft, and he said, 'Oh, I've got a rattle in the back of the car. You get in the back and we'll go for a trip round, so we can see what's rattling.' So I found out all right what it was and I looked round to tell him and the first thing I saw was a

Jim or Leslie Light seen in later years in retirement when his hobby was model engineering. (*Geoffrey Light*)

A brochure picture of a 13/70 Coupe, seen by the Thames at Maidenhead, with Brunel's bridge behind. (*Author's collection*)

ruddy car coming head first at us. He was on the wrong side of the road going round a corner down Blackmore Lane, down there Sonning way. What'd the old man do—he flicked the wheel and he was through. It was a while before I got in his car again. The other poor bloke, you could see 'im thinking ...

[Jim Light:] If you ever went out with Marendaz or Kaye Don you really had a ride. I was telling you he used to take me with him every Saturday working on the aircraft at Barton. We were coming back, I don't know if you know Denham or not, but there's some bends in the road there, you know the A40, a smooth road and he was belting down and he came round one bend, and he was only doing the best part of ninety and we had a full slide round the bend! And he looks at me, grinning all over. I don't know if he was trying to frighten me, but he didn't. But he looks at me and says 'D'you know, Light, I think I took that a little too fast. But you needn't say anything to anyone.' I never felt nervous with him. He was real mad with a car, all racing changes.

[Jim Light:] He had a near one, one day, came in, it was on the 17 hp maroon car. The rear wing and the front wing both had dents dead in line about ½ inch deep and 1½ inch wide, just as if you'd laid a 1½ inch bar across and hit it. Dead in line—God knows what he'd been under!

[Stan Duddington:] He came in one day with the bonnet all dented—he'd run it under the back of a lorry and it had been all pushed down. Another time I was with him on the Great West Road, I've forgotten where we'd come from and we were towing a chassis. It had been to some body place and we were probably doing over sixty, and the Police, when they had Hillman four-cylinder cars with a bell on the front—ting-a-ling. We had to stop. 'What's up?' 'You're doing sixty with a four-wheel trailer'. This wasn't allowed in those days, you were only supposed to do thirty, I think. It was classified as a four-wheel trailer, with this chassis behind, rigmarole and all that. I think he got fined for that.

[Jim Light:] Then there was the time he got fined £50 down at Oxted in Surrey, wasn't it? The original fine was £100 and two year suspension. I think he appealed and he got it cut down to one year's suspension and £50 and the old judge down there told Marendaz that if he ever saw him in his court again he would have no hesitation in putting him in jail. He was only doing ninety in a built-up limit with a thirty speed trap. That was about twenty week's wages. He had a bloke drive him about after he'd lost his licence, a bloke named Ken Base. At the time when he'd lost his licence, when you went in to the works on a Monday morning every corner round the building had the gravel pushed up where Marendaz had been going round testing a car. They say they hated him in the village of Bray.

A Marendaz Special brake pedal. (*Author's collection*)

10

THE 1931 MARENDAZ SPECIAL: PRODUCTION AND THE PEOPLE

There was no official handbook on the cars, so work on the cars was by instruction only, both for construction or repair: for example, the valve timing was exhaust valve closed three teeth on the flywheel after top dead centre. There was no timing mark or anything like that. For owners who had trouble with their cars, they were meant to ring the works and bring the car back.

There were sales catalogues, all broadly similar with photographs of the cars by the Thames around Maidenhead. The location for the cover photograph of the car outside the half-timbered pub is unknown, as is the lady driver, allegedly someone Marcus Marendaz just encountered. The car is probably the 'old rose' car with the spotlight on the screen, GW 2382, a Brixton Road-built car.

Production was always around one car a month. There might be two on the go at once with all told about four chassis laid out for building up.

Building up the bodies was another interesting tale as there was no wood-working machinery in the works. Stan Duddington commented:

> There was a fella called Clarke, 'Nobby' Clarke, who was an experienced body builder and he went away to Aston Martin's for a bit and then Marendaz got him back again. Him and a young fella who came from Reading and the two used to do the bodies between them with all the woodwork. The tricky bits were cut round by bandsaw, but Marendaz didn't have a bandsaw, in fact there were no machine tools at all in the bodyshop, so all the tricky bits, like corner bits, came over from Camden town. I had to go over to fetch a load of them once, all funny shaped little bits that you glued and screwed and then went over with a spokeshave. Then a cockney chap would come over and cover it. Of course there'd always be this argument with Marendaz and people would come and go.
>
> [Jim Light:] Nobby Clarke used to do all the bodywork, he was the foreman. He lived at Feltham so he left and went to work at Aston Martins, who were there. Then Marendaz got him to come back part time and he used to send me over to his house on a Saturday morning with a car to fetch him so that he could work the weekend at the Marendaz works. The trimmer was the same as the bodybuilders. One old fella, bloke with glasses, did it all and he lasted a long time. He would go away and do other jobs, all working on piecework. As Marendaz was only doing one car a month or every six weeks there wasn't enough work to keep some people on full time.

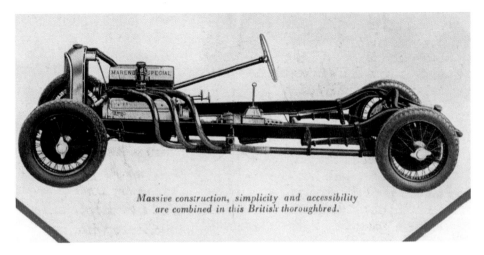

A brochure illustration of the 13/70 chassis and running gear. (*Author's collection*)

[Stan Duddington:] I remember the trimmer would be finishing a car and it would be on axle stands and while he was working on it the painter would come and spray a brake drum and if you were under the car you'd get your hair sprayed as well, or your sleeve or your trousers or overall. Then when you put your head back on the floor there'd be tacks lying there, the floor was covered in them. I got one stuck in my head one day and had to crawl out from underneath so as to get it out again. As the car was nearly built everybody was on it. There'd be fitters, trimmers and painters all working together, all in each other's way and this went on for several days at the time the car was getting to its finishing stages. The painter would grumble at you if you leaned on something where he'd sprayed it all. You'd be filling the rear axle and it would be 140 oil and the weather would be cold and you couldn't get it to go in and you'd put it in a pot on the oil stove in the stores. There was no heating in the works—he wouldn't pay for it as he reckoned that you'd work to keep warm.

[Stan Duddington:] He was an Irishman, the sprayer, Mac something. The cars were always finished off in the paint shop, near the door, and if you were working on it, he'd be spraying a brake drum under the wings and he'd spray all over you as he went past. He used to have that bucket of water with a bit of wood floating in it and two electrodes to warm the water. Just plug it in. Try putting your hand in that!

[Jim Light:] Before you were there, Stan, when he started at Maidenhead we used to have an old car, one called an ambulance, an old Sunbeam two-seater. They used to tow cars up the road to be sprayed, with the front axle lifted up on the ambulance. Mind you that old Sunbeam that was the only time Marendaz got caught. He really got caught—the old Sunbeam came in as part exchange—it was a big open one, grey wasn't it? When he phoned up the customer and told him to come and collect his Marendaz, that car came in as part exchange, in through the big door, and it turned straight round and stopped dead. Well, it stood there a long time, then Marendaz decided to start using it to tow this ambulance. When they went to start it up, do you know there wasn't a tooth left on the back axle. How the hell they drove it in that door, all the gearbox was in pieces. Had to buy gears, but we never made out how it had come shooting through that door. I reckon somebody must have driven another car towing it, then pushed him quick so he could swing in the door and stop. Old Marendaz did his nut, but it's the only time I remember him being caught.

Inside the Maidenhead works, showing around forty machined hubs, almost certainly the work of Jim Light. (*Marendaz Special Cars*)

When the move to Maidenhead was made, the cars were fitted with the Marendaz-designed gear box. While these were pretty robust, they had their problems largely solved by the purchase of a Laycock box, fitted to the later cars. Stan Duddington said:

> There weren't many people wanted his own box which had the propshaft going right up into it. We used to put them on a lathe, keeping pouring carborundum paste in them and running them in for a week to get them quiet. Do you remember the TT car—you could hear it right down at the gate on the main road. It had to have a Marendaz box in it, as they hadn't made enough cars with the Laycock and hence it wasn't listed in the catalogue. He slipped up there a bit. Unfortunately with his own box you could get two gears at once, such that if you changed down from third into second the selector would slip back again. I had one on the road to Bray like that—locked the gearbox and back axle up solid. In spite of this the Marendaz box was a solid box, ever so solid and you'd never break it. Once you got used to changing gears on that you could do some lovely changes, just changing on the revs.

Regarding the Laycock box, Kenneth Hurst who worked for Laycock in Sheffield had this to say when writing in *The Automobile*, April 1991: 'I recall seeing a Marendaz Special in the factory yard, and our own works director and the fiery little D. M. K. Marendaz having a stand up row (with hindsight, probably over the non-payment of accounts?)'.

Although advertised in the sales literature throughout the Maidenhead era, there only seem to have been two supercharged cars: one the stripped works car JB3702 and the other Marcus Marendaz's own long chassis car JB4300, both fitted with Zollers. Stan Duddington commented:

Inside the Maidenhead works, showing a 13/70
engine block being machined, undoubtedly
one not produced by Continental but a
Marendaz copy. (*Marendaz Special Cars*)

The Zollers had a big concentric vane in them, about a thou clearance on the vane and if it wore then
your efficiency dropped. And you had a little oil tank under the dash and a filtering pump on the
top going to the oil inlet. I remember Marendaz saying on his car, the big blue one, that the blower
was taking more oil than the engine. We had to make solid copper head gaskets for the supercharged
engine and when you annealed it, it twisted if you weren't careful. You could make it very accurately,
but directly you heated it with a blowlamp it went off. Do you remember the supercharger on the
competition car (JB3702), you'd start it on the Friday when it was going out Saturday and keep
revving it and then the knocking would appear which was the pistons touching the head. Then you'd
have to take them all out and get them machined down a bit, take so much off the top of the pistons.
[Marcndaz was planning to try a double engine and got as far as mocking one up in the works.]

… He was going to use two of his own side valves engines somehow in a car, which would make
it a twelve cylinder. There were some cylinder blocks being got ready, two engines side by side, but
there never was much done to them. He was going to build a record breaker. There were two gears,
the blanks were about ten inches with another one to match up with them in a central position, all
with helical teeth. Never came to anything, although he had a special left hand camshaft made for it.
I don't think they were ever put in the chassis and bonded together, but they stood there for months.
[Once cars were on the road there still remained a certain amount of road testing to be done, mostly
concerning back axle noise and low oil pressure.]

… The axles were E. N. V. crown wheel and pinion, bought in and they used to have a lot of
trouble with the noise so we'd do a lot of testing up past Kimbles. The axles used to be noisy very
often when they'd been built, but they used to sort of settle down, and we'd be up and down there
with no floorboards in, Marendaz driving, Chapman who was the foreman but who didn't do any

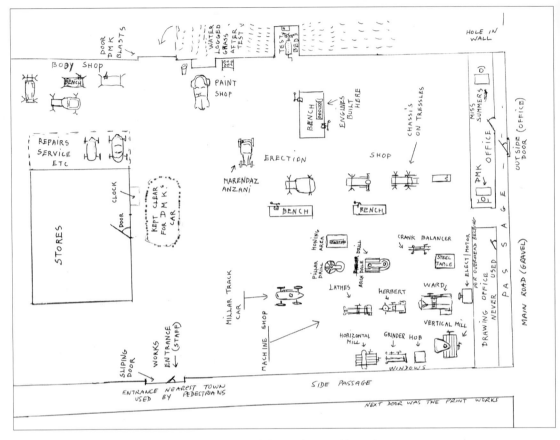

Stan Duddington's drawing of the Maidenhead Works layout. (*Stan Duddington*)

driving, and me hanging on the back axle like trying to feel it and listen to it and sit in the car. They took me more or less as ballast, I think. They'd have to stop and there'd be a bit of a to-do and we'd have to go back and have the diff out and re-set it.

[The differential casings were manufactured in the works as Jim Light recalls:] D'you know it was one of the worst jobs on that car and don't forget I used to make everything, was the two diff halves. It was a devil to get the machined part to lie flat enough. Yes, we actually made the diff halves, in other words the complete diff housing.

Presumably the problem was the marrying of the bought in parts with the Marendaz casing. The whole back axle, torque tube, and gearbox was a single unit, hung on the swivel joint at the front of the gearbox, with two sliding pick-ups on the rear axle onto the quarter elliptic cantilever rear springs, which only stuck out about an inch. This could sometimes cause a problem as any derangement could lead to the axle dropping off a spring at one side. One owner reported that a bump in the road on a tight bend at speed could cause this to happen, rendering the car uncontrollable. The usual reason was the torque tube clamping into the rear of the gearbox which if weak caused the tube to pull out of engagement slightly. This same weakness could also lead to the gearbox swivelling against the torque tube, so that the whole gearbox rolled over sideways, only being arrested by the floorboards. The problem casting was aluminium on the early cars being changed to cast iron later—an effective cure. This was not a problem Marcus Marendaz readily acknowledged, but as Stan Duddington said:

> You couldn't have more of a test than Marendaz driving one, could you? Nothing ever happened to his car like that. He never had any trouble. Marendaz claimed that it was the only fully floating back axle made in the British Isles other than Rolls-Royce. You could still push it about with no shafts in, you still had your two bearings each end.

The low oil pressure was found on bends due to starvation as a result of slosh and the lack of baffling in the sump, one assumes not a problem with the engine when fitted to the sedentary Erskine. Stan Duddington spent a lot of time testing the cars and checking the solutions:

> The early ones were different—the oil pump on the side, with a little priming pump and Marendaz's own ones had the submerged one driven off the camshaft. We used to have a lot of trouble with oil pressure, you were forever taking the sump off and stretching the spring or putting some washers behind it to get a bit more pressure—it must have been the bearings slackening. Start the engine, 'What's the oil pressure?' Oh, so-in-so; low. Rev it and fiddle with things. Chapman was the chief in the engine assembly area, a very nice chap, and he worked with Hagan, an Australian, just the two of them. Chapman didn't drive as he'd had an accident years ago on a motor-bike and if he wanted to go out I had to take him. Hagan was officially the foreman and Chapman was one of the mainstays of the fitting shop. A lot of people had been running big ends going round fast bends, the oil was surging away as there were no baffles

A Marendaz-designed gearbox, with ball joint at the front and troublesome torque tube clamp behind. (*Author's collection*)

in the sump, so a tin box was fitted inside the sump fitting round the oil pump. Then Chapman and I had to go out and test it at night, it was always at night, ever so late, with me driving and Chapman with pencil and paper writing down the temperature and the oil pressure, going round different bends at different speeds. It all turned out that that did the trick. The only snag was that we'd put a ¼ bolt through the bottom of the sump to hold the box with a fibre washer each side to stop it leaking, but it used to drip a bit; it was a bit crude, but at least it stopped the big ends going.

[Lack of oil pressure was an obvious concern, but it was the cause of another major problem. Stan Duddington:] Do you remember the chap who used to build the engines, Claude Hodgkinson, he used to work for M.G. and was supposed to have built George Eyston's motor?

[Jim Light:] Yes, I tell you what, I never seen anybody who could scrape bronze bearings like that bloke. But he got the sack. There were three engines seized up, right, if you remember. Used to have the oil hole come in, you had a main groove, and a channel about a ¼ in long from the oil hole into the groove, and he forgot to put it in.

[Stan Duddington:] One car seized up at Newcastle under Lyme and I had to go and fetch it. They sent me up there, two fellas came in an Essex Terraplane and I had to go back with them and I stayed the night in the pub. The car was in the pub yard and in the morning I had to take the sump down and take this bearing out and put some insulating tape and a jubilee clip round the crank and put the sump back up again, all on my own like and drive it back on five cylinders. There were about twenty-five bolts on those sumps and dropping it on your own when full of oil was no joke, as I'd nothing to drain it into.

[Jim Light:] Same thing happened once before. Do you remember when he dropped that little cotter pin down in there.' [The valves didn't have collets, but were retained by a pin]. 'Yes, he dropped one and it went down into the sump. He said 'Oh, it'll be all right'. By a thousand and one chance it got into the oil pump and when they got the engine back it was ruined! ½ inch long, about ⅛th diameter, couldn't be bothered!

[There was always a problem buying the components, as the radiators were ordered up one at a time and collected individually. It was the same for the Lucas components. Stan Duddington:]

The Laycock designed gearbox fitted to later cars. (*Author's collection*)

If you went anywhere at all you nearly always ran out of petrol and you had to go and get some in a can and you had to get a bill and show it to him and take it in again to get your money back. Then he'd tell you to go somewhere to fetch something. He used to send me to Lucas's about a quarter past five and he'd say 'They shut up about six, be sure you get there'. And of course Uxbridge road, Acton was slow and when you got there there'd be all this argument 'You haven't paid for the last lot, can't have any more', because he'd be buying one set at a time. So there'd be this big argument and they'd get on the phone to him and tell me to hang on and wait and there'd be all this argument and this, that and the other and then eventually they'd say 'Oh, all right you can have them', one starter motor, one dynamo, distributor, two headlights; complete electrical gear for a car, you see.

MOTOR SHOWS

Although Marcus Marendaz had exhibited at the motor shows in the early twenties with his Marseal cars a disagreement meant that during the thirties he exhibited elsewhere, usually nearby. He did have his London showroom at 3 Blenheim Street off New Bond Street as well (see *Autocar* advertisement, 22 September 1933), which was believed to be manned by Mr Bailey. *Autocar* for 15 December 1933 carried an advertisement from Marendaz Special Cars seeking a London salesman. Stan Duddington commented:

Of course, he didn't belong to the Motor Traders Association. When the Motor Show was on he had a little show of his own generally as he never ever exhibited at the Motor Show. He wouldn't belong to the Motor Traders Association, or they wouldn't have him, one or the other. One was at a little place at the end of Warwick Road or was it Holland Road, where it joins onto Hammersmith Road at the end of Kensington High Street. It was Bristol's latterly for a time. This was in the 1930s, and then another time he put some second-hand cars in the Agricultural Hall at Islington. He used to have a second-hand car show up there. He wasn't the only one as Fords didn't exhibit in the Motor Show either and used to go to the Albert Hall.

… After one of his little London Motor Shows at the Agricultural Hall there was a car that hadn't sold and he was taking me up there one night to bring it back to Maidenhead. It was the times that they had trams at Chiswick, trams used to run to where the Chiswick roundabout is now. There was this fella on an Ariel Square Four motor bike having a bit of a do, like, I think he must have looked at Marendaz and if anyone looked at him, that was enough. Well, this fella belts off full blast on this Ariel on the left hand side and Marendaz after him, but Marendaz can't get past him, so he goes out on the right hand side and belts down the road absolutely flat out and when we came to Turnham Green where the Chiswick Empire used to be he was just level and then all the way up to Hammersmith like this, one against the other. But we had to keep stopping at the traffic lights, so there we were at the traffic lights, broom, broom. But Marendaz had strained or broken the handbrake cable with him tugging at it doing a racing stop with some hectic braking. So we lost the chap on the Ariel but when we get to Kings Cross going up Pentonville Hill there, you know the old trams had a pick up in the road. Well, the handbrake wire cable must have dropped into the slot and was touching the live feed, and the angle-iron bits on the side, 'cos there were great big flashes coming out, like an electric train on a wet day. Great big flashes coming out from underneath. I was terrified in the back, thought I was going to get electrocuted. It wasn't bothering Marendaz at all. The wire dropped down the old tram thing-me-do with great big flashes going up Pentonville Hill!

Cars were delivered with this Union Jack badge, courtesy of Price's Oils. (*Author's collection*)

OTHER EMPLOYEES

Stan Duddington and Jim Light have provided a wealth of information about their life and times at Marendaz Cars, but they were not the only ones employed there who wrote about their experiences.

Mary Jackson, writing to the author on 18 January 1992, not long after the death of Marcus Marendaz, worked in the office and drove Marcus Marendaz around at the time he lost his licence:

> Reading about the Marendaz works today I feel a sense of loss that I didn't realise more, understand more of what was going on. I was an ignorant young woman, merely thinking that motor cars were wonderfully exciting and glamorous—which of course they were! My part was very minor.
>
> I was a young actress, out of work, out of cash, living in a London bed-sit and scouring the *Telegraph* jobs column. There didn't seem to be anything I could do, then I noticed an advertisement for a driver for a car manufacturer: I suppose it was intended for a man but why shouldn't it be a woman, I thought. In fact the more I thought about it the more it appealed to me. I wasn't exactly qualified as my driving experience was more or less my mother's Austin 7, my father not allowing me to drive his Calthorpe. Still I was desperate for a job and decided I would go for it and get it! I spent my last shillings on a red jersey and a black beret and appeared at the advertised address, a showroom in Bond Street with a gorgeous Marendaz Special in the window. I was interviewed by Mrs. Marendaz who took me out for a driving test. Of course the controls were very strange to me and my timing of the gear changes unfortunate to say the least. On our return to the showroom Captain Marendaz

A brochure illustration of the 17-hp long-chassis Saloon-bodied car, it is believed, by Abbots of Farnham. (*Author's collection*)

asked how I had fared. Mrs. Marendaz was somewhat doubtful but suggested that he took me out. This time I did a little better. 'Your gear changing isn't very good, is it?' Marendaz said. I remember my reply was something like this 'Oh, I'll be all right when I get used to it. Your gear box is different to any I have known.' He agreed that it was rather different and his own design. I think I must have willed him into giving me a job—perhaps the red jersey and black beret helped!

They arranged that I should live with them in their Maidenhead house and drive Captain Marendaz between the house and the works and anywhere else he wanted to go, his licence being endorsed for speeding. I should also take potential customers out and I should also clean and grease the cars. I remember making desperate calls to my brother who was training as an aeronautical engineer at De Havillands, 'How do I grease a car? What does this dial on the dashboard indicate?' and so on. I think my father's engineering genes had all been inherited by my brother, not me!

Anyway it was thrilling to drive those beautiful motor cars and everyone was very kind to me but a small domestic problem cropped up. Mrs. Marendaz left the office early each evening to prepare the dinner and instructed me to see that I got Captain Marendaz home by seven thirty. But that wasn't easy. Each evening I'd have to drive him and his manager to the local pub for a whisky. I used to say weakly, 'I did promise Mrs. Marendaz that we'd be home by seven thirty'. 'Oh, come on Mary—there's no hurry'. And it was always a number of whiskies after seven thirty before we made it.

I used to drive too slowly for Marendaz and he would goad me on, so we tore around the roads near Maidenhead at what seemed to me unbelievable speeds. One day I pulled up before turning from a secondary road into the main road where a lorry was approaching on my side. Marendaz made some impatient remark so I shot forward but not fast enough and the lorry caught the back of our car, swivelled us round and pretty well smashed our stern. Nobody was hurt but Captain Marendaz shouted at the lorry driver—hadn't he got any brakes—and that the poor man replied that they weren't working very well! Marendaz then ordered me to return to the office and ask the manager to give me a letter to take to Leicester and bring back a reply and to use the big car (which scared me to death). I've since realised this was to prevent me having an accident reaction and I've always been grateful to him.

When I returned from Leicester a letter was waiting for me. It was from J. B. Priestley's agent offering me a job in a Priestley play about to be produced in the West End. I showed the letter to

The clutch pedal showing the servo arrangement and simple adjustment.

Captain Marendaz and asked him, under the circumstances, if he would very much mind releasing me from the job with him. I still remember how he smiled and said 'Well, I didn't know you were a professional actress but I knew you weren't a professional driver.'

Some years later, during the war I was playing in one of the few theatres still functioning. A letter reached me there from the Marendaz's saying they had seen my name in a newspaper and would love to see me again. They were now making aircraft instead of cars and lived in Buckinghamshire. They invited me to come and bring a friend to a party they were giving. The play I was in flopped and I tried to find a friend with a car and petrol as I was now free to go. A Dutch journalist finally took me and I was given the warmest welcome by the Marendaz's. Captain Marendaz hugged me, gave me a cushion on the floor and a pile of banknotes. 'Mary will play with me', he said. The game was poker.

All my life I've kept an eye open in case I should still meet one on the road. I remember how in those days if you did meet another you both hailed and waved as you passed. If you ever stopped to ask the way the police showed you immense respect and you were immediately surrounded by crowds of admiring boys. No other car I've driven in my long life has thrilled me as they did.

John Midford-Millership, who worked there between 1933 and 1935, wrote to John Shaw in April 1993:

It's hard to recall events of some sixty years ago, I expect them to be sketchy, but hopefully accurate. I joined in 1933 as a trainee, with the possibility of driving for Captain Marendaz at some future date if suitable—such was the agreement made by my father. The works at Cordwallis was indeed a modern one by the standards then existing and at the same time sparse and simple.

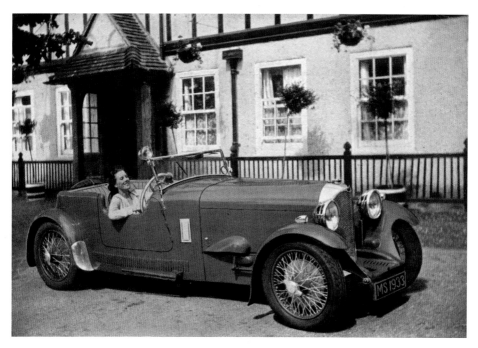

A brochure illustration of the 13/70. The location and young lady are unknown—apparently a happy find by Marcus Marendaz. The car is believed to be GW2382. (*Author's collection*)

My tasks started with the bare chassis which had to be drilled for the mounting of spring hangers, shock absorbers, bodywork, gearbox, radiator and so on and then assemble it all, not forgetting the copper pipework from the dashboard to each shock absorber for independent hydraulic control. The chassis were fitted with an old set of wheels to facilitate moving them from bay to bay. The work was exacting and meticulous, quite often assisted by lurid comments from THE MAN.

I cannot remember names—I was but a junior—with the exception of Mrs. Summers, secretary and housekeeper to Marendaz. He had so many convictions that he was banned and Mrs. Summers drove him about, to and from work. Not a good driver, very good at stalling and I found her an acerbic lady, ideal perhaps for the man. I took cars to Brooklands and Donington and on one occasion going to Donington, I found the oil pressure dropping and told her we must stop and find the cause. We were driving fast because we were late and in spite of my insistence she ordered me to keep going. Surely enough, the most awful noise I had ever heard started and a conrod broke near the gudgeon pin, thrashed around breaking the side of the block and carved into the sump, oil, steam and chaos. That resulted later in my stripping the engine out in the works, getting the block and sump welded, reassembly, all this in my own time without pay. As I said, a dreadful man.

I delivered a car to Brooklands, had the pleasure of a circuit with the course steward, the car was then in a Ladies Amateur Race, Mrs. Summers driving. At the off, they all got away and she was left on the line stalled.

On another day I took a car to Brooklands on Trade Plates, taking a friend with me. On my return journey I was passing through Staines and was pulled in by a policeman on a Ariel Square Four, booked for carrying a passenger on Trade Plates on a Bank Holiday and later fined £5 with 8 shillings costs.

Stan Duddington in the back seat, John Midford-Millership in the passenger seat, and John Shaw driving. (*Author's collection*)

One morning THE MAN said get in the car, we're off to Leeds to pick up a car and you will bring it back. Mrs M was driving to bring him back and I was wedged in the back. The Marendaz we were picking up was a bit of a mess and I had to retime the ignition, finishing about 9 pm. The man gave me a pound note, for me to fill it up and meet him outside Leeds Police Station at 11 pm. I put 16 gallons of petrol in the tank, had a meal and met him. He then said if you get back before me I will give you a pay rise, rousing words. I got back to Maidenhead about 3 am and, seeing a policeman on a cycle, asked him to give me a leaf from his notebook stating the time. I explained why and he even knew of the man and he did so. The next morning Marendaz said he'd arrived back at 3.15 am and I told him I'd won, but he did not accept my word. I then produced the chitty and the next week I received a rise of a halfpenny an hour.

One morning I'd tested a car for braking, was coming into Maidenhead down the hill, rather noisily, Marendaz was being driven back to work and as I turned left he came across from the crossing, the horn blaring. I therefore pulled in, he pulled up alongside, stood up in the passenger seat and started swearing and cursing. I was thinking about leaving his employment at that time so I shot off at speed, entered the works at enough speed to make a tyre burn mark in a perfect circle around the stores and got out of the car ready for anything. He came in and looked round the floor and to my amazement said 'A nice spot of driving, Millership' and walked off.

I decided to join the RAF and in January 1936 did so.

11

THE 1931 MARENDAZ SPECIAL: CARS, CUSTOMERS, AND CLOSURE

SOME OF THE CARS

Marendaz had a deal going with Prices Oils (later part of Shell) to supply Union Jack badges with their name on for the instrument panel. Stan Duddington commented:

> The Union Jack badges were supplied by Prices Oils and fitted from 1933 onwards, in other words whilst I was there. Marendaz was a bit of a wangler and he'd get some free oil or something like that for fitting them; he was getting something out of it. He was always a bit concerned by his 'foreign' name so he had a spare wheel cover made for the back of his own car that had a Union Jack in the centre with the slogan THE ALL-BRITISH MARENDAZ SPECIAL round it. All a bit of publicity.

13 HP COUPÉ

Stan Duddington stated: 'The 13 hp Coupés all had a straight back like a M.G. Magnette, a close-coupled thing with no room in the back seat at all, but there were only two or three built and I took one of them up to Leeds on trade plates, to Appleyards'.

LONG CHASSIS SUPERCHARGED AND LONG CHASSIS SALOON

> [Stan Duddington:] There were only two 17 hp long chassis cars ever made, his own car a four-seater with supercharger, which was the prototype (JB 4300) and a saloon. His supercharger was a Zoller driven at a forty-five-degree angle across the front of the crankcase off a special crank, so it had a different timing cover. It was called a 17/90 and was light pale blue. [Photographic evidence suggests that there were at least two long-chassis saloons.]
>
> [Jim Light:] The 17 horse long-chassis was the one that frightened the life out of Mrs. Moss. It always used to stand in the front of the stores, you see. She was arguing with the Captain to let her have a go in it and in the end he said well alright, we'll go together. I can see him now. She got in his car, the big doors to the works were opened and you know you had just the width of the road outside.

JB4300 Marcus Marendaz's own supercharged long-chassis car. It is believed that the lady is Rita Don. (*Marendaz Special Cars*)

She got in and started it up and she went out of that door at full whack, I can hear it now and how the hell she got round there without hitting something, I don't know. She came back in and said 'I can't be getting on with anything like that.'

[Stan Duddington:] There were only the two supercharged cars. I know, the 13 horse one which we used in the trials and Marendaz's own big blue one, 'cos I don't think the other one could go in a rally, it wasn't really a road car, it was an experimental thing. There was no paint on it or anything. Lots of things that wouldn't comply with regulations.

This car did in fact run in the 1934 RAC Rally, driven by S. R. Mitchell. Possibly a first, Marcus Marendaz's Supercharged Long-Chassis Tourer appeared on the stage at the Cambridge Theatre in August 1935 in a production of *Man and Superman* by Bernard Shaw, featuring in Act II, 'The Avenue to Mrs Whitefield's house, Richmond'. The programme for the play noted 'We are indebted to British Marendaz Special Cars Ltd of Maidenhead, for their kind co-operation in supplying the British Marendaz Special Car'. Marendaz did not miss a trick and an advertisement in the programme by Cook and Palmer Ltd (184-188 Great Portland Street) included notice of the car at £495, with 10,000 miles on the clock.

THE 17 HORSEPOWER

The 17/80 or 17/90 had radiator slats, which were thermostatically controlled, so the 17-hp cars can be identified in the photographs by these slats. One of them had a problem before it even left the works. Stan Duddington commented:

> There was the car that went to Edinburgh, a blue 17 hp with the radiator slats, that we had to squeeze the pistons up in a vice. It was going to Christies of Edinburgh who had one as a demonstration car. Claude Hodgkinson worked for us having come from MGs where he'd worked on George Eyston's car. He was a bit of a perfectionist and there were a set of pistons, just machined, all ready to be put in an engine which he micrometered up and found that they were oval in the wrong direction. Jim had turned them up and put them on the marking off table. Well, when he pointed this out to Marendaz, who said 'Can't you squeeze them up in the vice?' and Claude said 'That'll never work' and Marendaz said 'We haven't any other pistons, give it a try'. So when we ran the engine it was the quietest ever and also the fastest. One reason for this might have been because when we cut the timing gears there was no precision on where the locating keyway was cut, it being either opposite a tooth or between a tooth, so the valve timing could vary slightly with hit and miss results, but with that car it was a good result. 'Cos they all used to rattle a bit, didn't they?

DROP HEAD COUPÉ

Stan Duddington commented:

> The Drophead Coupé was yellow with a blue hood, the only one he made. It took years to get that one finished, 'cos the chap from Wilmot Breeden had to keep coming round about the door locks and hinges and the hood frame and all that and he'd want a bit here and a bit there and the little fiddly pieces and they could never seem to get them right. Then he'd go away, then he'd be back a few weeks later and it went on and on until it was kind of perfect. They were always in trouble with the hood frames and there had been a lot of argument, not surprising with the Captain. This was the car we went down to the Torquay Rally in and which he turned over on the way back.

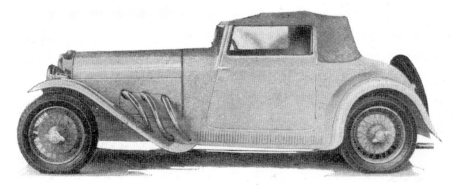

The drophead coupé in yellow and blue that Marcus Marendaz turned over. (*Marendaz Special Cars*)

SOME OF THE CUSTOMERS

Brinkwoods

Stan Duddington stated:

> The one at Brinkwoods at Taplow was green and it had a JB registration. I remember Mr Brinkwood coming in one day and I heard him say to Marendaz, 'There's only one fault with these cars, Marendaz' and Marendaz looks at him, odd like. 'Whenever I leave it somewhere there's always a ruddy crowd round it when I come back! I left one in Swindon and there were boys even getting underneath to look there; they were all over it'. Cars in the 1930s were all a bit square looking—so a Marendaz was racy with all those exhaust pipes. Only Invicta and Mercedes had those at that time.

J. A. Welch

Stan Duddington commented:

> Their biggest competitors at that time were Aston Martin and if you didn't buy a Marendaz then you went out and bought an Aston Martin. I remember a fella who had an Aston who came in and eventually bought a 13 hp Marendaz. He was called Welch and raced at Brooklands. It was in the works one time for some adjustment and I had to take it over to Brooklands and hand it over to him. 'Mr Welch will be in the paddock,' Marendaz said 'Drive it in there and hand the car over.'

This car is AMB631, which survives, and was illustrated in *Motor* for 9 January 1934.

One that has not survived. JB2536 looking rather tired and with an undersized stone guard. Last known in Essex at the end of the war. (*J. V. Bowles*)

FINAL DAYS

Marendaz Special Cars Limited as a company, was wound up the paperwork being dated 24 June 1936. Stan Duddington had left several months earlier and Jim Light moved across to International Aircraft Limited, a few hundred yards away, on a full-time basis. Given the times, it seemed a little strange that the company closed at this date, having survived intact through the depression of the early 1930s. There was every impression that a war was coming and the necessity for manufacturing concerns was ever greater. Marcus Marendaz was making luxury cars and given the number of similarly inclined newcomers trying their hand in the mid-1930s, it seems strange that he stopped at this juncture. It is possible that he saw a better opening with aircraft, having already started along this line in a building next door to the cars, possibly with potential extension into much-needed general engineering as a sub-contractor. His start with the aircraft was again into a luxury market, so it has to be said that his overall business objectives have to be considered unclear. Remaining stock was sold to R. H. Collier of South Yardley, Birmingham, whose business interests included buying up the residue of collapsed companies, Swift and Clyno being amongst their 'clients'. They then offered support to car owners with spares and whatever. According to *Old Motor* in 1969, the Marendaz Special stock was bought for £250 but was found to be a mixed blessing as no two cars turned out to be alike. At least one Marendaz Special was completed by Colliers following the factory closure at Maidenhead.

PRODUCTION RATES

In reviewing his success, it is probably worth looking at his production rates. These cannot be ascertained with absolutely certainty, but chassis numbers and registration dates do give a clue. It does not look as if Marendaz ever sold a car abroad that was brand new from the factory and there is no indication of him ever advertising abroad.

Production rates averaged out between the years 1932 and 1936 at about one car a month, namely seven in 1932, sixteen in 1933, nine in 1934, twelve in 1935, and seven in 1936, with two cars registered after the factory closure. There does not seem to be any obvious tailing off, or even a step increase with the advent of the 15/90; possibly because the 15/90 did not increase sales significantly, Marendaz may have decided that his future lay with aircraft.

HOW MANY WERE BUILT?

The figures noted above can be added up to give a rough idea of production numbers. At least five 13/70s were built in London, the rest in Maidenhead, giving estimated totals as follows.

Chassis numbers for 13-hp and 17-hp cars run between thirty-one and seventy-four, with the chassis numbers generally presented doubled, for example 3131, so forty-four cars, plus two un-numbered cars to make a total of forty-six. Chassis numbers for 15/90 ran in a sequence starting at 7401 to 7429, but only using every fourth number, meaning eight cars, plus a prototype and a late number 7445, were made, giving a total of ten cars. There was therefore a grand total of fifty-six. To this has to be added the estimated thirty Anzani-powered cars built in London, so for the marque all told, perhaps eighty-six cars were built.

The six cars, left to right, of Messrs Bremner-Smith, Hodge, Urry, Arney, Spiers, and Skillen in Oxfordshire, 2006. (*Peter Arney*)

HOW MANY SURVIVE?

It is believed that at the time of writing there are twenty-three surviving complete cars, namely one 11/55 (Anzani), twelve 13/70s, three 17/80s or 17/90s, and seven 15/90s. There is no specific club for the owners of the cars, although ties between owners are moderately close, providing some technical support. In 2006, Dick Hodge, an owner at that time, organised and funded a Marendaz Special gathering in Oxfordshire, the only time since the war that as many as six cars have been together.

12

TECHNICAL DESCRIPTION

T he seating in the 13/70 is comfortable with two bucket seats in front on sliding rails with a rear seat behind. This is nominally for one person but could take two at a pinch. The restricted rear seat comes about because of the folding hood, which stows into a box inside the body, thereby restricting the available space. A selling point for the cars was this hood stowing arrangement complete with zip fastener, referred to as the 'disappearing hood'. Later models had a faired metal cover, hinged at the back. Footwells at the back are box-like structures, one either side of the torque-tube tunnel dropped neatly below the chassis level. The steering wheel is adjustable for height but requires spanners to accomplish this. The wheel itself is a four-spoke Blumels item with white celluloid covering. It seems to be specifically a Marendaz item, the identical wheel not being found on other marques. Lights, hand throttle, and advance and retard are controlled by levers operating a concentric rod system to the base of the column and the horn likewise is wired from a centre push to the column base. Instruments are variable depending on customer options, but speedo, tacho, timepiece, and oil pressure gauge are black-faced marked Marendaz Special. The ammeter is not so marked.

The handbrake is of the fly-off type and is slightly to the left of the gearbox; it operates a single cable to both the rear brake drums. The gearbox is either a Marendaz or Laycock item. The Marendaz box is four forward and reverse, reverse being achieved by a lift up baulk on the top of the box and pushing past the position for first gear, all in a 'reversed H' layout with first and reverse right and forward. The Laycock box also has first right and forward with reverse further to the right and forward, second right and back, third left and forward, and fourth left and back. Both boxes are non-synchromesh in all gears, which are straight cut. Steering is by Bishop cam and the lock is poor. The foot throttle is central between the brake on the right and the clutch.

The 13/70 engine of whatever origin is a side-valve unit. Specifications vary according to source, but the factory brochure gives 59-mm bore by 114-mm stroke, a capacity of 1,869 cc and 12.8 hp. Carburation was originally by Amal downdraught, but most cars today use S.U., 1 ⅝th (42 mm). There are two air inlets to the engine, split between cylinders one to three and four to six and three exhausts each from two cylinders, the centre exhaust providing a doughnut round the downdraught inlet tract. The triple exhausts curl out and down and are joined in a collector box just under the forward bodywork. This box is un-silenced and was the only one

A 13/70 panel layout. (*Author's collection*)

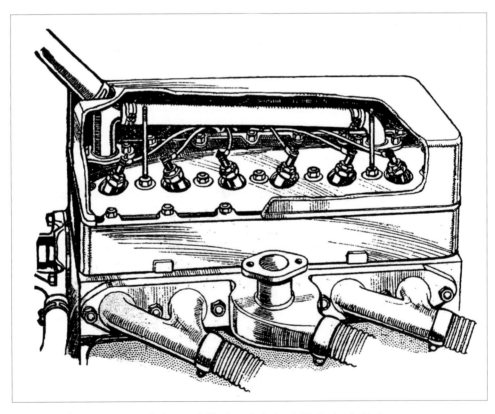

The curious plug arrangement with them angled in the cylinder head. (*Author's collection*)

fitted to the cars from the factory. Today, most owners have fitted a supplementary silencer box downstream. The camshaft and dynamo are driven by toothed chain off the crankshaft, with the distributor driven off the remote end of the dynamo by skew drive. The ex-Erskine engines have a side-mounted oil pump that requires priming if there has been a long period of inactivity and feed to the main bearings and big ends is by internal copper pipe. The Marendaz manufactured engines have an improved oil system with pump in the sump and internal oil galleries in the block. These differences are visible on the left-hand side of the engine. The Marendaz cylinder head is identifiable by the mounting of the sparking plugs at an angle of forty-five degrees and referred to in the sales publicity as the 'anti-pinking high-efficiency head'. The benefits conferred by this arrangement are unproven. The compression ratio is stated to be 6:1. New engines in the factory were fitted with special low-compression heads for running in. These were economically manufactured in two parts by being split horizontally, thereby opening up the water jacket space. Various compressions could be used by changing the lower part of the casting. In the casting process for these 'half' heads no core plugs were necessary, as for making hollow castings, so the casting process was much simplified and very economical. The cylinder head, plugs, and plug leads are hidden under a dummy rocker-box cover. The larger-engined models had a bore of 67.5 mm and a stroke of 114.3 mm, giving a capacity of nominally 2,500 cc, 16.9 hp. The 15-90 model with the Coventry-Climax engine had a bore 65 mm and a stroke of 100 mm, giving a capacity of 1,991 cc, 15.7 hp.

Marcus Marendaz was very proud of his 'disappearing' hood. Later cars used a metal cover. (*Marendaz Special Cars*)

The clutch is dry plate operated by a 2:1 gear on the pedal—a Marendaz innovation, giving lighter loads but longer travel. A further 2:1 gear is fitted to the brake pedal, equally reducing foot loads, operating directly on the Lockheed master cylinder to all four wheels. The brakes have 14-inch drums with a single leading shoe and a single training shoe.

All electrics were originally 12-volt Lucas pattern, headlights L170 Biflex, single dipping. The wiper motor is mounted at the top of the windscreen on the passenger side, operating two blades. The battery is located in the bulkhead under the bonnet. Twin Altette horns are fitted.

The radiator is by the Gallay Radiator Company of the attractive Bentley style. As originally designed, they are regarded as slightly undersized, but an additional radiator can be fitted horizontally underneath out of sight. There is a water pump and belt-driven fan.

The transmission chain only contains one universal joint, located inside the large spherical bearing at the front of the gearbox. The gearbox, torque tube, and rear axle are one unit, with the propshaft for the Marendaz box extending from the gearbox into the differential. The rear axle is fully floating.

The chassis is standard C-section front and back, but at the centre is deeper and of L-section, the top flange of the 'C' not being present. The floorless body is attached outside the chassis and extends below it and the separate body floor sits inside the chassis on the lower flange. This is what gives the car its attractive low line. Front springs are semi-elliptic, with rollers at the rear. The rear springs are cantilever quarter-elliptics, with a roller shoe at the rear pick-up on top of the axle. Shock absorbers are from Hartford.

The petrol tank is of 12-gallon capacity, carried at the rear and a S.U. fuel pump is used.

The preceding description is broadly applicable to all models excerpt where noted, although some owners of surviving cars have effected modifications that are regarded as almost standard, for example the additional radiator and a S.U. carburettor. Unsurprisingly, most cars were non-standard in some details, for example, Peter Mercer describing his black 17-80 Convertible Coupé, JB2601previously owned by Alfred Moss, stated that it had 'ice-box calf upholstery and trim with thick pile carpets to match and limed oak dashboard. It had Andre Telecontrol shockers and a chromed louvred auto radiator shutters and a white steering wheel'.

13

MARENDAZ SPECIAL IN COMPETITION: 1931-1936

BROOKLANDS AND TRIALS

Marcus Marendaz's endeavours were changing, 1931 being largely a fallow year without competition, but undoubtedly with major effort on revamping his design ideas, which eventually emerged in late 1931 as the Model 13/70. The development mule that later became BGW770 was around and may well have been tested on the track at Brooklands, but seemingly all was under the radar until the launch in October 1931. At least five cars were produced at the old Brixton Road establishment before the factory move to Maidenhead; one of these—GW2382, painted in an old rose colour—appeared at Brooklands in March and June 1932 driven by both Marcus Marendaz and his cousin Altair Kelway. Marendaz was reported to the stewards at the June meeting for having the name of the car displayed using too large lettering on the bonnet sides, being told by the Clerk of the Course that if he had been entered for another race, the markings would have to be of regulation size or be blotted out. Away from Brooklands, there were three cars entered in the 1932 RAC Rally, driven by Marendaz, Colonel F. H. Windrum and A. Milburn. The June meeting at Shelsley Walsh saw Marendaz in a 13/70 where he obviously had problems, recording a very poor time. It has to be said that the cars now being built and selling quite well were tourers and not racing cars, so competitively Marcus Marendaz had to adjust his appearances to more trials-type events.

There were thirteen cars registered in 1933 so one can conclude that Marcus Marendaz was pretty busy and consequently did not run at Brooklands that year, but elsewhere there were four cars entered in the RAC Rally, which that year ran from London to Hastings. Drivers were Marendaz, W. A. Silcock, C. E. Coppen, and Aileen Moss, mother to Stirling Moss, all driving 13/70s. The Moss car was JB1477, the first of four Marendaz Specials Aileen and Alfred owned, and was specially adapted for hill-climbing having a secondary gearbox. They elected to run this car in the concours events initially before the condition deteriorated to the point where it would only be fit for use on trials. In an appearance at the Scarborough Trial and Rally, Aileen Moss was first in Class and won the concours but was unrewarded at the similar Ramsgate Concours d'Elegance a few weeks later. Entries for the Sporting Trial and the Gloucester Trial towards the end of the year, saw JB1477 in serious action, but retired from both. After a clutch failure and with Aileen Moss not willing to give up, Stan Duddington was summoned to Gloucestershire to attend to the car as told in Chapter 14.

An early 13/70 on Beggar's Roost in a 1932 trial. The driver is not known. (*National Motor Museum*)

Aileen Moss (left) with Alfred Moss during the 1933 RAC. Rally with the black 13/70. Note the turn-with-the-wheel headlights. (*Author's Collection*)

The year 1934 saw D. G. Silcock and Mrs Moss at a J.C.C. event at Brooklands early in the year and, in June, S. R. Mitchell turned up at a J.C.C. Members Day with a supercharged car. There were two Zoller supercharged Marendaz Specials, Marcus Marendaz's own amethyst-coloured car, JB4300, and a lightweight works car that remained in a stripped and tatty state, JB3702, built in 1933 and run on trade plates until registered in March 1934. S. R. Mitchell was a works driver entered into various sprints, hill climbs and other competitive events, so it seems likely that this entry was JB3702.

> [Stan Duddington knew him:] Do you remember the supercharged 13 horse?
>
> [Jim Light:] Yes, that was the one they put in against the twin cam Bugatti at Brighton. It just beat him on distance.
>
> [Stan Duddington:] That chap Mitchell used to drive it. He had a lot of yellow hair.
>
> We used to have to go out Saturday morning with that to the Brighton Speed Trials, Shelsley Walsh and the like. That was the supercharged one and I generally used to go with him sitting on my toolbox, because there was no trim in it. We sheared the water pump one time, on the end of the fan spindle. Had to come back keeping switching the engine on and off.

Two cars ran at the BARC summer meeting at Brooklands in July, both entered by A. G. Bainton, one supercharged, probably Marcus Marendaz's JB4300, the other being a 17-hp car driven by Dorothy Summers. At the August meeting, Rita Don (Kaye Don's sister) put in an entry for three races all for a 17-hp car, one race each to be driven by S. R. Mitchell, Dorothy Summers, and Rita Don herself. For Marendaz Special cars, the Brooklands season ended spectacularly in October when Dorothy Summers blew up the engine of her car. Stan Duddington was there:

> She drove in one race and when she was leading and doing about 80 a conrod bolt broke and it cut the whole engine in half almost. It broke all the oil gallery pipes, smashed all the pistons with a big hole in the side—made a terrible mess of it. 17 hp engine.
>
> [Jim Light:] I'd never seen anything like it. She was on the last lap and she was leading.

Away from Brooklands, the 1934 RAC Rally, which ended in Bournemouth, saw entries by Marendaz, D. G. Silcock, T. McCabe, S. R. Mitchell, and the Mosses, who won a coachwork prize with Alfred's 17 hp car, JB2601. S. R. Mitchell was, as usual, driving the works supercharged 13-hp car, road registered a few days earlier and unlikely to be a candidate for the concours, but retired with supercharger failure. Jim Light commented:

> D'you remember the supercharged one we put in a rally where the supercharger blew at Cambridge? I don't know who was driving it, but it started from Newcastle, I remember that, and we were getting ready for work one morning, when Chapman in overalls came round and the phone was ringing like hell and Reg dashed round to the office and it was this bloke who was driving the car ringing up from a phone box in Cambridge. The supercharger had blown up.

Aileen Moss got a bronze award on the Land's End Trial that year and D. G. Silcock earned a first-class award on the Barnstaple Trial. Marcus Marendaz recorded a best time of 57.4 seconds at Shelsley Walsh in June but failed to better it in September.

JB3702, the works stripped supercharged 13/70 at the 1934 Amersham Hill Climb. The supercharger can be seen sticking out of the left-hand bonnet side. (*National Motor Museum*)

The year 1935 saw only two Marendaz Specials appearing at Brooklands, one in the hands of J. A. Andrews in the Junior Car Club Fourth Brooklands Rally and J. T., Jack, Thorowgood in the Middlesex Car Club second one-hour trial. Further afield, Marcus Marendaz gained a third in his 17-hp car in the RAC Rally which ended in Eastbourne, having started in Leamington. A. G. Bainton was also entered, starting from Yarmouth, also in a 17-hp car. Marcus Marendaz was undoubtedly very busy planning the emergence of the 15-90 Model, the main difference from earlier cars being the adoption of the Coventry-Climax 1,991-cc six-cylinder engine. Two of these cars were completed in the late summer, the fully finished demonstrator (JB7140) and the utilitarian stripped car planned as an entry for the Tourist Trophy race in Ulster on 7 September.

THE 1935 TOURIST TROPHY RACE

Stan Duddington stated:

McCalla drove the T.T. car with the Coventry Climax engine. We built it one weekend, started the Thursday night. Shenck, the works manager, took the T.T. car to Euston to put on the train and I had to take his Lancia there to come back in. When I got there still in overalls he phones up Marendaz to tell him, yes, the car's there, we've put it on the train, all right. Marendaz then tells me to wait on the station as I'm going over to Ireland with it. You see, I didn't know that and I had to wait on the station another hour while he comes in his car and brings a bit of my stuff he'd collected from my digs. I think Schenk was German or Austrian or something. He came as a works manager, but he didn't do

The first Moss Marendaz Special, JB1477, on the 1934 Land's End Trial. Alfred is driving with Aileen 'bouncing' in the rear. Note the external handbrake. (*National Motor Museum*)

much, talk to you a bit. I went over there with the car, but we had ever so much trouble there getting it ready. Mechanically it was all right, but there was this trouble with it being tight getting it into gear. You had to have the selectors screwed down tight to stop it jumping out of gear. McCalla, who drove it found it was too much of a push so he had to have an extension put on the top of the gear lever. So I turned one up, screwed it and threaded it. Then we found the mudguards were at the wrong angle. They had to be so much out of the vertical and so much horizontal. Then we'd trouble with the screen which had to be 3 or 5 mm copper mesh. There was something wrong with the spare wheel carrier, we had to alter that. Mechanically it was all right, I think I did the tappets. It finished the race, 12th or 13th. I remember I drove it back to the garage in Belfast from Newtownards. He'd run over the kerb somewhere and broken the front shock absorber bracket, I know. But on the first lap he came into the pits and we had to take the top off the gearbox. We had to tighten or slacken the selectors, one or the other. McCalla used to drive at Phoenix Park in Dublin and was very well known. He owned Seagrave's old Sunbeam at the time and had it in this garage, which used to do jobs for him. The mechanic would work in the garage but was his own personal mechanic, so when his car came in he dropped everything else and worked on his car. I got fixed up by this mechanic with digs and we were there a fortnight, fiddling about. I remember we came back on the Sunday morning. When he went over the pavement he made the top joint of the radiator leak. It was leaking badly and I had to tie my handkerchief round it. We got some mustard and went to a little shop that was open and bought a tin of Colman's mustard, put it in and that froze it up and stopped it. As we were motoring on—we did 102 along the Coventry bypass. I think that was the fastest I'd been in those days.

Schenk ran the works when Marendaz was away. He had this Lancia Lambda car, one of those long low things, like a bath. He told me when we were setting out for Euston 'Follow me up and if I

W. T. McCalla driving the 15/90 Marendaz Special in the 1935 Ards TT. He was unplaced but Marendaz claimed a Class 'E' win and lap record. (*Ulster Folk and Transport Museum*)

disappear just drive at your own speed. Round about 63–65 the steering wheel will get a wobble on it. Well, either accelerate or slow down, just ignore it.'

The gearbox trouble with the T.T. car was possibly because it had a Marendaz box, rather than the later and better Laycock item. This was because of homologation regulations not allowing a non-production item to be fitted.

As far as Marendaz was concerned, he rather felt that he had been handicapped out of it. He was classified in Class 'E', for which there was a very small entry so stood a good chance, but he did have the consolation of seeing W. T. McCalla break the Class 'E' lap record twice at 72.74 and 73.07 mph, with the car still running at the end, having done thirty-four laps. The winner was Freddie Dixon in his 1,496-cc Riley at 76.90 mph.

[Jim Light:] I tell you the scruffiest racing driver I ever came across, he was round at Marendaz one day trying to get a drive with Marendaz, somehow, Freddie Dixon, the old Riley chap. He was a scruffy so-in-so with his collar all twisted round him. But he could get twelve to twenty mile an hour more out of a Riley than Riley ever could. D'you ever see him? He wasn't sober when he came round our place.

[Stan Duddington:] Oh, yes, he was over in Ireland when I was there for the 1935 TT. He won that race. He seemed half drunk at the time, swearing and cussing. Of course he went to prison for doing something, getting drunk. He was in prison for a long time. He was a good tuner but such an awkward sort of fella. I have a friend in Acton who was born in Cumberland and Freddie Dixon lived about

Marcus Marendaz driving his 15/90 with *élan* at Shelsley Walsh in August 1935. (*D. M. K. Marendaz*)

two miles from him. Freddie Dixon used to test engines and he had a water wheel running round off a river coming down the mountain and he connected this engine up as a test brake, driving the water wheel in the reverse direction and he reckoned you could hear this thing all over Cumberland for miles around when he was testing it. You wouldn't call him a gentleman.

Marendaz's 1935 season ended with a very successful outing to Shelsley Walsh where he entered his own 15-90 tourer with the Coventry-Climax 1,991-cc engine, with a time of 57.0 seconds, good enough for a Class 4B win and the award of a very nice silver rose bowl.

The 1936 season at Brooklands commenced for the Marendaz establishment at the BARC opening meeting in March, where the works new competition car, the 15-90 that had run in the 1935 T.T., appeared in the hands of Dorothy Summers. She missed the start of the first race, her engine not being started, but leapt away in the second race to win easily by 300 yards at 89.03 mph. This win was lauded in the national press with headlines such as 'Shy Miss Wins Race and First Day of Women's Car Racing Freedom' and the nuances of the words caused argument and discussion into the 1980s. The late Michael Sedgwick, a most careful historian, said 'Miss D. Summers was the first woman to win a race at Brooklands after the fair sex had been admitted on equal terms as the men'—a complete and accurate statement. She was not the first woman to win a race there, but previously for various reasons, BARC had imposed fairly trivial restrictions that were completely removed in 1936, thereby creating a rather ambiguous impression. Anyway, it was to Dorothy Summers advantage and capital was made.

Dorothy Summers with Marcus Marendaz alongside her on the start line at the 1936 Brooklands Opening Meeting. She did not have her engine running for the first race, seen here, but won the second easily. (*Autocar*)

THE 1936 RAC TORQUAY RALLY

Elsewhere, Marendaz Specials continued to appear at sporting events until the demise of the company and thereafter in the hands of the Mosses. The RAC Rally, ending this year in Torquay saw entries of Aileen Moss in her new short chassis white car, DPG7, recording the best time on the hill of 19.4 seconds, Marcus Marendaz driving, it is believed, his very pretty drop-head coupé and Mrs A. C. Lace in a red Marendaz Special. Mrs Lace and her husband were well known in the Brooklands firmament and she was undoubtedly friendly with Marendaz. Unfortunately, her entry for this event did not go well as the clutch failed:

[Stan Duddington:] We got the message that the clutch had gone so I had to go down to the West Country with Captain Marendaz in the drop head coupé. It was a very pretty car, only snag was that it was enclosed and the roar of the exhaust was tiring. He picked me up around six o'clock one evening and I hadn't had much to eat and with Marendaz driving like mad on the corners, I was never still always bracing myself with him driving like a fanatic and of course he belts along and all the time I'm sliding this way and that and with the hood up there's this great droning noise. He stopped somewhere and got me a bag of cakes, and if you hadn't had much to eat, cream horns aren't the thing, so with all the whipping around corners I got ever so sick and had to get out near Newton Abbot and be sick and sit for a minute. Lovely countryside and me feeling ever so green. He took me down with Jim Clark. We were down there two days. Mrs. Lace, d'you remember Mrs. Lace, a brilliant blonde, who used to drive?

[Jim Light:] Was she another of his flames?

Mrs A. C. Lace, who drove a Marendaz Special in the 1936 RAC Rally, seen here on the pit counter at Brooklands in August 1938. (*Brooklands Society*)

[Stan Duddington:] Well, I never really knew. She was a very brilliant blonde and they all used to be thrilling around her. She was well known at Brooklands. We got there eventually and Marendaz got me fixed up in a place and he went to another big hotel himself near my boarding house. There was a bit of a scandal when we got back to the works as Miss Summers reckoned he'd been staying there with Mrs. Lace or something. Bit of an upheaval domestically, like. She'd run the car into a garage at Honiton and Marendaz said we've got to go and rescue Mrs. Lace, so we'd belted down there, full bore, and by the time we get in this garage there were about six or seven chaps all in white coats. They'd taken the floor boards out and were looking at it, hadn't started on anything mechanical and Marendaz strides in and says 'What are these men doing on my car, get them out of the way, my man will see to this'. I felt ever so embarrassed as I was all scruffy in these old overalls and with all these chaps in white—it was a posh garage. 'Get these men out of the way, my man'll see to this!' He was always like that, very peremptory towards everybody.

[Jim Light:] Not too difficult a job.

[Stan Duddington:] It didn't take very long. You can change a clutch in about half an hour. You just take the four bolts off the coupling, six bolts round the clutch shaft, pull that out, and you're at the flywheel and that was it. I had to do the same job at Birdlip for Mrs. Moss. When we came back from Torquay he turned that yellow coupé over.

[Jim Light:] I wouldn't be surprised.

[Stan Duddington:] It was foggy and we kept having roads where one went round a bend and another went off at an angle and there were two roads like that with an A. A. box in the middle. Well, he came to an A. A. box on a bend and the road went left but there wasn't one to the right and he

The second Moss trials car, a short-chassis 15/90, DPG7, on a Club event in 1936, Aileen driving. Note the '7' number plate and entry number, favoured by Stirling Moss in later years. (*National Motor Museum*)

thought there was and he went up the bank and rolled over—it was the wrong A. A. box. Mrs. Moss was with him and I was in Moss's car behind with Mr Moss. So it lay there and we had to pull the hood down and pull Mrs. Moss out and when Marendaz got out of it he'd broken his ribs, so he sat there as a passenger and I had to drive him back. And for that week I had to drive him, fetch him and take him and he kept going on about his ribs.

[Jim Light:] Did he go to hospital?

[Stan Duddington:] Yes, I had to drive him—a miserable job.

Mrs A. C. Lace was born Phoebe Elizabeth Mylchreest in 1914, but apparently was known as Betty. She married a Mr McQueen in 1931, but in her time was known as Mrs Lace and later Mrs Williams but was married to Mr Brian Carberry between 1940 and 1948. In later years, she was still calling herself Mrs Lace, a reflection of her days racing at Brooklands.

Aileen Moss ran her new car in various trials, the Land's End, the Brighton-Beer, the Blackpool Rally, the July Rally at Torquay, the Mid-Surrey Automobile Club's Barnstaple Trial (where she achieved a first), the Scottish Trial (where she was fourth), a silver at the M.C.C. Sporting Trial at Buxton, and others—a successful year indeed.

THE 1936 FRENCH GRAND PRIX

The Marendaz Special swan song in competitive terms was the French Grand Prix in June 1936. This was a sports car event and the T.T. car was entered with Earl Howe to drive. How this came about was that the press was giving Earl Howe a bad time for always driving foreign cars, to which he replied that he would drive a British car if there was one good enough and it was made available. Marcus Marendaz responded and Earl Howe was more or less obliged to accept. It did not go well. Before the race, Earl Howe had taken the car down the Portsmouth Road having collected it from Guy Griffiths's tuning establishment at Molesey, Guy and Alfred Moss having taken the car from the Marendaz Special works. He got as far as Cobham where there was a pub on the roundabout; he stopped and got out, then asked Guy to drive it back. Guy said it was awful and his hand was raw with the gear change after driving a short distance. A stiff gear change had been a problem at the T.T. The car, white in the T.T. was, unsurprisingly, repainted British racing green. Guy also said that Earl Howe had crashed early on in the Grand Prix running into a bank due to the very heavy steering. He drove it back to the pits for a hub change, using a hub taken from Alfred Moss's car in the car park. Earl Howe 'cleared off' and Tommy Wisdom was left to carry on trundling round at 25 mph to get the starting money. This wasn't the story from the works:

[Jim Light:] I remember the T.T. car in the French Grand Prix and I worked on a set of pistons for it.

[Stan Duddington:] Well, I'd left then. I think I'd just left by about three weeks. Lord Howe drove it. His front hub seized up, didn't it? His mechanic over tightened the bearings. He didn't know they were taper races.

[Jim Light:] I got back in at 10 o'clock. It was rattling, the roof. The old man came back about 10 o'clock with a set of pistons, seven he'd had made and I worked all night to turn them up. Louis Giron came over about 5 o'clock in the morning to fit them and I went back to help him. What happened was I went over the hubs and wheel bearings, got them just right, but for some reason his mechanic went and did the nearside front again, the one that seized up. You wanted to have seen it, the taper races were just melted, absolutely melted. The old man had taken his car over and they took the stub axle off his and got Lord Howe back in the race. That's what happened. Giron was a Bugatti specialist, bit of a loud bloke.

Earl Howe driving T. T. 15/90 repainted green for the French Grand Prix in 1936. (*Author's collection*)

As it is right and due, perhaps we should permit Marcus Marendaz the last word on this sequence of events, as written to Anthony Blight on 3 September 1987:

> On the night before the 1936 French Grand Prix I wanted the car to make an adjustment. Lord Howe insisted on his mechanic Williams had the car to screw his Toddy Can to the front floorboards and screw his clip for the mouthpiece to the solid walnut facia board ... and other unspecified adjustments.... The race commenced with Howe driving, but very shortly he was missing and hobbled into the pits with a buckled front wheel and bent stub axle, the driver having collided with a gate standard.... Alfred Moss who had come over with Aileen to see the Grand Prix in his own 15/90 gave permission to take off the part from his car parked in amongst thousands of others—if we could find it. Among the people congregated in and around the pit and our gallant effort to get going were many drivers, among them Wisdom; I chose him although he had never driven the car before. Soon the Marendaz Special commenced circulating never varying a second and some time later a packet arrived for me from the Automobile Club de France enclosing the times for each lap proving, as they said, the car's extraordinary consistency.

This was an eighty-lap, 1,000-km event at Montlhéry, the Marendaz Special being twenty-six laps down at the finish. This ended the competitive history of Marendaz Special cars, although as the years pass they continue to appear from time to time in VSCC events and elsewhere.

14

THE MOSS AND DON CONNECTION

THE DONS

Both Kaye Don and Rita, his sister, seem to have been close to Marcus Marendaz and Dorothy Summers through the late 1920s and 1930s. Kaye was mixed up with the Miller-engined Lea Francis, this engine being restored to the Miller chassis in the Marendaz works in 1929, and he helped with the record breaking at Montlhéry in February 1928.

It has to be said that the Maidenhead works seems to have run more smoothly whenever Marcus Marendaz was away, as Stan Duddington relates:

> When he arrived in the morning he'd belt into the works and slam his brakes on—there was plenty of space, you see. Then he'd come over to me and say, 'Just check the so-in-so' or 'Just check the brakes.' The clutch, or something like that, and you'd think, 'Oh, he's off to London,' which was good news. Jim would come and ask me 'Is he going out today?' and I'd say 'Yeah, I've got to do the so-in-so, he going to London.' It was peaceful when he was gone, but while he was there he was always coming out and interfering with something, but when he went out for the day you could work more. He asked me one day to adjust the brakes, which I did, but I didn't test them, just told him they were done. So he backs the car into one corner and puts his foot down, going up to about forty, straight at the wall and slams the brakes on hard! I thought, I'm for the high jump here, but they worked. It was a silly thing to do, really, ask somebody else to adjust your brakes and then do that, I'd have thought.

This peaceful atmosphere in the works was extended to a week when Marcus Marendaz went over to the Isle of Man to act as an expert witness on behalf of Kaye Don, who was in court following the death of his riding mechanic on Monday, 28 May 1934. The Mannin Beg race for which Kaye was entered was to be held on Wednesday the 30th, being a preliminary to the Mannin Mor race scheduled for the following Saturday. Official practice was on the day preceding the race, Tuesday, but following work on the car, an M.G. Magnette, the mechanic Francis Tayler advised Kaye on the Monday evening that the car was ready for test. Kaye took the car out on test, with the mechanic as passenger, towards dusk on the public roads, not closed for official practice, the car not being insured for road use and not carrying lights, horn, or number plates. The racing car hit a taxi coming the other way, a wheel was dislodged and the

Kaye Don seated in the Miller Lea-Francis at Brooklands, April 1928. (*Brooklands Society*)

car overturned, both driver and mechanic being seriously injured, with Francis Taylor dying in hospital the following morning. Stan Duddington commented:

> Kaye Don was often in and out of the works. If you remember Kaye Don had that accident in the Isle of Man, he killed someone, his mechanic, he was practising on the open roads instead of closed and someone was killed. There was a big court case over on the Isle of Man. Marendaz had to go over there as friend and supporter of the accused and he was over there for over a week, then he was going back and forward. We were glad to get rid of him for a rest as normally he used to hover around you like a big dog.

The trial on a charge of manslaughter was held in July 1934 when Kaye Don was still suffering the effects of his injuries. Marcus Marendaz was called as an expert witness regarding the marks on the brake drum where the wheel had come off. If the brake drum had contacted the road the wheel must have been completely detached and not collapsed, rendering the car un-steerable as Don alleged. Notwithstanding the fact that something had broken or given way on the M.G. Don was found guilty and that the death of Francis Taylor was 'due to the culpably negligent driving of Mr Kaye Don'. The sentence was four months, reduced from a potential six months due to Kaye Don believing that he was allowed to practice on open roads as he had been allowed to on a previous occasion. An appeal was lodged on the grounds that Francis Taylor may have said something before he died that was common knowledge and prejudicial to Kaye Don's case but was unsuccessful.

In happier times, both Kaye and Rita Don were to be seen at the Marendaz works and with them at motoring events, such as the Shelsley Walsh hillclimb.

Dorothy Summers after winning the Second March Short Handicap, 14 March 1936, with Rita Don congratulating her. (*Author's collection*)

[Stan Duddington:] I used to do a lot of going around to hill climbs and so on, in the orchard at Shelsley in the rain. You'd have oil on your overalls and the rain would wash it through onto your shirt and you'd be in a terrible state by the time it was over. Once we went to Shelsley, it was with Mitchell, wasn't it, I don't think Marendaz was driving. Kaye Don's sister, Rita, used to drive a lot in the concours but she'd turned up at Shelsley and wanted a lift home, because she lived near us down Ray Mead Road, Maidenhead, so I had to sit in the back of the Marendaz on my toolbox, because this was the blown thirteen horsepower and there were no back seats and naturally she had to sit in the front. She'd a whacking great scarf on and she kept looking round at me, then she said 'You're cold, aren't you?' And I said 'Yes.' So she took off her scarf and tied it round me—a really big thick one—but it made me look like Wilfred the Rabbit with the two ends of the scarf sticking up like ears. Every time we stopped in a town like Worcester and Oxford and all the other towns everybody was laughing at us with people saying 'Look at that silly so-in-so.'

… Another time we went over one Saturday when Kaye Don was racing an Alfa, Marendaz was pit manager and I had to go along and give him a hand, put the oil in and so on. We did quite well in that race, changing four wheels in twenty-one seconds, which was going some in those days.

[The Dons were well liked by the works staff. Jim Light:] She used to have all make-up on, more'n you'd have in a shop. Talk about a dolly.

[Stan:] Kaye Don was always coming in and out, like. Rita would borrow the yellow drop-head coupé with the blue hood and drive it in these concours. Kaye Don was always immaculate with his clothes.

[Jim:] I know Marendaz was very thick with the Dons.

THE MOSSES

It is not very clear when Marcus Marendaz picked up with the dentist Alfred Moss and his wife, Aileen. Alfred Moss and his family lived at Thames Ditton in the early 1930s but moved to Bray on the Thames around the mid-1930s, a very short distance from Marcus Marendaz and Dorothy Summers, 'Mrs' Marendaz. It seems very likely that he backed Marendaz when he made the move from London to Maidenhead, as it seems unlikely that Marendaz's tuning establishment would have generated the funds for this move.

Consequently, all the Moss family were a familiar sight at the Marendaz works, including a very young Stirling Moss—not always to the comfort of the 'troops'. Jim Light noted:

> I tell you what, Mrs. Moss used to wear the trousers, she was the boss over Alfred. He was funny, old Alfred, you'd be down there beside his car and he'd come up and spot a grubby mark and say here, give it a rub. But if you used an old dirty towel—he wouldn't hold with that. I remember Stirling, he brought him round there one day, must have been about six or seven years old. Nosey, I'll say! I was turning some pistons up for Tom and he comes to watch and he was arguing, arguing this and that, I would have clipped his ear off, if he'd had anything to do with me.

Aileen Moss's first Marendaz Special was JB1477, a black 13/70 with an interesting modification, namely an additional two-speed gearbox with a lever lying flat on the floorboards, doubling up the ratios for sporting trials. Apart from this it was a standard car, which later had chromium-plated wheels, fairly unusual at that date. Later again, the front mudguards were modified. Stan Duddington commented:

Aileen Moss seated in her Singer Le Mans with her silverware, much of it won with her two Marendaz Specials. (*Pat Moss*)

I remember we had turn-with-the-wheel front mudguards on Mrs. Moss's black car. Put on with three-eighth bolts and when they went out and drove around a bit they'd come back all floppy and loose. We couldn't stop them and eventually we had to put longer bolts and short stiff springs with washers, like clutch springs, and then split pin them, so that they could move around on the road, but didn't come loose.

Stan Duddington had to change a clutch for Aileen Moss on this car at Birdlip in Gloucestershire when engaged in a trial, probably the Gloucester Trial in December 1933. The Marendaz Special does not have the clutch in a bellhousing, but externally between engine and gearbox making it particularly accessible. As usual, he got the call out late and emerging from the local cinema was met by the Moss's chauffeur and their red Hudson Terraplane. Having collected his tools and a clutch plate, they set off for a location that was on the tip of the chauffeur's tongue, 'Bird-something'. Fortunately, his memory was jogged by some unfamiliar signposts and the car was eventually found in a garage with a water-filled pit, the proprietor thoughtfully providing an oil drum to stand on. Stan worked through the night, the chauffeur meanwhile sleeping in the back of the Terraplane, the Moss's asleep in the local hotel. In the morning, job done, Stan was invited into the hotel for breakfast on the Moss's. Alfred Moss seeing Stan wolf it down said, 'You looked as if you enjoyed that, would you like another one?' to which Stan said 'Yes, please!'—customer support, followed by a supporting customer.

Alfred Moss ran his own Marendaz Special, a black 17-hp tourer, JB2601, which he entered in various rallies along with other cars that he owned.

Aileen Moss ready for the off in her Coventry Climax engined short-chassis Marendaz Special, during the 1936 RSAC Scottish Trial, June 1936. (*Autocar*)

In 1935, when the works had built the first 15-90 for that year's T.T. on the Ards circuit, Stan Duddington remembers:

> Going in the T.T. car with Marendaz. Mr and Mrs Moss were following in a car of theirs. They were so impressed with the T.T. car in the mud that they wanted something similar, you see. They had got something like this in mind and of course when they saw the T.T. car, they wanted something built like it. As far as I know their short-chassis special was built as a copy of the T.T. car and if you look at the two cars side by side they look much the same with no doors, except that one has a shorter chassis.

So that was the gestation of the only short-chassis Marendaz Special, DPG7. The engine was standard, but the car was lightened significantly by having a chassis, shortened by 18 inches and specially made, not cut and shut and a doorless body fabricated in square section steel tube with fabric covering. Stan Duddington commented:

> When they made it they saved all they could on weight, but it ended up too light at the back and spun the wheels. So we had to shift the battery to the back and add some lead and a second spare wheel; the lead must have weighed half a hundredweight, cast and put in the battery carrier behind the seat.

The fourth Marendaz Special that the Moss's owned was the T.T. car, which they came by in rather more difficult circumstances. This car was not built for them or anything like that, but it was acquired by Alfred Moss at the time of the collapse of Marendaz Special Cars. After the T.T., the car was generally used as a works hack, being seen around Maidenhead on Trade Plates and painted white with red wheels. It was removed by Alfred Moss and Guy Griffiths one Sunday morning after the closure of the works, but whether Marcus Marendaz knew about this is a moot point, Guy intimating to the author that they essentially had to force entry so that Alfred Moss, a major creditor of the firm, could remove this car and the Miller racing car, the only assets worth taking. The Marendaz Special was eventually sold off and road registered.

15

THE MOVE TO AIRCRAFT BUILDING

ollowing the inevitable demise of Marendaz Special Cars and its winding up on 24 June 1936, Marcus Marendaz moved smoothly 100 yards west inside the Cordwallis industrial estate to the old factory site of G.W.K. cars, his office now being on the corner of the building where Arthur Grice had run things before the Great War and during the twenties. In keeping with the aspirations of Marcus Marendaz, the business was grandly named International Aircraft and Engineering Limited. Some of the machinery went as well, with the plan being to design and manufacture aircraft. When he'd owned his own aircraft, Moth G-EBOT, he had flown it from Woodley and quite possibly met the Miles brothers at that time. By 1936, he knew them well and was a regular visitor to their aircraft factory also on the grass airfield at Woodley. So it is not surprising that his design ideas were not dissimilar to the Miles types, although what the Miles brothers made of this is not known.

Late in 1935, just before the final change over, Marcus Marendaz and Marendaz Special Cars started running down the car activity and made a move to aircraft. Stan Duddington, seeing the writing on the wall, jumped before he was pushed and left in early 1936. Some of the staff, such as Jim Light, worked for both companies at the changeover period, for although the aircraft were to be built mainly in wood there was enough work for a machinist and metal worker. Of course, Miss Dorothy Summers was also involved. When Marendaz Special Cars closed, only two shop-floor employees were retained: Jim and Eddie Long.

THE FIRST MARENDAZ AIRCRAFT

Work commenced on a prototype of the Marendaz monoplane in 1935, the fuselage being sufficiently complete by February 1936 to appear as a *Flight* illustration. Although the concept was undoubtedly by Marcus Marendaz, he had need of a proper aircraft designer, familiar with working in wood who could size the elements, stress them, and do the necessary aerodynamic calculations. Marcus Marendaz took on the Australian Geoffrey N. Wikner, better known of course for the later design produced under his own name: the Foster–Wikner Wicko. The Marendaz monoplane followed the general constructional principles of the Miles' types but was to be powered by a 90-hp Pobjoy 7-cylinder radial, not an engine favoured by Fred and

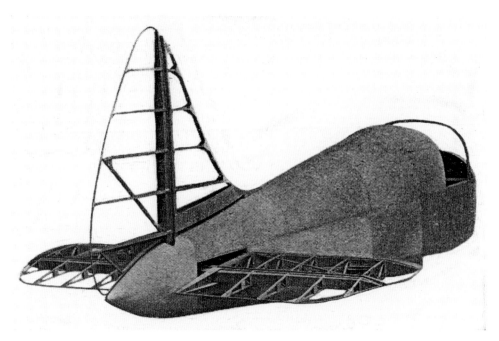

The first Marendaz aircraft seen partially built in the Maidenhead works. (*Flight*)

George Miles for a two-seater, who probably regarded it as being of insufficient capability. It is a feature of aircraft designers that they believe that their skills are such that their new design will slip though the air on a zephyr of power, the rude awakening coming shortly after the first flight. Not helping the performance was the fixed undercarriage and the wire braced wing, the latter feature being anachronistic for the date. No photographs of the side-by-side two-seater aircraft exist with the engine fitted, and the photograph that does exist shows some variance from the arrangement drawing, notably the cut down cockpit side not being adopted, presumably in the interests of weight saving and structural simplicity. If the data sheet is correct, flaps were conventional (although see later) and the rudder unbalanced. According to *Flight*, Marendaz had patents pending on the differentially operated brakes and torsion shaft undercarriage springing and although the author has not succeeded in verifying this point, the later Marendaz Trainer appears to have made use of these ideas. Before construction was finished, Geoffrey Wikner walked out the day *Flight* magazine published an item on the aircraft in February 1936, which credited design to Marendaz. Wickner had agreed the text of the item with Marendaz beforehand clearly stating his own name as designer, but this was changed before publication. Although the later Wicko aircraft was high wing, initially with an 85-hp Ford V-8, but later a conventional 130-hp Gipsy Major, there are design similarities and the Marendaz Monoplane can be regarded as an antecedent. Geoffrey Wicker did not hang around once he had parted with Marendaz as he flew his Wicko prototype around September 1936, a mere seven months later.

Depending on the source of the information and the stage of design, stated seating capacity varied between two and four. Working on aircraft was a new departure for Jim Light, as he recalls:

The Marendaz was definitely a three-seater with dual control, because Marendaz wondered in the end how he was going to work his controls, because the whole arrangement wasn't ideal for it. I made the best part of the fittings for that aircraft. What happened there was the usual, the bloke that was doing the fittings, Bill Evans had made about half of them, all the wing flap hinges and so on. Well, Marendaz came over one day and said, as I could do anything, 'Light, in your spare time and when held on the machine, better get on and make some of the fittings, the so-in-so's bin and left'. And I said 'I don't know anything about metal fittings' and he said 'Ah, you can do it'. But as you know some of the fittings before they're bent they look like a butterfly—they don't look anything like that when they're folded. But I got away with it, put in a bit of overtime, and when I'd got so many ready Marendaz would send for the A.I.D. man [Aeronautical Inspection Directorate, Ministry of Transport]. He only scrapped two pieces, one of them was a little flat hinge and had two or three marks on it—you could hardly see them—and the other one he scrapped 'cos I'd scribed a line too deeply. Probably done to make sure I kept my standards up. The only other thing he scrapped was the bracket for the tailwheel spring assembly. Marendaz had sent it down to Hampshire to someone who specialised in aircraft welding, but the Aircraft Inspection Department man said they'd burned the welding. So the old man had to make another one, but he made the people in Hampshire pay for it. Then the retractable undercarriage, which came in and back, was all worked by hydraulics with a two-way reversing valve. All the main castings were duralumin, which he got hammered out somewhere. They were a terrible job to work on. There was one pawl where the legs fitted in and another pawl that went off to the lever. Then they ran on a steel stamping about that long milled on the angle. I had to do all that in my spare time, in overtime. Don't tell me about Mr Marendaz.

In April 1936, as his interests turned to aviation Marcus Marendaz took an option with ABC Motors Ltd (All British Engine Company) for the manufacture of their Scorpion II, 40-hp, ultra-light aircraft engine, commonly used in the home-built and frequently crashed Flying Flea. Jim Light recalled:

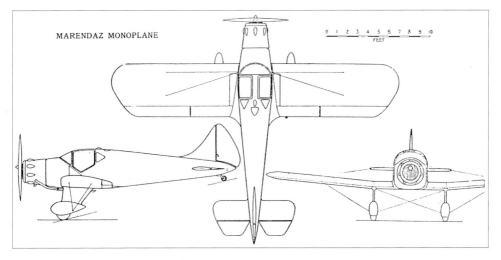

The initial design with fixed undercarriage, braced wing and a Pobjoy engine. (*Flight*)

[They were] dangerous things … Well, he was going to manufacture the ABC flat twin engines for ABCs. He sent for me one day and said 'Strip that engine out and see what's in it'. I took a look at it and the big end in it was out of this world, I'd never seen one like it. I've never seen a piston, big-end or conrod to touch that. It was a needle roller thing. The finish on it was amazing, it was polished all over. Well, it never came to anything.

The Scorpion has not gone down in history as a 'good little engine'. The weekend before the winding up of Marendaz Special Cars in June 1936 everything was taken out of the works and put down in the old G.W.K. toolroom. Jim and Eddie had just about got everything ready for running when as Jim Light recalled:

Well, I dunno what happened, but all of a sudden Eddie and Marendaz were having a hell of a row and Eddie he was very quick, but he was threatening to spread the Captain all over the wall. He said that, yes! The Captain sacked him.

So Eddie left, leaving Jim as the sole survivor from the shop floor at Marendaz Special Cars.

FIRE IN THE WORKS

Marendaz Special Cars were wound up in June 1936 and International Aircraft and Engineering Ltd was formed to carry on the aircraft work, Mr C. F. Allen, late of Faireys and Westlands being appointed chief draughtsman in March 1937. Also, there was Ted Hillier on the design side and skilled in woodworking, who later worked for the Miles brothers. However, disaster struck on the evening of Saturday, 5 June 1937 when the factory and the nearly completed first aircraft were burnt out. The *Maidenhead Advertiser* reported that the fire was discovered in its early stages, the Fire Brigade arriving shortly after 8.30 p.m., discovering that the workshop and stores were a mass of flames. The fire was contained to this one area and was under control in about fifteen minutes, but considerable damage was done to the plant and stock. Jim Light remembered:

He had a fire, one Saturday night, nobody ever found out what started it. I only salvaged one thing out of that fire, a steel ruler lying in the ashes, so burnt I had to straighten it up. The aircraft was about three parts built. After the fire on the Saturday night, someone told me Sunday morning so I got on my coat and went down there. The old machine tools were a bit black. But that wasn't the end of International Aircraft as far as Maidenhead was concerned, because they carried on and we got started on another 'plane. We weren't really allowed to re-use the metal fittings after the fire as they'd all been annealed or heat-treated, but we did. Made some new ones but cleaned up a lot of the damaged ones. No one noticed or complained.

The reason for the fire was never determined and it was not established whether arson was to blame; no blame was attributed, and it remains an enigma today. Such a serious setback did little to dampen Captain Marendaz's aspirations and work recommenced on an improved Mk III, still on the Maidenhead site adjacent to the burnt-out workshops. As Jim noted, Marendaz asked him to rescue various heavily heat-treated metal items from the workshop floor for cleaning up and re-use, completely contrary to safety standards and also to get the

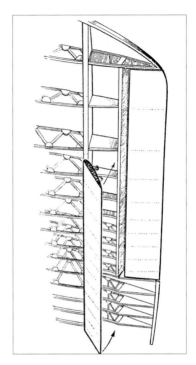

The Marendaz patented flap design, showing an unusual arrangement of flap ahead of the aileron. (*Flight*)

smoke-damaged and blackened lathes back into operation. The rescued items were duly presented to Aircraft Inspection Department of the Air Ministry as newly manufactured.

So, with the second aircraft under way, the hiatus caused by the fire and the lack of an airfield was obvious and precipitated the inevitable move. Later in 1937, Marcus Marendaz purchased from Mr C. H. Latimer-Needham the establishment at Barton in the Clay, Bedfordshire, which at the time contained the remnants of various Luton aircraft which were eventually moved to Gerrards Cross. The hangar was very modern being of welded steel construction, unusual at the time. Jim Light recalled:

You know when the cars packed up, I was telling you, I was working for him for about two years after that. Well, after the fire he was moving up to just outside Luton, Barton. Well, I took all the machinery up there on the back of this gravel lorry. It was overloaded by hundredweights. The last thing we took up was the damn great miller. I hired three tent poles from Edwards tent works, big ones, got the machinery on with that with a 2 or 3 ton block and tackle, and do you know when I got that miller on the old gravel lorry it went down at the back, nearly frightened the life out of me.

The hangar was along a road, on the Bedford road, then you turned down a rough old lane down to the airfield. The hangar was a totally open sided building – it was a new type of building at the time, single span, all welded. The airfield was all grass with grass runway, they were a bit limited 'cos there was the Luton Road and a hill that went up and it was difficult for aircraft getting over the hill on take-off that way, so it had its limitations. You could see the Luton Road going along on the ridge. The village had one old pub there, 'cos I went in there when I was waiting. What done it was after the last load that I took up on a Friday, I was going to stay up there and he was supposed to have some lodgings for me. I went round to these lodgings and they didn't want to know, did they.

The Marendaz Mk III, G-AFGG, at the 1938 Royal Aeronautical Society Garden Party, Heathrow 1938. It was delivered to the event by road. The rudder looks unfinished with an added tab. (*Author's collection*)

They started to do absolute pantomimes—they hadn't got time for lodgers. Well, I spent that night in the hangar. There were two lovely little aircraft and a glider. I had to sleep on the old couch and it was very cold and I was fed up. So I went over to his house at Bray one Saturday morning, just as he was coming out of his house and drove into the drive just as he was coming down. When he saw me he nearly fell out of the car. When I told him I'd packed the job up, Oh, dear, he went mad. I'd weighed it over anyway—you never knew if he was going to go broke and I didn't want to get stuck up in Luton. There were two other people at Barton, Oldwright or Holroyd and another. Marendaz went in as manager, running things, but I think I ran it more than he did.

Installed at Barton by November 1937, construction work continued on the second aircraft, the Marendaz Mk III, as well as other engineering tasks. To keep things turning over, he had a contract with Napier engines as a small item in *Flight* reports on 16 December 1937.

Actually, for some time past the International Aircraft and Engineering machine shop has been active and in every Short–Mayo upper component that flies the Atlantic there will be sixty-four rocker-boxes completely machined by them using twenty-seven different operations, sixty-four push-rod yokes and four gas distributors all from their shops.

Jim Light, who was a weekly traveller to Barton at this time, remembers this work:

When we were doing the job for Napiers, Marendaz asked me one day 'What shall I charge them?' so I says 'Ang on, that's your job, I'm having nothing to do with that.' Talk about ... I said 'I'll give you what I think the machining time is and anything like that'. He was getting the manager's money—I wasn't! We used to do the rocker cases, it was all milled out with tight clearances and a very fine thread. He had to get special plastic taps to do that, which was the first time I'd seen them, where you get a die and box that clips over. That tap did the same thing, but cost lots of money. They weren't half funny that Napier lot.

The Short–Mayo aircraft was a piggyback concept using a light float-equipped mailplane atop a flying boat, the combination being flown to an initial cruising altitude where the upper element was cast off to fly to New York, conventional flying boats on their own not having this range. The top half of the combination was 'Mercury', G-ADHJ, powered by four Napier Rapier engines. Napier were working on a family of H-layout engines: the Rapier, the Dagger, and the wartime Sabre fitted to the Hawker Typhoon, the Rapier being the smallest, designed by Frank Halford, having sixteen cylinders and a capacity of 8.55 litres. These engines were compact, smooth running with a high rpm, and very noisy. The principal user of the Rapier was the Fairey Seafox shipboard floatplane, sixty-six being built, so total production of the engine was probably under 100. It is not known if International Aircraft's contract with Napier was extended to the later Dagger and Sabre engines; it is unlikely the Rapier rocker boxes were common to the other engines. There is a surviving Rapier engine to be seen in the Shuttleworth Collection today, which is not from *Mercury*, but nevertheless the rocker boxes may well be the product of International Aircraft.

THE BEDFORD SCHOOL OF FLYING

Marcus Marendaz's attentions were diverted to a degree by his formation on 1 January 1938 of the Bedford School of Flying, opened under the aegis of the Government Flying Scheme. He obviously had previous wartime experience in the field and in 1940 claimed that he had restarted the Midland Flying Club at Elmdon, Birmingham prior to the Bedford School of Flying venture, but there is no evidence to support this. The airfield for the Bedford School was, unsurprisingly, Barton in the Clay, although the suitability of this site was questionable given the ridge of high ground to the South. Some 20 acres were levelled, hedges and trees

Avro Avian IV G-AAHK, used by the Bedford School of Flying between September 1938 and January 1939, when it crashed. The location is not known but may be Barton in the Clay. (*A. J. Jackson collection*)

uprooted, and drainage dug. About this time, Marcus Marendaz had the inevitable brush with officialdom in that the local authority cut off his water supply following a dispute, his response being to sink a well. Directors of the school were Dorothy O. Summers, secretary, with Leslie C. Hilditch as flying instructor, later assisted by A. E. Hill. A clubhouse was built and instruction was given using Moths and Avians, which by 1938 were getting rather long in the tooth. By the end of the 1930s, the standard biplane trainer was the mid-1930s D.H.82 Tiger Moth, usually supplemented by training on monoplanes such as the Miles Hawk series of aircraft, *ab initio* military training being broadly similar. So, looking at the equipment used by the Bedford School of Flying is rather an eye-opener. The oldest listed was Avro Avian III G-EBWK, granted a Certificate of Airworthiness in March 1928 and acquired by the Bedford School of Flying in October 1938. It was grounded when the Certificate of Airworthiness expired in June 1939 and was eventually sold in parts in December 1940. Another Avro Avian IV G-AAHK, first C. of A. issued in June 1929 crashed around late 1938 and Avro Avian IVM G-AAVM, first C. of A. March 1930 was another one of the School's aircraft grounded when the war started. Picketed outside at Barton it was damaged beyond repair in gales in 1940. G-AAKE was a D.H.60G Gipsy Moth dating to August 1928, whose C. of A. expired in July 1939 and was later scrapped around 1940. Another Moth, D.H.60M G-AAMU dated from January 1931 was sold in 1940 and survived the war to be scrapped in 1948. A sister Moth G-AAMW suffered a broadly similar fate. D.H.60G Gipsy Moth G-AAGM, another throwback to April 1929 spent a lot of its life abroad but was re-imported for the Bedford School of Flying in January 1939, but after failing to get a C. of A. was broken for spares in 1940. One of the early trainees was Marcus Marendaz's cousin Altair Kelway and another was John Sproule, very well known in gliding circles. Flying rates were £1 15*s* for Dual, £1 10*s* Solo.

Marcus Marendaz with glasses and pipe (left) inspecting a Piper Cub at Barton in the Clay. (*Don Summers*)

Standing back from the goings on at Barton in the Clay, we have the words of Jack Willmot in conversation and in correspondence with the author. Jack learned to fly at Barton and knew Marcus Marendaz well. He found him a complete mystery man, very touchy, an extremely clever engineer, and very inventive but always in trouble with authority as, for example, when falling out with the Council over the water supply to the point where he drove a well at Barton's Farm. Dorothy Summers was his 'lady friend', but actually had more control over him than anyone else. Jack said that he liked Marcus Marendaz and for some unknown reason they got on very well together. He did not pull his punches, once accusing Jack of making an 'aerobatic landing' on one of his machines. Of the aircraft at Barton, Marcus Marendaz tended to fly the Aeronca G-ADYS (possibly known then as *Gladys*, as it was in later years), but the aircraft of the Bedford School of Flying were elderly Moths and Avians, in spite of which Jack regarded the Bedford School of Flying as a progressive organisation. At some point after the war, writing from Bergh Apton in Norfolk, Marcus Marendaz tried to buy back the Aeronca once again when it was owned by Jack.

THE SECOND MARENDAZ AIRCRAFT

Returning to the Marendaz Mk III, which was a pretty aircraft, Marendaz had an artist's eye and his products were stylish, as can be seen from both his cars and aircraft. It was registered as G-AFGG on 23 March 1938, described as a three- or four-seater monoplane and largely complete by May 1938 when it appeared at the Royal Aeronautical Society garden party at Heathrow. Overall appearance was as for the earlier Marendaz monoplane but with a slimmer and longer rear fuselage, three or four seats much in the style of the cars, a 200-hp Gipsy Six (nearly three times the power of the initially planned Pobjoy), a retractable undercarriage, and wheel brakes. The wire-braced wing was abandoned, but the Marendaz-patented flap system was to be retained. Patent Number 490850 was granted to Marcus Marendaz in August 1938 for 'Improvement in Aircraft Flaps' and detailed in the usual incomprehensible patent style but explained more clearly here below. Another feature was dual spectacle controls, and the cockpit door shows the cut down sides of the original general arrangement, although the transparency is conventional. An estimated top speed of 200 mph was claimed. The Marendaz Mk IV, which was not built, was planned to be similar but with two seats, a fixed undercarriage, and a 130-hp Gipsy Major.

The Marendaz Mk III and possibly the planned Mk IV had the Marendaz flap system for increasing lift and drag. A full description of the system appeared in *Flight* in May 1937, just before the disastrous fire. It comprised a conventional split flap arrangement but moved forward allowing the flap to be extended spanwise in front of the aileron. History does not relate a similar successful arrangement and this may have been the death knell of the Marendaz Mk III. The late Terence Boughton, a well-respected author and aerodynamicist, looked at this system in conjunction with the author, the conclusion being that a split flap is really only effective at the trailing edge of an aerofoil, where it increases the camber and hence the lift coefficient. Moving it forward will probably increase its drag effectiveness (much like a downgoing airbrake on a glider) but do very little to increase lift. With selection of the Marendaz flap, a slot was opened as with a Fowler flap, the intention being that the air passing just over the flap was going to keep the aileron in business. The volume of air reaching the lower side of the aileron would have been greatly reduced, so with the flaps down aileron control must have been seriously

The Marendaz Mk III, G-AFGG, at the 1938 Royal Aeronautical Society Garden Party, Heathrow 1938. The landing gear was retractable, but what look like gear fairings are actually display notices. (*Aeroplane*)

reduced. On a conventional trailing edge flap, not a split flap, the air would follow the upper surface re-energising the flow, but on the Marendaz system, it must have merely 'filled the space' between flap and wing, increasing drag but doing very little for lift. The concept of a flap ahead of an aileron does not sound good either and with the benefit of hindsight it is believed that no other designer has attempted this. The trailing edge of modern aircraft tend to have more flap spanwise with smaller ailerons and no overlap, but with upper-surface spoilers in front of the outboard flaps to help the ailerons. When the aircraft appeared at the 1938 garden party at Heathrow, it was roaded there as an unflown prototype and in another photograph of it at Barton in the Clay, it looks much the same but showing the much vaunted and patented flaps deflected. In both photographs, a moderately large fixed tab on the rudder is visible; this would almost certainly not have been designed in, but rather added after test, the smallish fin and rudder possibly demonstrating inadequate directional control. Its presence indicates that some flight testing, possibly a hop, might have been attempted on the rather short grass runways of Barton in the Clay, but as these were short enough to have almost certainly required the use of a flap giving more drag than lift, and if the ailerons were then found to be inadequate, the prospect of testing might have been abandoned as being too risky. Given a longer and more suitable runway, a flapless take-off would have been successful, but as Marcus Marendaz never claimed that the aircraft flew, one has to assume that it almost certainly never did. The cost of development and the redesign (or abandonment) of the curious flap system probably put Marcus Marendaz off, with the added realisation that a war was likely, meaning a time when recreational aircraft would be of little value.

Anyway, in 1938, the Bedford School of Flying was enjoying success and no doubt Donald Marendaz's thoughts were there. He took up flying again at that time and usually flew the Aeronca G-ADYS (a survivor later with the Cooper family). Again, at this time, he took to

Marcus Marendaz, wearing his 'teddy-bear' coat in front of the Marendaz Mk III, G-AFGG. Note the deployed flaps—the possible reason why the aircraft never flew. To the left is his 15/90 Marendaz Special. The other people are not identified. (*Don Summers*)

flying further afield usually with a professional pilot and using one of the faster monoplane Moths. His visits were to Germany where he studied the training methods in connection with his position as an SBAC (Society of British Aircraft Constructors) representative on two government committees of inquiry on the production of aircraft and the training of pilots. In the course of these visits, he certainly met Göring and probably Hitler, an association that was shortly to be used against him, the details of which appear in Chapter 16.

A FLYING MARENDAZ AIRCRAFT—AT LAST!

Marendaz's interest in training and building training aircraft (he claimed the Marendaz Mk III to be the first trainer with retractable undercarriage) culminated in a further effort to produce a Marendaz aircraft. Happily, this was successful and the Marendaz Trainer, G-AFZX, registered 31 October 1939, constructors number ABT.1 and built by Marendaz Aircraft Ltd, was flown shortly after the outbreak of war in November 1939 by Mr R. A. Wyndham. Given the prohibition on most civil flying, authority for a very limited flight programme must have been given, probably only extending to showing that it did actually fly. It was conventional in nearly all respects having a 90-hp Cirrus Minor, tandem two seats, no flaps, and outboard leading-edge slots for better lateral control. Construction was of wood and like the earlier aircraft was intended to be aerobatic. The undercarriage was unconventional having a very wide track. It was made having a chrome-vanadium stub axle connected to the front and main spars by pivoting square section steel links, with lateral splay resisted by a radius rod having landing and rebound springs all connected to the front spar and centre section. So, on landing, the wheel track varied slightly with the load. The tail skid was mounted on a cantilevered leaf spring, just like the rear axles of his cars. G-AFZX was painted all red and had a most basic fit of instruments and then only to the rear cockpit. Credit for the design in general is likely to rest with Ted Hillier.

The Marendaz Trainer, G-AFZX, in the air. (*Philip Jarrett*)

The Aeronca C-3, G-ADYS, the only aircraft owned by the Bedford School of Flying that survived the war. (*Malcolm Clarke*)

It is of no consequence whatsoever, but it is of interest to speculate what the initials 'ABT' in the constructor's number signify. Here it is suggested that they stood for the 'All British Trainer' on the very slight association with Marendaz's publicity by-line for his cars, 'The All British Marendaz Special'.

The Marendaz Trainer was a private venture, the government having made it clear that no *ab initio* trainers not already in production would be adopted. Strangely, the government in September 1939 were advocating the export of aircraft, presumably to capitalise on the need for allies also to rearm and expand militarily. Marendaz applied to produce the Trainer for the overseas market, seeking assurances regarding raw materials. In December 1939, he was told that it was most improbable that materials would be available and that in any event difficulties were likely to arise with regard to the supply of engines. This ended the prospects of the Marendaz Trainer, given the lack of adequate production facilities and no government support.

EXPANSION TO EATON BRAY

On 19 October 1938, General Airports was formed with Dorothy Summers and S. Shaw as directors to carry on the manufacture of motor and aeroplane engines and also to cover some aeronautical changes. This resulted in June 1939, just before the outbreak of war, with Marendaz expanding his activities from Barton in the Clay to include the nearby site of Eaton Bray, between Leighton Buzzard and Dunstable. The intention was to replace Barton in the Clay because of complaints from that area regarding low flying and also the shortcomings with regard to obstacles, not to mention threats from the ministry regarding Barton in the Clay's suitability. An application to licence the site at Eaton Bray was made by Dorothy Summers in June 1939, wherein she stated she was the owner and intended it for training under the

The Marendaz Trainer, G-AFZX, at Barton in the Clay. (*Author's collection*)

The wide-track fixed undercarriage of the Marendaz Trainer, a design by Marendaz that he hoped to patent. (*Aeroplane*)

Civil Air Guard scheme, taxi work, joy-riding, and charter, with a wooden club house and hangar to be built in the north-west corner. A survey of the site rated it 'excellent' with some trees to be felled, hedges grubbed up and a ditch to be levelled. Officialdom initially replied positively, but an input to them caused doubt concerning the proximity of the new RAF Wireless Telegraphy station on the outskirts of Leighton Buzzard, 1.5 miles north of the proposed airfield, with the possibility of radio interference. It was established that legally no objections could be made, but the airfield owners could be encouraged to avoid flying too close to the radio station, so an acceptable compromise was reached. August 1939 was spent in various negotiations regarding the detail, with a request from Dorothy Summers for the licence to run from 31 August, a date almost coincident with one of the most momentous events in the history of the United Kingdom. Needless to say, the outbreak of war brought the correspondence to an abrupt halt, but by early October, with all civil flying at a standstill, the director of Home Civil Aviation wrote to Dorothy Summers asking if she wanted her £1 5s fee returned as her plans were now nullified. Nevertheless, the airfield was licensed in October 1939, but obviously was not capable of being used by her for training. It should be noted that the controlling authority for the airfield was General Airports Corporation, with a registered address at Barton Airport and it was to them that a Ministry Annual Inspection Report was sent in April 1940 by the inspector, John Branson, who reported that his Magister had become bogged. Notwithstanding the initial report that the airfield was 'excellent', the underlying impression was one of a piece of land bounded by waterways and comprising the famous Bedford clay underfoot. When one combines this report with a note by Dorothy

Marcus Marendaz with a lady outside the Clubhouse at Barton in the Clay. (*Don Summers*)

Summers that the RAF seem to use Eaton Bray as a turning point, the subsequent history and downfall of Marcus Marendaz initiated on this site seems inevitable.

Before we get to that point, a short valedictory note on the success of the Bedford School of Flying is necessary, the salient points of which were published by Marcus Marendaz on 1 September 1939. His review after twelve months of operation stated that 2,774 hours were flown, sixty-five A-licences were obtained, and ten Civil Air Guards had transferred to the military. A similar summary of all civil club flying was published in *Flight* for 7 September 1939, a few days after the outbreak of war, where for the Bedford School of Flying Dorothy Summers was named as secretary; T. A. Evans-Freke as senior instructor; and E. H. Peet, G. D. Garnett, and E. Knight Bruce as assistant instructors. A. R. Sarup was chief engineer and the flying rate had risen to £2 per hour.

THE END OF CIVILIAN FLYING

Once the war started, in very broad terms civil flying stopped unless specifically authorised. At Barton, the fleet was grounded with immediate effect, a devastating blow to Marcus Marendaz, essentially depriving him of any income. Although this seems draconian, it was a by-product of the need, for security reasons, to know that aircraft in the air not readily identified as 'ours' could be shot at. Club pilots wandering over RAF airfields in times of war were not to be encouraged. It did presume that the Ministry had a plan to replace the immediate loss of useful pilot training, their solution being to militarise some up-and-running organisations into Elementary Flying Training Schools and presumably to increase the intake at such schools to meet the military need, the civil need having evaporated. So flying clubs with the relatively modern D.H.82 Tiger Moths had their aircraft impressed into military service, being repainted and given military serial numbers. All other aircraft were assessed with regard to value to the services and many touring aircraft were impressed for communications purposes. No Avians were taken over, other than for ground instruction, but the better Moths were impressed. Whether those belonging to the Bedford School of Flying were just in too poor a state to be useful or whether the hiatus concerning Marcus Marendaz influenced any decision is not known, but all the aircraft at Barton were left to moulder, those outside suffering from the winter storms. All the effects of the Bedford School of Flying were put up for auction on Thursday, 19 December 1940 by the Agents Swaffield and Son at Barton. The sale comprised the workshop effects and materials and the aircraft, Avro Avians, de Havilland Moths, the Aeronca and two Marendaz Special aeroplanes, plus Gipsy I and VI engines, Cirrus III, and Hermes II. As noted above, some of the aircraft were broken for parts and none other than *Gladys* flew again. It rather appears that buyers were not thick on the ground and the little red Marendaz Trainer was given to the Halton Squadron of the Air Training Corps where it disappeared without trace or record. It seems the ill-fated Marendaz Mk III was broken up at Barton some time after the sale, the very final end of Marcus Marendaz's aeronautical aspirations.

Avro Avian IVM G-AAVM, used by the Bedford School of Flying from March 1939. (*A. J. Jackson collection*)

16

18B OR NOT 18B?

In the dark days of the summer of 1940, when the Battle of Britain was raging, a note crossed Winston Churchill's desk giving a list of people detained under the Category 18B Defence Regulations. It included the name Donald Marcus Kelway Marendaz, owner of two airfields in Bedfordshire. In vernacular terms, these detentions were seen to be a rounding up of Fifth Columnists, whether justified or not.

Regulation 18B of the Defence (General) Regulations 1939, as it was correctly termed, was part of a wider regulation introduced to cover immediate tasks necessary in the event of war breaking out, as normally there would not be time to pass appropriate laws: 18A, which introduced restrictions on the movement of aircraft, was invoked in late August 1939 and 18B, a suspension of *habeas corpus*, on 1 September 1939. To use a term familiar in more recent years, this meant internment. Initially, only a small number of people were detained, but in the spring of 1940, the success of Quisling in Norway alerted the government to the potential of a right-wing coup by Fifth Columnists working in conjunction with the German frontal attack, then at its height. This resulted in a much wider cull of people alleged to have sympathies with our enemies.

The Regulation was the responsibility of the Secretary of State for the Home Department, Sir John Anderson (from 12 May 1940) and said:

> If [he] has reasonable cause to believe any person to be of hostile origin or associations or to have been recently concerned in acts prejudicial to the public safety or the defence of the realm or in the preparation or instigation of such acts and that by reason thereof it is necessary to exercise control over him, he may make an order against that person directing that he be detained.
>
> … For the purposes of this Regulation, there shall be one or more advisory committees consisting of persons appointed by the Secretary of State; and any person aggrieved by the making of an order against him … under the powers conferred by this Regulation, may make his objections to such a committee.

While *habeas corpus* was suspended, the law allowed you to object, with a rider that the detainee had to be told of this right and afforded the 'earliest practicable opportunity' of doing so, should he so wish.

The badge of the Bedford School of Flying
showing an aircraft similar to a Marendaz Mk III.
(*Author's collection*)

The other little nugget was that there was no requirement for preliminary notification or warning of your status, so it was the knock on the door at dawn, detention, and a chance to argue your way out of goal.

Turning to Captain Marendaz, his *curriculum vitae* was not that of a subversive and in his field, he was well known. As we have seen, he was born in 1897 and attended Monmouth School, before serving an apprenticeship with Siddeley-Deasy in Coventry. He flew with No. 35 Squadron, Royal Flying Corps, in the Great War, afterwards starting his own business manufacturing cars under the name Marseal and later Marendaz Special. He weathered the Great Depression in this trade, supplementing it by a career motor racing at Brooklands and elsewhere. By 1936, he had moved his interests back to aviation, building several aircraft and running the Bedford School of Flying at Barton in the Clay and nearby Eaton Bray. This was a successful and much needed adjunct to the defence of the realm by training pilots under the Civil Air Guard scheme, part of a Government plan should war break out.

As a person, Marcus Marendaz could be charming or abrasive and many people found him difficult to deal with, others saying exactly the opposite. His status obviously mattered to him and he was not easily approachable, it would appear. Stories abound of his brushes with authority, both civil and with, for example, the Clerk of the Course at Brooklands. He seemingly was a supporter of Oswald Mosley, but then many people were, although there is no evidence of any deep involvement. One has to say that he suffered by having what was generally considered a foreign name. Although it originates in Portugal, Marcus Marendaz's antecedants settled in South Wales in the seventeenth century, his father being a farmer at, variously, Margam and Chepstow. One of the bylines he used when selling his sporting Marendaz Special cars was 'The All-British Marendaz Special', thereby overtly offsetting to some degree the foreign-ness of the name.

So, Marcus Marendaz had a good war record and was British, but seemingly not British enough. Any good Regulation usually has interpretive material supporting it or working documents that provide the powers that be with guidelines. In this case, there does not seem to have been any, so the phrases 'reasonable cause' or 'hostile origin' were the bald texts that the rounders-up had to use. Yet who nominated someone as being hostile, or what had you to do to be considered hostile, or who informed on whom? This was not a good situation, but then there was a war on and at times it rather looked as if we were not winning it.

MARCUS MARENDAZ IS DETAINED

John Anderson on 25 June 1940, signing his name over the title 'One of His Majesty's Principal Secretaries of State', directed that Donald Marcus Kelway Marendaz be detained, the citation being that there was reasonable cause to believe that Marendaz had recently been concerned in acts prejudicial to the public safety. The order was served on Marcus Marendaz at Leighton Buzzard on the 26th by Frank Kitchener, Detective Inspector of the Bedfordshire Constabulary. He was taken to Brixton Prison and 'received along with criminals from the Old Bailey' as he later wrote. He was then taken by van and entrained for Liverpool. In a letter dated 27 June, Marcus Marendaz wrote to Sir John Anderson asking for his detention to be terminated, having never been concerned in prejudicial acts.

This letter, obviously written from the heart of a rather concerned and possibly frightened man, terminates with the note that it was being 'Written on the train to Liverpool Prison, from which I am told I am being transported to Isle of Man with numerous aliens & fascists of which I have never been a member nor associated'.

The Manor House, Little Tring, Hertfordshire, the home of Marcus Marendaz and where he was arrested in 1940. (*Don Summers*)

The letter does admit the he had been fined for photographing a seven-year-old training aircraft on his own aerodrome but ends with a statement of his war record and of his current war work, namely the training of pilots and the development of the Marendaz–Bowman transmission for machine tools and tanks. During his journey, he was fed a beef sandwich but nothing to drink.

At Liverpool, he was housed in a small cell with a tiny window and remained there for a number of weeks, living off food parcels and initially deprived of his baggage containing such luxuries as pyjamas and shaving gear. His routine allowed him two half-hour exercise periods, but he was locked in his cell between 4 p.m. and 6.30 a.m. In return for sewing mail bags, he was allowed more time out of his cell and at the end of his time at Liverpool was paid the sum of 4 shillings and 2 pence for his efforts.

At this point, Marcus Marendaz wrote a further letter, this time to the Advisory Committee which, given the detail of the law, was the possible route to freedom. It detailed, once again, his CV complete with upstanding family background and great detail of his war work. He noted that at the start of the war he had offered to the RAF the results of observations from an earlier visit to Germany and he also pointed out that, being the operator of a civilian flying school, his activities had been brought to an abrupt halt by the war, such that his airfields were idle. Nevertheless, he maintained that he had kept his organisation intact at personal expense so that they could more easily be put to government use. He continues in National Archive. Reference HO 45/23722:

> On May 27th arrested for it was alleged photographing on May 5th a 7-year-old training aircraft on my own aerodrome ... Film developed by Police—no photograph. At hearing prosecuting council stated no question of espionage or ulterior motive arose. I was fined and afterwards I was detained for 'an act prejudicial to safety of realm', etc.

Thus the story slowly emerges. Captain Marendaz is accused of photographing a training aircraft, fined, but re-arrested immediately afterwards as being hostile. The charge and the penalty clearly seem inconsistent, so was there more to this 'Fifth Columnist'?

On 27 June 1940, two days after the detention order, Dorothy Marendaz wrote an impassioned letter to the Secretary of State. It will be recalled that Marcus Marendaz had married Dorothy Evans in 1918 and had three daughters, but by 1922, around the time their third daughter was born he employed a secretary at Marseal Cars, Dorothy Summers, with whom he formed an attachment that lasted until the wartime period. It was Dorothy Summers who wrote this letter, noting that Marcus Marendaz was at the time of writing in Brixton Prison and, having quoted his recent history regarding war work, asked 'Please, does this look like a man who would commit acts prejudicial to the welfare of the country or public safety?' She went on to outline their 2,000-mile tour of Germany in July and August 1939, after which Marendaz reported to Group Captain Cochrane of the Intelligence department, who advised him to talk to Major Heaton of the War Office.

Their house at Tring had been searched on the night of Monday 24 June, one can assume with the intent to provide supporting information for the impending court case for allegedly photographing an Oxford aircraft. Papers were removed, such as a review of the Marendaz Trainer by *Flight* magazine, a résumé of the previous twelve months' Civil Air Guard training by the Bedford School of Flying and Marcus Marendaz's 1939 Christmas Card. A telling rider was added to the effect that the Marendaz's solicitor's opinion was that the recent trial and fine was a complete farce and, had it taken place in London, it would have been dismissed without even calling witnesses. One of these had been a small boy who had told a corporal that he had seen Marendaz take a photograph.

A telegram to the Home Office from Dorothy Marendaz (Summers) in July 1940 pleading for Marcus Marendaz's release. (*National Archive*)

From HM Prison Liverpool on 1 July 1940, B532 MARENDAZ wrote again to the Advisory Committee concerning the reasons for his detention. It is written calmly, but his frustration and anger seem to lie near the surface. He pleads that, other than motoring offences, of which it has to be said there were a few, the recent act is the only one alleged against him. He then goes on to outline the course of events, the arrest by Tring Police on 27 May, a charge of photographing an aircraft on 5 May, to which he responded by pointing out that postcards of this aircraft could be bought for twopence. He was brought before two magistrates the following day, the 28th, where the chief constable of Bedfordshire opposed bail and he was remanded until 12 June, although this was rescinded and he was released on bail on 4 June, after seven days' imprisonment, to stand trial on 26 June.

Describing his trial, Marcus Marendaz again notes that the prosecution stated that there was no question of espionage or ulterior motive, that the camera film was taken and developed by the police and 'the film did not have an aircraft on it' and that the only evidence that a photograph had been taken was given by a fourteen-year-old boy, who was trespassing. The outcome was a fine of £20 and £6 12s costs.

Marcus Marendaz then went on to describe the aircraft in question, a twin-engined Airspeed Oxford, averring that a photograph of which with reference to an act prejudicial to public safety would not even deceive a reader of *The Boy's Own Paper*. He ends by saying 'I have never and do not now belong to, nor am I associated with, any fascist, communist, Peace Pledge, Link, Anglo-German or any other Union, association or political organisation whatsoever', noting that Supt. Paton of the Berkhamstead Police in searching his house found 'no book, paper or thing prejudicial or contrary to the Defence of the Realm or the highest traditions of an Englishman, as he said, not even *Mein Kampf*.

A will written by Marcus Marendaz on the back of a solicitor's letter, when imprisoned in July 1940. It is a bitter document wherein he left his wedded wife one shilling. (*Don Summers*)

Marcus Marendaz was undoubtedly a worried man, uncertain as to his future, so to put his affairs in order he wrote a will on 8 July 1940. It is a bitter document. He left his possessions to Dorothy Summers but only one shilling to his wife. In the event of Dorothy Summers pre-deceasing him, his estate was to be split between his mother and his daughter Ann Summers, with one hundred pounds set aside for the education of Donald Summers, his son. His other three daughters by his wife were only to receive a piece of Swansea china because no reasonable communication with their father had been made.

At this point, to return to legal matters, I suspect you will agree that the case for the prosecution seems weak in the extreme, but as we have only heard so far a rather garbled case for the defence, it is only half the story, so what was really behind the arrest and detention? Writing to the Home Office from Shire Hall in Bedford, the Chief Constable of Bedfordshire, W. J. A. Willis, notes that the Detention Order was executed at the end of the hearing at the Petty Sessions under Regulation 5(1)(b) of the Defence Regulations, 1939, and under the Control of Photography Order No.1, 1939. More tellingly, he notes that he had reported this action to MI5.

THE DUKE OF RICHMOND AND GORDON ENTERS THE STORY

On 13 June 1940, two weeks before the detention order was served, the Duke of Richmond and Gordon made an unsolicited statement to the Chief Constable of Buckingham, who, no doubt registering it as a 'hot potato', passed it on to the 'new boy' Chief Constable of Bedfordshire, responsible for the county where the offence of photographing an aircraft had taken place. Presumably, the Duke's action came about as a result of him hearing of the impending summonses and, coming from a Lord of the Realm, the Chief Constable felt obligated to pay attention. In summary, the Duke's statement notes that he knew 'D. K. Marendaz' at Brooklands and that he recollected him being in the motor trade. Furthermore, he noted that, 'with no particular interest', Marendaz was transferring his engineering activities to civil aeroplane construction.

The Duke of Richmond and Gordon was also in the motor design and construction business, also at this time transferring his interest to aircraft, so his statement is rather disingenuous as Marendaz was well known to the Brooklands aficionados, the Duke counting as one. He qualifies his remarks by saying that Marendaz was not blessed with a first-rate reputation amongst the Duke's motor racing colleagues. He then noted that at the beginning of May 1940, he met Marendaz driving his Rolls-Royce near the Duke's factory, which made propellers at Haddenham and recorded the exchange that took place. In it, Marendaz had enquired about the Duke's trouble with the Air Ministry, the Duke noting subsequently that these dealings were most confidential, such that he could only have gained such knowledge by seeking to find out. The conversation then moved to the war where the Duke quotes Marendaz as saying among

The Duke of Richmond and Gordon in his racing days at Brooklands when he was the Earl of March (left). The car is an MG C-type and the event is the BRDC 500-mile race, October 1931. (*Brooklands Society*)

other things, 'It's all up with us and you only have to study how they do things ... in Germany'. In fairness, he concludes 'It is no proof of anti-British action but as an attitude of mind combines with the offence with which he is apparently charged to raise distinct suspicion'.

Documents emanating from MI5 are not headed by the Department's address nor signed by a readable signature, all no doubt part of the mystique surrounding them, but because of these traits they can be identified. The case against Marcus Marendaz was gathered by them and given in a note dated August 1940, signed by a G. Pilcher, marked 'secret' until later declassification. As well as repeating the photography story Marendaz is noted to be apparently a somewhat aggressive individual and that MI5 had little information in this case additional to that supplied by the Chief Constable of Bedfordshire but noting that it included a recommendation for detention. So seemingly Mr Willis, the Chief Constable, started the ball rolling, by taking the statement from the Duke of Richmond and Gordon and passing it onwards with this endorsement.

The chief constable backed up the Duke's statement with another from a Mr George Fuller, a quantity surveyor who knew Marendaz and his company the Bedford School of Flying. This contained quotes from Marcus Marendaz referring to his German tour, summarised by the words 'In short (Marendaz) saw and knew far more than one would expect him to know and learn from a simple holiday tour'. It has to be said that MI5 were not totally convinced by the whole story and proposed to 'leave this case to the Committee without recommendation'.

Turning to the statement by George Fuller, quantity surveyor, presented by the Chief Constable we find a malicious diatribe against Marendaz and his colleagues that defies rationality. Mr Fuller received flying lessons under the Civil Air Guard scheme at the Bedford School of Flying, Barton in the Clay, where he noted 'D. K. Marendaz' as manager (note the identical mistake in the initials to that of the Duke of Richmond and Gordon) and had constant contact with Marendaz and hence ample opportunity to assess him. He first 'fingered' a Mr Gallagher, an Irishman who he alleged stayed overnight at the club house every time there was an IRA outrage in England.

Next came a 'dangerous' ground engineer employed at the Bedford School of Flying, an Indian who was openly anti-British and pro-Hitler. Then Mr Evans-Freke, a flying instructor, was merely accorded the epithet of 'peculiar', and had got lost flying but flew quite a lot in the districts where our air stations were situated, the implication being that he was snooping on the RAF. Shaw, a director like Evans-Freke, was 'definitely a dubious character who knew Lowenstein, the man who disappeared from an airliner over the Channel'. He concealed his political views but had been heard to make pro-Hitler comments in unguarded moments. Another, Pilot Sergeant Chater, 'should be checked up,' as should Mr Welch, Mr Mallinson (being a Yorkshireman was enough to damn him), Mr England, and two cousins: H. M. and W. E. Kendal. Mr Crawley (aero engineer), two unknown but foreign aircraft designers who helped Marendaz build his Trainer and a Mr Chaminex got the treatment.

Then in a fit of misogyny, Dorothy Summers got the full works. According to George Fuller, she had the most highly developed faculty for memorising that he had ever encountered, she did not look English, and in moments of excitement seemed naturally to fall into a foreign tongue, believed to be German, leading him to state 'that this woman is very dangerous. She accompanied Marendaz everywhere and appeared to be the controlling figure'. Dorothy Summers was born in Warwickshire in 1900 of humble origins and seems innocent of these accusations. Fuller suggested that the foregoing was evidence of a clearing house of some sort at

Airspeed Oxfords over Bedfordshire around 1940. They are from No. 14 Service Flying Training School, Cranfield. (*Philip Jarrett*)

Barton, a point he went on to amplify by detailing the Marendaz's trip to Germany in July and August 1939. Leaving these minor details aside (his words), he went on to the really suspicious meat describing his professional business regarding buildings to be turned into a club house at Eaton Bray. Marendaz had ignored his recommendations and had built using white bricks, hence making it a useful landmark for (presumably German?) airmen and indicating to George Fuller that a carefully planned landing ground for some other purpose was the intent. Fuller seemingly fell across the disabled and non-photographed Oxford at Eaton Bray, but decided that it was there to indicate wind direction to the said approaching airmen.

This whole document defies reason and the fact that it was believed by the Chief Constable is incredible; possibly he felt obliged to react to the Duke of Richmond and Gordon's statement, tugging his forelock as he went, and needed to scrape up further ammunition to support a thin story.

HIS APPEAL TO THE ADVISORY COMMITTEE

The events rolled on, the case against Marendaz now having been made. At this time, Marcus Marendaz was being held at Ascot; he was never actually interned on the Isle of Man and his hearing had been delayed due to the bombing of the Advisory Committee's offices in Burlington Gardens. It was now to be heard at the Berystede Hotel, Ascot, near the detention centre which was housed in the winter quarters of Bertram Mills's circus, between 2 and 4 October, 1940. The Advisory Committee comprised Mr Norman Birkett, KC, Chairman, Methodist preacher and a Liberal barrister, The Right Honourable Sir G. R. Clerk, GCMG, CB, a retired diplomat, with Mr G. P. Churchill, CBE as secretary.

Reading the papers, one concludes that the hearings were conducted in a constructive and friendly manner, with in many cases the Committee leading the witness. This seems surprising, given their quasi-legal nature. Marcus Marendaz was called first, the only other person called being Dorothy Summers, referred to throughout as Dorothy Marendaz. He was cross-examined about his background, war record and career leading up to his recent war work, training pilots, and manufacturing rocker boxes for Napiers. Marendaz said that as a result of the case, he had put together a war diary of events and dealing with Ministry officials since the start of the war. He had offered both his airfields, Barton and Eaton Bray, and also his manufacturing facilities to the Ministry, but only Eaton Bray had been accepted.

It has always been a slight mystery why Marcus Marendaz started operations at Eaton Bray, as the land was poorly drained and not completely suitable as a grass airfield, but it came about because the Ministry asked him to extend the runway at Barton. None of the land-owners thereabout were prepared to sell, possibly because of earlier bad feelings, so Marendaz elected to move his flying operations to Eaton Bray, with the consequent need to build facilities. In the hearing he was cross-examined about his relationship with the Ministry, which he declared to have never been anything other than good. However, the question of camouflaging the hangar at Barton was raised, it being alleged that he had refused to do so, a point that the Committee returned to later.

Given his prickly nature, Marcus Marendaz was never in complete accord with authorities of any sort and without doubt bodies dealing with him found him difficult. This certainly caused them, not only to be cautious but almost certainly not go out of their way to smooth his bureaucratic path. Marendaz was never one to be pushed around, so problems were rarely smoothed over.

The Committee turned to his visit to Germany in July and August 1939. At no point has it ever been stated that he was accorded an audience with any of the German hierarchy, but it has been alleged in recent years in the most general of terms that he had met with Göring and possibly Hitler. None of this was suggested by the Committee, Marendaz explaining that as an owner of a training establishment he was interested in seeing how the Germans trained their pilots, taking a letter of introduction from the Royal Aero Club with him to show to the Aero Klub in Berlin. They gave him permission to see over a military training school, which impressed him enormously, as did the general level of working conditions and the apparent fact that the people 'worshipped' Hitler. Asked if this made him feel pro-Nazi and anti-British, he replied 'no' and neither did it make him think Germany would win the war. Norman Birkett then led him by asking if his feelings were that he had been impressed by the German preparations and was saying 'If our country does not look out and get down to it, well, there is a bad day ahead for us'. Unsurprisingly, Marendaz replied, 'Yes'. In among the case for the prosecution was the statement that Marcus Marendaz spoke German well, so when the Committee asked him this, he said he spoke no German at all and that when buying petrol, he had been obliged to write the numbers down.

After the problem with continuing to use Barton without expansion and the need to buy land at Stanbridge for the airfield at Eaton Bray, one of allegations against Marendaz was that his choice of land was because it was near RAF Leighton Buzzard, a wireless station, the implied accusation being that this would facilitate his listening to military communi-

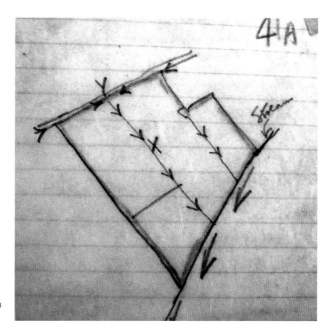

The inspector's sketch map of the Eaton Bray airfield site. (*National Archive*)

cations. Once they had clarified the fact that the land at Eaton Bray was not immediately adjacent to the RAF wireless station, the Committee moved to the assertion that Marendaz had refused to put obstacles on his airfield to render it unusable to an enemy landing assault. Marendaz denied that he had even been asked to do so.

The airfield had been licensed as a civil airport on 1 September 1939 and offered to the Ministry on the outbreak of war, who turned it down. Marendaz then elected to plough it up and sow wheat to get some use out of it, but after an expenditure of £900 and no sooner than the ploughs arrived, the RAF at Leighton Buzzard rang up to inquire what was happening as they might need the airfield. The upshot was that he was prevented from ploughing it up and, just as he was about to get the hay crop off it, the military dumped 120 old cars on it to render it unusable for aircraft. It transpired that having been denied use of his land for either flying or agriculture, Marcus Marendaz read the situation as being equivalent to someone renting his land, so he demanded payment of £200 a quarter from the Ministry. When questioned as to this, Marcus Marendaz explained that the company had a mortgage so had to have income of some sort, a position apparently agreed with by a Mr Fish at the Ministry, there being compensatory rights.

The Bedford School of Flying had been solvent at the outbreak of war but having had their income removed and their aircraft impressed they currently owed £2,000 against a value of £11,000 for the impressed machines. The Committee assessed these developments as indicative of a pugnacious attitude towards authority, putting people's backs up, and possibly why the Detention Order had been served, to which Marendaz replied 'Extraordinary!' To the suggestion that there was vindictiveness by a Government official, as a result of Marcus Marendaz's actions, he replied 'It was what he was doing to us'.

They were at an impasse, unsurprisingly, Norman Birkett noting that it looked as if Marendaz had been getting across all sorts of people. The discussion returned to the question

PLAYER'S CIGARETTES

AIRSPEED "OXFORD" ADVANCED TRAINING AIRCRAFT

This cigarette card was produced by Marcus Marendaz in his defence in 1940, illustrating the ease of obtaining information on military aircraft. (*Author's collection*)

of camouflaging the hangars at Barton, Marcus Marendaz denying repeatedly that he had ever been asked to do so, under considerable pressure from the Committee. One has to say that Marendaz's position was that no written instruction had ever been received and no evidence that one had existed was tabled. A number of officers had inspected the site with regard to the defence of it but apparently had not mentioned camouflage; Marendaz's thinking was that if it were not camouflaged, the Germans would waste bombs on it to no useful effect, thereby saving some other site. His implication was, very much, that if the government wanted it painted, they should arrange it and pay for it themselves as they had summarily terminated his income.

Given that the main accusations against Marendaz had seemingly been instigated by a statement by the Duke of Richmond and Gordon, the Committee then asked for Marcus Marendaz's interpretation of the fateful meeting outside the propeller works. He said that the meeting had been quite friendly and denied knowing about any of the Duke's negotiations with the Ministry, and that the talk was about business and the locality. Stonewall.

Dissatisfied with this answer, the Committee returned to the subject and Marcus Marendaz went a little deeper into the discussion. From this he said that he had enquired after Sammy Davis, March's co-driver at Brooklands (the Duke of Richmond and Gordon was the Earl of March at the time he was driving at Brooklands), then discussed the shortage of skilled labour and the German 'push' when the Duke said, 'Well, I'm not a defeatist yet,' and Marendaz replied 'It's not much use being like that anyway.' Interestingly, he then said that earlier he had been round at the works and finding things were not going along well spoke to one of the directors, offering Barton as an alternative, an offer that was not accepted, as the hold-up had been temporary. Undoubtedly, this director was the source of the confidential information, of which the Duke was suspicious when it emanated from Marcus Marendaz.

THE OXFORD AT EATON BRAY

Apart from innuendo, the only substantive evidence of subversive activity was the alleged photograph of an Airspeed Oxford trainer, resting on Eaton Bray aerodrome, under RAF guard, with a damaged propeller. Turning away from the troubles of Marcus Marendaz, it is worth looking at the arrival of Oxford II N4828 from the RAF College, Cranwell. It was piloted by Flight Cadet (LAC) T. R. N. Wheatley-Smith; he was lost on 3 May 1940 on a cross-country flight from Cranwell to Abingdon, one assumes with a turning point well to the east of his destination, and elected to force land, choosing Eaton Bray. The wheels sank into soft ground, a ditch filled with soft earth, the general area being prepared for a landing ground and the Oxford tipped on its nose. This shortcoming at Eaton Bray had already been noted and although the airfield was licensed it seems unlikely that any significant flying ever took place there. Wheatley-Smith was flying solo and had a princely total of fifty-two hours total flying time, thirteen of which were on Oxfords. In his defence, this was obviously a minor blip in his career as he retired from the Air Force as a wing commander in 1965.

Returning to the case against Marendaz, it would appear that the 120 cars were not the obstacle they were intended to be, as they do not feature in the discussion. A lengthy wrangle then ensued, going over much of the ground already elaborated, but with some of the details filled in. The whole photograph or no photograph issue had been gone into at the Petty Sessions court and the Advisory Committee went through these proceedings carefully and, it has to be said, generally agreeing with Marcus Marendaz's and his solicitor's position that it should never have come to court.

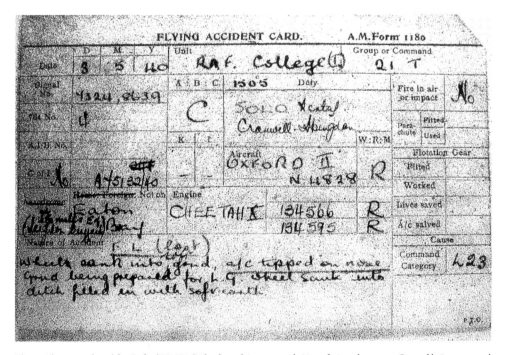

The accident record card for Oxford N4828. 'Wheels sank into ground. Aircraft tipped on nose. Ground being prepared for landing ground. Wheel sank into ditch filled with soft earth.' (*RAF Museum*)

The guilty outcome rested on the fine distinction that Marcus Marendaz had gone through the motions of taking a photograph, although no actual photograph could be produced. No actual photograph was necessary as the regulations stated that it was an offence to attempt to commit anything contrary to the regulations. Norman Birkett summed up by saying that the feeling among officialdom seemingly was 'The behaviour of Mr Marendaz is something we are not going to tolerate any longer', with the added comment, 'Why in the world was all this police machinery brought into being over a simple matter like that?' Marcus Marendaz's attitude was undoubtedly provocative. As recorded he was practising with his new Zeiss Contax 3 camera, bought at a price of £88, quite possibly when he was in Germany. Quite why, when informed of an Oxford on Eaton Bray airfield, he chose to drive over two days later and then start practising photography is anyone's guess. It's quite possible that he did indeed take a photograph, given that the subject was benign, but when challenged discreetly opened the back of the camera thereby destroying the image. Marendaz having produced a camera, a small boy informed the RAF guard, a Corporal Kenneth Harrison, who asked Marendaz if he had an authorized permit to take photographs, to which Marendaz replied 'Have you permission to be on my land?' Marcus Marendaz denied this exchange took place, saying that any exchange was almost friendly, the Corporal willingly helping him open the sunshine roof on the Rolls, which had become stuck.

When asked about his relationship with the Chief Constable of Bedfordshire, Marcus Marendaz said that he had only met him in the course of the case. At the time of his arrest he was allowed to ring up Sir Thomas Keynes a JP for the County, asking 'Can you possibly do something with the Chief Constable, to be told "He is a new one, he has only just been appointed and if I do anything it might be considered it was against the public interest."' During the earlier summons, Chief Constable Commander Willis, said 'I have no wish to speak to Mr Marendaz' regarding his bail request, so it seems that whatever relationship existed it was unlikely to have been good.

DOROTHY MARENDAZ AND THE ADVISORY COMMITTEE

In all of this, Dorothy Marendaz had been a most stalwart supporter. Right from her first letter her tenacity was notable. On 13 July 1940, she asked for an interview with Lord Beaverbrook, citing her husband's recent history of war work. The same day another letter went to Sir John Anderson, followed by a telegram on the 23rd saying: 'Please Sir John will you now release Captain Marendaz who is all British'.

Inspired by the slogan of the Minister of Supply, Herbert Morrison, 'Go to it' encouraging production for the war effort, Dorothy Marendaz wrote to him, saying that interning Marcus Marendaz was not helping. The National Council of Civil Liberties was approached by her as well, their legal department writing to the Under Secretary of State for Home Affairs on 7 August on the matter. Sir John Anderson received a further telegram on 7 August asking that Dorothy might visit her husband at Ascot and on the 20th, a letter to him was handed in by her at the front desk asking when his appeal will be heard, Marcus Marendaz by this time having been interned for eight weeks. The appeal process was grinding slowly along and, as noted above, Dorothy Marendaz finally had her say on 4 October 1940.

In the intervening months before the Advisory Committee hearing, Dorothy Marendaz had been assiduously collecting the personal and business paperwork supporting her husband's case. She was able to produce the letter from the naval *attaché* in The Hague, whom they had

Dorothy Summers and Altair Kelway, Marendaz's cousin, seen during the war with the family Rolls-Royce, a 1934 20/25 Gurney Nutting Saloon. (*Don Summers*)

visited on returning from Germany to offer information on German preparations that would be of interest to the War Office. He had given them contact details, that they had followed up on their return, not the overall actions of a fifth columnist and his wife, one would say.

On being asked by the Advisory Committee about the by now infamous non-photograph, she gave a reasoned and lucid account of the two-and-a-half hours spent at Eaton Bray, first of all the encounter with the RAF corporal, then being asked about the photograph, which was denied, then talking to the farmer about harrowing some land, then having lunch and finally getting the sunshine roof open on the Rolls. 'We went away ... and it was twenty-two days before they arrested him. I think he was flabbergasted, he was taken aback'. She ended her appearance, having been asked about the German trip with the following words in National Archive Reference HO 45/23722:

What he says and what I say too is they [the Germans] are frightfully thorough. Their largest flying school was the last word in efficiency. It was marvellous and it was that that impressed him so much and that is the kind of thing he would talk about, but he would never in the wide world say they will beat us or this, that and the other because he would not believe it anyway.

Dorothy Marendaz was not the only overt supporter and many people wrote to the Committee in support of Marcus Marendaz. Today, there is only one supporter's name that has resonance, one Alfred Moss, father of Sir Stirling Moss. He had been a consistent financial supporter of Marcus Marendaz during the early 1930s, both he and his wife Aileen driving Marendaz Special cars. The collapse of the car business in 1936, leaving Moss a significant creditor seemingly did not end their friendship. Of all the people offering support to Marendaz, Alfred Moss was the only one offering to put up a surety for his release.

This ended the hearing and true to their word and no doubt burning a bit of midnight oil, the report by the Advisory Committee was dated Monday, 7 October 1940, just three days later, having been written over the weekend. Interestingly, they obviously discussed their findings with MI5 as a note dated Saturday 5 October by the Secretary George Churchill says that Mr Pilcher agreed to the proposed release of Marendaz. The report, having stated the case as put to them then states 'This is a very remarkable case, which has caused the Committee grave concern.' Without going over all the specific detail again, where the Committee essentially take Marcus Marendaz's position, they specifically commented on the report by the chief constable of Bedfordshire, Commander Willis in National Archive Reference HO 45/23722:

> Those are the matters which were contained in the report of the Chief Constable of Bedfordshire, on which the Order of the Secretary of State was made. When they are examined and all due allowances made for errors in recollection or misunderstanding of the purport of conversations and the contradiction of the facts which undoubtedly exist, it will be seen that it is extremely difficult to say that MARENDAZ had been guilty of acts prejudicial to the national safety in any ordinary understanding of those words.

FREEDOM OR NOT FREEDOM

Given the urgency indicated by the Advisory Committee's report, one would have assumed that Marcus Marendaz would have been released immediately, but this was not to be. Commander Willis was not prepared to accept the criticism levelled at him in the report and wrote to Sir Alexander Maxwell at the Home Office on 15 October 1940. Like his earlier efforts, it was a rearguard action based on character blackening and, once again, unsubstantiated evidence. One cannot see how the powers that be would see it as a reason to reopen the case.

Apparently, a constable had informed Marendaz that the hangar at Barton had to be camouflaged; the people of Barton were concerned about the overt visibility of the hangars, fifty-six cars had had to be purchased by the Air Ministry to block the landing ground at Eaton Bray; an unidentified but credible citizen of Luton regarded Marendaz with suspicion; Marendaz was only a charge hand at Alvis in 1921 and had been sacked; and, finally, his interview with the Ministry following his visit to Germany imparted no important information.

It does seem incredible that in a period of significant social disruption that the chief constable was prepared to waste resources on checking on the career of Marcus Marendaz twenty years earlier. Among this litany, he managed to squeeze in that Marendaz was a man of violent temper and 'cannot be reasoned with and that he has been regarded with suspicion'—all hanging offences it would appear. He also noted that the original statement by the Duke of Richmond and Gordon had not been made to him but to the Chief Constable of Buckinghamshire who, with great good sense it would appear, had passed it on to the new boy in Bedfordshire.

While that spanner in the works was being digested, Dorothy Marendaz, having met her husband during the hearing, was concerned as to his health, as the period of detention, now over three months was affecting him. She wrote to Whitehall once again on 9 October requesting that a doctor and family friend visit Marendaz to assess him. Dr John Sophian, of Harley Street, duly did so and his report of 18 October suggests that as well as being suicidal, listless, apathetic, lacking concentration, and suffering from insomnia and amnesia, he was apparently on the point of complete breakdown.

On a slightly lighter note, another letter arrived at the Home Secretary at this point, signed Dorothy Marendaz, but this time from the still-married Mrs Marendaz from South Wales, enquiring as to why her weekly allowance from Marcus Marendaz had stopped, having read of his arrest in the papers. It is understood that this Mrs Marendaz, being a Roman Catholic, was against divorce, so remained only separated, and had lived a life apart from him for nearly twenty years. The Home Office, disconcerted by this turn of events, quickly passed the buck 'but naturally Home Office wish to keep out of this tangle'.

The whole affair was finally brought to a conclusion when Herbert Morrison, Home Secretary, revoked the Detention Order on 23 October 1940, Donald Marendaz having been interned for just short of four months.

Not guilty but hit very hard by a blunt instrument, his hard-won reputation was destroyed. He was undoubtedly a damaged man, whatever you may think about his character and demeanour towards his fellow man. The whole case against him, while not fabricated, was tenuous in the extreme. It rested on an event that did not happen, the cautionary word of a Duke being taken verbatim by a new chief constable and the underlying threat of invasion. In many matters, Marcus Marendaz was his own worst enemy; in his dealings with officialdom at any level, he was suspicious, unhelpful and antagonistic. Had he been a German sympathiser, fifth columnist or Quisling welcoming the invaders to his brightly marked landing ground, I have absolutely no doubt that he would have been kicking against the newly-established German government in Britain just as readily.

Marcus Marendaz spent the rest of the war in relative seclusion. One could not say house arrest, but he played no part in the events that followed after 1940. One assumes that he was told to keep his head down. He did write for the *Daily Express* about his experiences, very much in the vein of an injured patriot. His company at Barton was put into receivership and the aircraft together with the effects remaining being sold off at auction, the aircraft being broken up. His own Marendaz aircraft were similarly disposed of and eventually destroyed. He spent some of his time writing a slim volume *You Can Fly* and studying Worcestershire porcelain. After the war and having parted from Dorothy Summers, he elected to start a new life in South Africa. Needless to say, this ended in controversy and in 1972, he returned to retirement in Lincolnshire, where he died in 1988, aged ninety-one.

17

AFTER THE WAR

In late 1940, Marcus Marendaz was undoubtedly a somewhat shaken man, the world events unfolding around him having passed him by. The glorious summer of 1940 was ruined by the murderous aerial battles over southern England, the threat of invasion by hordes of Germans, and the start of a night-time terror bombing campaign on the cities of the United Kingdom. Emerging from his seclusion at Ascot, he must have wondered what was next. He was undoubtedly a marked man, whether there was justification for this or not, and the prospect of carrying on as before was not an option. Before he was arrested in June 1940, he was wrestling with the problems of maintaining his businesses International Aircraft Limited and the Bedford School of Flying at Barton in the Clay with a fleet of retired and rapidly deteriorating aircraft of marginal use to the powers that be, prevented from making proper use of his land and his ability to provide training for much-needed pilots at a halt. Some flying schools moved smoothly into military units, for example the nearby De Havilland School of Flying at Hatfield quickly became No. 1 Elementary Flying Training School with their civil aircraft being given military marks. In some ways, this change was pre-planned and the fact that the Bedford School of Flying was not transferred was probably because overtures in the years leading up to the war may have been spurned by Marcus Marendaz or because his school, while doing a useful job, was on a smaller scale using rather old aircraft.

As described earlier, the effects at Barton in the Clay were auctioned in December 1940, not long after Marcus Marendaz's release and given that all the aircraft essentially disappeared off the aeronautical scene, seemingly in small pieces, it is unlikely that Marcus Marendaz made any money at all out of the sale. Remember that in 1939 and into 1940, things were at a poor ebb in Britain and the most wonderful cars could be had for a pittance, provided you had the vision to expect that sanity would one day return to the world.

During the time Marcus Marendaz was incarcerated at His Majesty's pleasure, in August 1940, a notice appeared in *Flight* magazine stating that a new company had been formed called Marendaz-Bowman Transmissions; this was surprising, but quite possibly a counter to the accusations being put about and an indication of Marendaz's wish to do productive work for the government. Their stated business was 'manufacturers, letters on hire, purchasers and repairers of motor cars, motor and aeroplane engines, motor cycles, motor bodies, sidecars, airships, etc.'—a position that seems to be backing most options for his continuation in the engineering

The book written by Marcus Marendaz during the war.
(*Author's collection*)

business. Note that transmissions as such are not listed, but in the Category 18B wrangles, Marcus Marendaz made frequent reference to his discussions with ministry figures regarding his designs for a transmission system for 'machine tools and tanks' that offered a 30 per cent improvement in efficiency. This move was not kite flying as a UK patent was applied for called 'Improvements in power transmission systems': No. 542126 dated 21 March 1940—in other words, on a date before he was arrested. The patent description talked about transferring rotary into reciprocating motion and being applicable to vehicle propulsion or to the actuation of pumps. Marcus Marendaz was stated to be living at the Manor House, Little Tring and his partner was Hugh Bowman, an instrument maker and engineer of 5 Beaconsfield Road, St Albans. What transpired from this collaboration is not known, equally whether it resulted in anything useful.

Flying did continue at Barton in the Clay, both as a relief landing ground for training at nearby Luton and for the Air Transport Auxiliary (ATA), but Marcus Marendaz was not involved.

THE MOVE TO BERGH APTON

In October 1941, he bought for £1,500 Holly Lodge, Loddon Road, Bergh Apton, six miles south-east of Norwich, where he remained until 1948. Apart from continuing with his design activities, he published in 1944 a slim volume *You Can Fly* for a princely two shillings. This was actually quite a useful and accurate summary of the whole business of flying, aimed at the light aeroplane pilot and no doubt based on the course notes handed out to trainee pilots at the Bedford School of Flying. The title page was rather overdone as it contained a Marcus Marendaz *curriculum vitae* in block capitals (as shown on page 1 of *You Can Fly*):

The drawing room of Marcus Marendaz's house in Bergh Apton, with a Titian on the wall. (*John Ling*)

A PILOT IN THE ROYAL FLYING CORPS IN THE GREAT WAR 1914–1918 DIRECTOR OF GREAT BRITAIN'S FIRST POST-WAR PROVINCIAL FLYING SCHOOL ONE OF GREAT BRITAIN'S FIRST PRIVATE OWNERS OF AIRCRAFT FOUNDER, DIRECTOR AND GENERAL MANAGER OF THE BEDFORD SCHOOL OF FLYING DESIGNER AND CONSTRUCTOR OF MARENDAZ TRAINER AND OTHER AIRCRAFT DESIGNER AND PATENTEE OF MARENDAZ FLAPS

His family record that he helped run the Bergh Apton Fire Service during his time there.

While maintaining his interest in aircraft, cars and machines at this point in his life, aged forty-eight in 1945, Marcus Marendaz expanded his interests in art and porcelain, writing a number of articles for *Apollo* (the fine art magazine) from 1944 to 1948. We are reliant on Marcus Marendaz's interview with the *Lincolnshire Standard* in January 1975 for some of the other details, for instance the receipt of letters from George VI, the German aristocracy and directors of the Louvre in Paris and the National Galleries in both London and Washington for his assistance in art research. The letter from an allegedly delighted George VI concerned Marcus Marendaz's identification of a picture by Zoffany acquired by George III in the late 1700s. His picture collection, which was to feature largely in his later life when he was resident in Lincolnshire, comprised works by Titian, Gainsborough, Murillo, Reubens, Gerard Dou, Metsu, Corregio, Frans Hals, Fantin Latour, Caspar Netscher, Constable, Francis Barlow, Cornelis De Heem, and others, plus a picture of Lady Hamilton by an unknown artist. Whether the attributions of the day are correct is a matter for the experts, given the time that has elapsed since their acquisition and recent developments in historical research. Whether Marcus Marendaz purchased them on the open market or inherited them from his family in Wales is not certain. It seems that his Welsh connections added to his interests in porcelain and he had a significant number of pieces from the Nantgarw and Swansea potteries, which in turn connected with Worcester porcelain, another interest. By good fortune, a sale catalogue for his house—Holly Lodge at Bergh Apton—survives from 1948, complete with photographs of the interior showing two of the pictures and the porcelain.

Marcus Marendaz's fertile mind was still very busy on mechanical devices and while his Marendaz–Bowman transmission seems to have fallen on stony ground, other plans were afoot. UK patents 582189 (December 1943) and 595767 (February 1945) were for control of a clutch or ratchet gearing and an improved differential mechanism using ratchet clutches respectively. Again, neither of these patents resulted in a design that made use of them commercially. One item produced by him was a neat and compact engine of 650 cc with vertical in-line cylinders and a chain-driven overhead camshaft. Its intended use was for small tractors or lighting plants, but it was referred to in the magazine *Sailplane and Glider* in October 1948 as a potential auxiliary power-unit for gliders. Having three cylinders in line, the cylinder block and crankcase was a single casting in light alloy with cast iron liners and a cylinder head also in light alloy with bronze valve seats. The three-throw crankshaft was mounted in plain white-metal bearings and there was a dry sump lubrication system. Power output was 18 bhp at 4,000 rpm, for a weight of 54 lb. Whether the engine seen in the illustrations was a development prototype or whether any were produced is not known. Alternatively, it may have been seen as the basis for production at a later date in South Africa—it certainly had the appearance of being a useful tool.

The three-cylinder two-stroke engine designed by Marcus Marendaz in 1948. (*John Shaw*)

THE MOVE TO SOUTH AFRICA

The lack of success with his design efforts and perhaps his general dissatisfaction with life in England and the way he had been treated may have prompted Marcus Marendaz to consider a move abroad. Coupled with a recommendation from a German consultant that his rheumatism might respond to a drier climate; that prompted him to sell Holly Lodge in 1948 and move to South Africa, where he believed his engineering talents could better be exploited. The house, cottage and land went for £8,150, five times what he had paid for it in 1941.

Given the lack of rapid communication, the first thing we learn about Marcus Marendaz in South Africa was the publication of his slim volume *Revelations of Old Worcester* in August 1950, printed in Cape Town. As slim volumes go, this limited edition privately published volume was very slim, running to only twenty-three pages, bound in boards and illustrated with photographs of his personal collection of porcelain and paintings. It seemed to be filling the role of correcting 'facts' alleged by 'authorities' dating from the late eighteenth century. Presumably to finance his other interests, it was reported by *The Times* in July 1958 that Captain Marendaz had sold his porcelain collection at Christies for £5,050, equivalent to around £80,000 in 2017 values.

A book on porcelain did not mean that Marendaz has abandoned his engineering exploits and according to a chance meeting by the author with Michael Strauss, Marendaz initially lived at Strandfontein, Gordon's Bay near Cape Town and was involved with growing lupins while developing a five-cylinder engine. His house was stacked with pictures and English bone china. A 2001 edition of the *Cape Vintage Engine and Machinery Society Newsletter* says that Marendaz built stationary engines in single and twin-cylinder form, rated at 6 hp to 16 hp at the Marendaz Engineering Corporation Ltd of Cape Province, but qualifies their statement by asking 'does anyone have one?'

Marcus Marendaz said that when he moved to South Africa, he settled in the area of Johannesburg, where he built a beautiful country house in the Dutch style, which made a fitting background for his collections of paintings, porcelain and Chippendale and Sheraton furniture. It would appear that his time near Cape Town was fairly short, before the move to Johannesburg and the Vaal triangle, the industrial heartland of South Africa, a more suitable location for his engineering activities. Here, according to his own notes, he produced his low-speed diesel engines for the farming industry, being made in four models ranging from 7 hp to 17 hp, and being the only engine designed, developed and manufactured, not just assembled, on the Continent of Africa. He allegedly employed about seventy-five people at a business address called Marendaz town, near Meyerton.

THE THIRD DOROTHY

At this point in the story of Marendaz, at the time when he lived in South Africa we should introduce the third Dorothy. As we know, he married Dorothy Robinette Evans in 1918 and is believed to have eventually divorced her in 1954 but lived with Dorothy Olive Summers between about 1922 and 1942. By 1970, the name of Dorothy Marie Marendaz appears: she was married to Marcus Marendaz, but we have no marriage date, although it probably dates to the mid-1950s in South Africa. She was born Dorothy Marie Austen on 23 May 1916 in Hammersmith, London, in other words she was about nineteen years younger than Marcus and married a Mr Perry in 1937 in Kensington. She died in Kensington early in 1996, so survived Marcus Marendaz, but we do not know when she moved back to London. It is believed that she was not living with him in Lincolnshire after he returned to England.

ENGINEERING AND POLITICS IN THE TRANSVAAL

Returning to Marendaz's industrial activities, in an undated document he was reported as being the managing director of Marendaz Diesel Engines Pty Ltd, controlling the company but holding no shares, the majority of which being held by Mrs Marendaz. The company was registered in April 1959 with a capital of £1,000 and at the unknown date of this document a factory was being erected at Meyerton, with the anticipated production of diesel engines within one month. He was regarded as being hard working and capable, but likely to be fully committed financially with the new factory.

Ken Hurst writing to Michael Worthington-Williams on 21 July 1990 gave a little of the background to this factory:

He started an engineering business in South Africa at Meyerton, supposedly manufacturing stationary diesel engines. Marendaz phoned my company, would not speak to anyone on my sales staff, demanding to speak to someone 'who could make on-the-spot decisions.' I went to see him at the Meyerton factory, I was on time but he kept me waiting. I examined the display of stationary engines in the reception area, all of the external pipes, etc., were in place but what was supposed to be the crankshaft projecting from the rear of the engine was in reality just a steel bar, there being

The overhead-cam Marendaz engine block and probably not put into production. (*John Shaw*)

nothing inside the engine. When I was at last ushered into his office he showed me a pile of letters from important people in the U.K. motor industry, one was from Hives at Rolls-Royce wishing him success in his new venture. All the letters were bland and non-committal but Marendaz tried to suggest that there was financial backing behind them. Marendaz was going to produce an agricultural tractor which would push all the other manufacturers out of the market (the company of which I was a director also manufactured tractors in a separate factory in East London). Well, the deal was that my company was to have the honour of supplying all the timing gears and gearbox, P.T.O. and axle gears on an extended payment basis for this world beating tractor. In other words we were to finance him. He was also going to manufacture the Marendaz car. I gave him my on-the-spot decision which made him cross and that was the last I heard of him, his company went bust and several right-wingers lost their money.

Controversy followed Marcus Marendaz, so it is not entirely surprising that his time in South Africa would be more of the same. Putting a personal opinion based on what he saw around him, Ken Hurst in writing to John Shaw on 1 November 1990 gave an overview:

The redoubtable Captain was all mixed up with the South African politics which were at that time convoluted. The dominant National Party was ruled by simple farmers, minor lawyers and Dutch Reformed Church predicants (ministers). They were so much in the majority that they controlled the press so that few facts ever got out and many dubious aspects were covered up. One member of this Government was Mr Carel de Wet, who had been at one time S.A. ambassador to Britain. The government then were pro-Nazi (B. J. Vorster, one-time Prime Minister was locked up for the duration of the war for acts of treason) and they were anti-British. Most of the big mining groups and most of the industry were British orientated so the 'Nats' hated us and wherever possible directed government contracts to Afrikaans owned businesses. The Captain cashed in on this situation, he did not have an English sounding name and he was pro-Nazi and he could claim to be an industrialist. Carel De Wet put money into the firm and probably some government funds were pumped in which Marendaz used for his own benefit. I suspect that this was the basis of the Marendaz Affair, but very little got into the news here, I think there was more information in Britain. Marendaz started up in Somerset West, near Cape Town, but the main industrial area was in the Vaal triangle which included Meyerton. I think the designs of the engines came from Czechoslovakia or maybe from Germany, I do not know how many were built, sales were handled by Afrikaans co-operatives and were mostly for agriculture. Frankly, I was not very interested, I had enough problems of my own as M.D. of David Brown. Marendaz was a colourful character, I don't think he was capable of running a straight business, the temptation to do a fiddle was always too much for him and it was this that eventually got him into trouble in S.A.

The 'Marendaz Affair' in South Africa was not trivial and caused Marcus Marendaz to quit the country. The South African *Sunday Times* carried an article in October 1970 reporting that Government ministers had attacked Captain Marendaz in Parliament, under parliamentary privilege, calling him a crook and a blackguard, knowing that he was in no position to command similar opportunities to put his own case. This situation provoked a letter from Marendaz to the British Consul General in Johannesburg, outlining the background and asking for help. A letter from the Embassy in Pretoria to the Foreign and Commonwealth Office in London asking how to proceed noted that Captain Marendaz had been a thorn in the flesh of the Embassy and Consulate-General for a considerable number of years, and that the alleged association between Dr de Wet, then Minister of Mines and Health, with Captain Marendaz was of some ten years standing. Pressure from the Opposition in Parliament calling on de Wet to resign had resulted in the Prime Minster, Mr Vorster, having to step in to defend him, resulting in him overstepping the bounds of parliamentary privilege. This 'hot potato' was handled by the Embassy by replying to Marendaz that the matter was receiving consideration.

In a sworn affidavit in 1970, Dorothy Marie Marendaz gave clear evidence that Dr Carel de Wet had accepted a directorship with Marendaz Diesel Engines on 15 September 1959, including copies of documents clearly in de Wet's hand. Also recorded was the transfer of £1,000 worth of shares to him. The association did not last as he resigned on 12 February 1960, 'due to circumstances beyond his control'. De Wet's involvement included a trip to Ghana looking for agents for the diesel engines and despite his efforts, including meeting President Nkruma of Ghana, the trip was unsuccessful, de Wet reporting that Ghana, despite all reports to the contrary, was 'back in the bush'. After de Wet's resignation, over the next number of years, he categorically and repeatedly denied that he had ever been a director in Marendaz's company, to the point that Marcus Marendaz was prosecuted and convicted in the 1960s for falsely submitting a Form 'J' to the authorities for Carel de Wet's directorship. Marendaz's defence was denied permission to present evidence on the grounds 'that his case was being sufficiently canvassed before the Court already.' Following the exchange in 1970 with the Consulate-General and the submission of Dorothy Marendaz's affidavit to various Government ministers and the *Sunday Times*, Marendaz was advised by all parties to 'play it cool' and to await developments from the authorities, at least for some months. In passing, the Embassy noted that Marendaz had admitted that he was an undischarged bankrupt and technically insolvent, but that he was taking steps to get himself discharged, his case to be heard on 8 December 1970. He also said that he was planning to develop land for industrial and residential purposes near Viljoenskroon in the Orange Free State, finances coming from 'the Marendaz family'. The matter was rested, but undoubtedly things had got too hot. He had evidence that a minister was guilty of fraud, but his chances of redress—a pardon, compensation perhaps—were essentially nil. There was absolutely no chance that anyone would now do business with him in South Africa and one has to wonder whether greater threats existed, so the best option was to cut and run.

A MARENDAZ SPECIAL CAR IN SOUTH AFRICA

Although Marcus Marendaz's time was occupied in establishing his agricultural engine business, he was still interested in restarting car manufacture. Possibly to that end, he repurchased one of his own 15-90 cars and had it shipped out to Johannesburg. By the late 1950s, it would have been a little 'old hat' and was, of course, a luxury sports car. Utilitarian vehicle production would have been useful, but seemingly an upgraded Marendaz Special possibly not. The car in question was first registered JB7776 in November 1935 and remained in the United Kingdon until about 1960, at which point it was exported, essentially complete and probably in running order. For whatever reason, either as a pattern vehicle or merely to effect restoration, the car was parted out and the elements scattered around many engineering works in the Johannesburg area for attention. Probably due to lack of finance, many of the parts were never reclaimed and the engineless hollow shell in poor condition was found by Peter Spiers in 1982. He expended

JB7776 as found in South Africa by Peter Spiers after being abandoned in a derelict state by Marcus Marendaz. (*Peter Spiers*)

many hours searching for the missing parts, thankfully finding many of them, and together with a replacement engine supplied by the author, put the car back together again. It is now running and back in the United Kingdom.

THE RETURN TO THE UNITED KINGDOM

As far as one can tell, this was Marcus Marendaz's last fling with cars, so together with his brush with the hot breath of South African politics and his 'escape' back to the United Kingdom in 1972, his life then took on a more placid routine with the exception of his occasional literary outbursts. He bought two semi-detached cottages in the village of Asterby in Lincolnshire, which he restored and enlarged to become the new Asterby Hall, which was then filled with his pictures and porcelain. His engineering enthusiasms continued and in 1975, he was developing a small, multi-purpose tractor that for economic reasons would be likely to appeal to farmers large and small. He alleged that prototype engines and transmissions had been produced at a cost of some £250,000, a figure that might have come from 'the sale of the Trust's pictures'. George Murray of Storrington, West Sussex, was employed by Marcus Marendaz to do the design and drawing for these engineering items and was resident at Asterby Hall for periods of time stretching to three to four months. The Marendaz transmission was hydrostatic and George also said, in passing, that engines had been built in South Africa, and had a pre-chamber built into the head.

It probably comes as no surprise that Marcus Marendaz's later life followed the pattern of earlier times, being regularly enlivened by stories from people he came in contact with.

John Aston, writing in the *Autosport* forum in 2008 told us that when he worked for Lincolnshire County Council in the 1970s, Captain Marendaz was a regular correspondent, to the point where he had to deal with reams of ranting letters about him being ripped off by some garage when buying a Mercedes-Benz 250. Apparently, he was also barred from most libraries in the county because he refused to return books or pay fines on them. With regard to a Jaguar car that he owned in 1974, he won a court case where a garage mended the brakes but failed to retain the parts removed from the car, as requested, throwing them away three months later. He conducted his own case in court, the Registrar congratulating him on his performance, and he was awarded £46.60 for his efforts. Reading between the lines, the garage was at fault in law, but must have felt rather hard done by.

CAPTAIN MARENDAZ IS ROBBED OF HIS ART COLLECTION

The *Horncastle News*, 17 November 1988, stated that the majority of Marcus Marendaz's paintings belonged to A.M.V. Trust and presumably had done so since the mid-1960s, but if his pictures were so protected, it seems unlikely that they could be used as a source of funds. Therefore, it is a little difficult to establish the extent of his art collection at any date. We know he sold some of his porcelain while in South Africa, but whether some paintings were also sold is not clear. Searches for the A.M.V. Trust and what they hold or held have revealed nothing. Yet as it happened, paintings that were not sold became involved in a much more serious matter, *The Daily Telegraph* reporting on 21 February 1986 that £1 million worth of paintings and jewellery had been stolen from an eccentric recluse in Lincolnshire, but that the thieves had left behind £10 million of antiques. Apparently, some of the raiders were dressed as policemen and

Asterby Hall in Lincolnshire, converted from two cottages and given a faux-barley-twist chimney. (*John Ling*)

Marcus Marendaz announced the robbery by leaving a note on his front door for the postman saying 'I have been robbed, call the police'. The robbery was on Monday 17 February and by 3 March, four men from a caravan site had been arrested. Some days later, he was refusing to admit that it had been his house that had been burgled.

For whatever reason, it rather looks as if the major paintings, such as the Titian that Marcus Marendaz had acquired in 1942, were elsewhere, as the list of stolen paintings was variously reported as five, six, or seven items including two Metsus, one Fantin Latour, one Caspar Netscher, an unknown of a woman kneeling, and the portrait of Lady Hamilton. Only two, not identified in the press, were recovered, the remainder of those stolen being believed to have been moved abroad. Also recovered were the jewellery and Captain Marendaz's medals.

HIS FINAL DAYS

According to Alice May Heseltine, his secretary and housekeeper since the mid-1970s, Marcus Marendaz was very affected by the robbery and it undoubtedly contributed to his death nearly two years later on 6 November 1988. The final straw might have been a bankruptcy order against him dated 16 October 1987. This was not the end of the story, as the previous publicity relating to the valuables in his house meant that it was broken into again after his death when a number of antiques were stolen as well as two paintings by Francis Barlow, two alleged small Constables and one by Cornelis De Heem.

Donald Marcus Kelway Marendaz is buried in the nearby churchyard and in keeping with his status in the world the gravestone bears his title and qualifications. It reads:

In memory of
Captain D. M. K. Marendaz, R.F.C.
M.I. Prod. E., M.S.A.E.
Died 6th November 1988, aged 91 years
R.I.P.

18

EPILOGUE: CORRESPONDING WITH THE CAPTAIN

Donald Marcus Kelway Marendaz was an inveterate correspondent in the columns of the motoring press, usually, to put it mildly, to take someone to task. Very few of his published letters are of a benign or conciliatory nature and it is largely because of them that the public's impression of the man has been generated.

THE ORIGINS OF THE TITLE 'CAPTAIN'

Many of them have been signed Captain D. M. K. Marendaz, M.I. Prod. E., M.S.A.E., referring to him being a member of the Institute of Production Engineers and a member of the Society of Automotive Engineers at some time in his career, both respected organisations. His title 'Captain' is rather more problematic. Going back to his days with the Royal Flying Corps and the RAF, 'Captain' is an army rank used in the RFC, but only one that Captain Marendaz aspired to rather than was promoted to. His RFC rank in his service records refer to him as second lieutenant, and his RAF record (the RAF being formed from the RFC and Royal Naval Air Service on 1 April 1918) refers to him as a lieutenant. This is not an RAF rank today but probably would be equivalent to flight lieutenant. There is a convoluted logic for him to justify calling himself captain in that for higher ranks, it was accepted that someone could use, as a title post military service, a rank one 'pip' up from that gazetted. In other words, a lieutenant-colonel could call himself colonel and so on. This was a not a right, but a generally accepted practice and not one generally extended to the lower commissioned ranks. This does not mean that no one called themselves captain after their military service, but it probably does mean that they were gazetted as such when in the service. No doubt Marcus Marendaz saw no reason why a lowly second lieutenant should be denied the privilege of enhancement.

Looking through the vast amount of material generated by and about Captain Marendaz, it rather looks as if he only started using this title around the time of the Second World War and his internment in 1940, and in a letter from him dated 29 June 1940 he adds 'Late Captain, R.F.C.' In other words, the need to emphasise his association with the United Kingdom was more urgent and one has to have sympathy with this position when seeing him rounded up with all the other foreign-sounding ne'er-do-wells. (See Chapter 16).

Plain Mr D. M. K. Marendaz's name appeared in the motoring press back as far as his Marseal days: for example, *Autocar* on 21 December 1922, responding to the suggestion that a practically standard light car could not lap Brooklands at 80 mph; he pointed out that such a Marseal, less wings, screen, dynamo, and spare wheel, had lapped at 76.75 mph from a standing start. In August 1928, he wrote to *Light Car and Cyclecar* complaining about the proposed handicap times for the forthcoming T.T. later that month, this probably being the reason he non-started.

Apart from the standard press articles about his cars, a further article, *Random Recollections*, by Marcus Marendaz appeared in the December 1930 *Motor Sport*, following on from an article the preceding September about his tuning establishment. Around this time, an interview with D. M. K. Marendaz by Alan Hess called 'My Greatest Thrill' was published in *Modern Boy*.

An interview with Captain Marendaz by Paul Irwin of the *Sunday Express* in November 1940, shortly after his release from Category 18B detention, gave him the opportunity to express how badly he had been treated, given his background (See Appendix I). Even though he was still only forty-three, after this, he seemingly played no great part in matters to do with the war, probably being advised to keep a low profile, although he did write his book, *You Can Fly*. The wartime motoring press kept going, filling their editorial pages with articles based on reminiscences and, of course, Marendaz Special cars were mentioned from time to time. In February 1943, J. V. Bowles (an inveterate Marendaz Special driver) wrote of his experiences of the cars, having first seen Aileen Moss's black and chromium JB1477 at the RAC Rally at Hastings in 1933. Interestingly, his article started the hare running that the later Marendaz Special cars had a Moss gearbox, when it was in fact a Laycock box. He also refers to the engines as being of American Continental manufacture, a point heavily disputed by Marendaz, and that head gaskets were obtainable from Studebaker in Camden Town. Whether Marcus Marendaz read this article we do not know, but curiously it evoked no response from him—unlike the article 'Talking of Sports Cars' written by Guy Griffiths (pre-war car dealer and latterly car photographer) in *Autocar* for 26 October 1945. Essentially, a whole-page reply was published correcting the points made by Guy, but years later, talking to him, he said *Autocar* at the time had received a threat of legal action, huge claims for defamation, and demands for an abject apology. When the very concerned Guy consulted *Autocar*'s editor, Sammy Davis, he was told not to be too upset as Sammy had the drop on the Captain and would draft a letter to go from Guy to Marendaz mentioning certain matters. *Autocar* was not troubled further.

The above reaction was typical of Marendaz and effectively stopped authors considering writing about Marendaz Special cars—positively or negatively. Marcus Marendaz's response to Guy Griffiths' review of an Anzani-powered Marendaz Special (YT1378) included the words that Marendaz Specials had something that a 1.5-litre Anzani had not, yet it is a fact that they all had a standard 1.5-litre Anzani, so if nothing else, he was playing with words. His further statement in this reply that he was the first British manufacturer to adopt hydraulic brakes is not considered correct: the author cannot twist the known facts to fit this assertion. He also says that his 13/70 was not first produced in 1931, though it was announced in *Autocar* 30 October

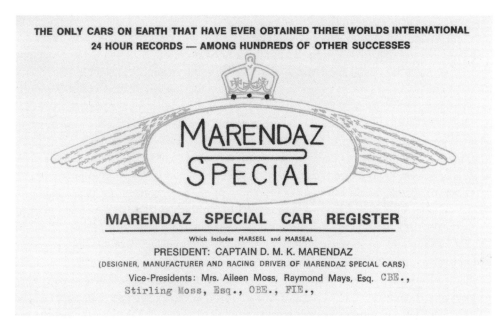

THE ONLY CARS ON EARTH THAT HAVE EVER OBTAINED THREE WORLDS INTERNATIONAL 24 HOUR RECORDS — AMONG HUNDREDS OF OTHER SUCCESSES

MARENDAZ SPECIAL

MARENDAZ SPECIAL CAR REGISTER

Which includes MARSEEL and MARSEAL

PRESIDENT: CAPTAIN D. M. K. MARENDAZ

(DESIGNER, MANUFACTURER AND RACING DRIVER OF MARENDAZ SPECIAL CARS)

Vice-Presidents: Mrs. Aileen Moss, Raymond Mays, Esq. CBE.,
Stirling Moss, Esq., OBE., FIE.,

Marcus Marendaz's letterhead for his correspondence. (*Author's collection*)

1931 and the five-car photograph is dated in Marendaz's own handwriting as 1931. He further says that the Maidenhead factory was not opened in 1932, yet the *Maidenhead Advertiser* for 16 September 1932 carries a picture of the first car produced being christened by the Mayoress on 13 August, albeit there is every chance it was partly built in London. The old chestnut 'No engine fitted into Marendaz Special cars by me was ever made by Erskine or any subsidiary of the Studebaker Corporation' also reappears. Like many of his letters redressing some calumny, he gives useful information such that Midland Motor Cylinders (Birmid) produced his cylinder block and head castings and Sterling Metals Ltd of Coventry some cylinder heads. He did, of course build engines but, indisputably, not every engine. Marcus Marendaz's reply was from his home in Bergh Apton, Norfolk, but his move to South Africa a few years later rather slowed down his ability to respond to criticism voiced in the United Kingdom, real or imagined.

With the increase of interest in old cars, reflected by the appearance of the magazine *Veteran and Vintage*, founded by Lord Montagu and edited by Michael Sedgwick, correspondence on Marendaz Special cars increased, but generally bypassed Marcus Marendaz due to his remote location. In March 1961, *V. and V.*, as it was commonly called, noted that a Marendaz Special car had been shipped out to South Africa to the Marendaz household. This was a 15-90 JB7776. Discussions between readers in 1961 and 1962, unsurprisingly, centred on the origins of the engines.

THE ALVIS SAGA

In 1961, Neville Hall wrote to *Motor Sport* concerning Buckingham cyclecars with Alvis-manufactured engines. In a reply written from Marendaz Town, South Africa, Marcus Marendaz 'stated I brought Alvis cars into existence, which was in 1919, and can say that Alvis had nothing to do with the manufacture of Buckingham engines'. As mentioned in Chapter 3, this sweeping assertion was soundly refuted by Alvis Ltd, in the form of G. H. Wiltshire, publicity manager, who not only said that Alvis had in fact made the engines for the Buckingham cyclecar, but added that Marendaz was an apprentice under T. G. John, chief engineer, at Siddeley-Deasy and later was employed by him when he formed T. G. John Ltd, later Alvis Ltd. The two disagreed and Marendaz left Alvis in 1920 and had nothing further to do with the company from that date onwards. The normally litigious Marendaz did not respond to this contradictory rebuttal, which is interesting in its own right, although he returned to the subject in 1973.

In 1964, Captain Marendaz had caught up with the presence of *Veteran and Vintage* and he wrote an article on his own cars, Surprisingly, this is actually quite well written and missing a lot of the hyperbole and absolute assertions of his usual writings. Several interesting details emerged: battery manufacturers withdrew their warranty for his cars because the batteries were mounted under the bonnet and if you think about it, not many manufacturers did this pre-war, although today it is commonplace. He also made clear his dislike of running boards on Marendaz Specials and in fact this extended to some of the cars of other marques that he owned, such as his James Young Bentley 3.5-litre in 1947–1948. The article ended with the assertion that he was about to reopen production in a specially designed factory in Europe. This was all very well, except for the enormous fly in the ointment. He had supplied printing blocks to the magazine to illustrate the article: these were obviously pretty sensitive to him as they showed his famous not-Continental engines being machined in the works, and *V. and V.* lost them. They were never forgiven and the echoes of this sin continued until his death. Of course, they should not have lost them.

The explosive Alvis saga reopened in 1973 when Peter Wright interviewed Harold Irving (an important player in the Alvis story) and, as he says, in conversation, the name Marendaz kept cropping up. Perhaps unwisely, John Shaw passed this article to Marcus Marendaz, presumably with the wish that some clarity would be added to the marque history. The response from D. M. K. Marendaz once again repeated the point essentially denied by the company that without Marendaz the company would never have come into existence and that he had been works manager at T. G. John. He offered to write the story for the *Alvis Register Bulletin* should they be prepared to publish it. The editor failed to take up on this offer, but Marcus Marendaz, never one to let go came back to them in 1982, a full nine years later, to re-assert the point and demand the publication of both his letters. By now, the *Bulletin* editor was Dr Adrian Padfield, a position he had held since 1974, who then in an effort to catch up offered to publish whatever Marendaz would write for him and even to interview him, should that be helpful. Yet he made a fatal mistake by addressing his letter 'Dear Marendaz', a familiarity immediately resented and leading to further demands to publish his previous letters. Adrian Padfield's measured response listing the facts as he saw them and quoting sources was not the oil on troubled water a reasonable person might expect but it caused a further retaliatory response demanding publication of the correspondence. Added to this was a demand for a reason why he had not been interviewed in 1973 (at that date, they probably did not know he was still around, but they did now); this was aside from the more recent offer to interview him. This last letter also noted that his previous letter by first-class post was replied to by Dr Padfield using second-class post, seemingly not good enough if you were dealing with the Doyen of Automobile Engineers. This was enough for Adrian Padfield and the correspondence was closed forthwith, although one has to say the scars did not heal immediately and a valedictory article on Captain Marendaz by him appeared in the *VSCC Bulletin* for autumn 2007, long after the Captain's death.

1446

A family crest used on Marcus Marendaz's
envelopes. (*Author's collection*)

Motor Sport published an item on *Marendaz Myths and Memories* in March 1970, largely based
on the reply by Marcus Marendaz to an article on the cars, both appearing in the *Manchester
Evening News*. One assumes Marendaz did not react to the *Motor Sport* article because he was
being quoted more or less verbatim by Bill Boddy.

Veteran and Vintage returned to the subject in 1974 with a very good article by John Wilkinson
who wrote about the road test he did on his near neighbour John Shaw's 13/70, JB1476. Perhaps
a copy of this article did not reach the Captain as the expected response never arrived.

MARENDAZ SHORTCOMINGS

The correspondence pages of *Motor Sport* were troubled once again by Captain Marendaz
in 1977, now resident at Asterby Hall in Lincolnshire, sparked by an innocent letter by H. D.
Brown-Kelly regarding problems with the torque-tube back axle, titled by the editor 'A Marendaz
shortcoming'. A further letter by Frank Annett emphasizing the concern provoked a reply not
surprisingly titled 'Not a Marendaz Shortcoming'. The editor of *Motor Sport,* Bill Boddy, had
been reeling under various 'inputs' from Marendaz over the years, both as editor and earlier
and had reached the point that he wrote and said as little as possible about the man as it always
caused ructions. His interesting series 'Fragments of Forgotten Makes' was never extended to
include Marendaz, nor did he ever publish a retrospective interview as he did with so many
of the other pre-war Brooklands names. He was always delighted to discuss the marque and
the man behind it but he did not want to publish Marendaz's name for fear of the certainty of
repercussions. Turning to the lengthy letter from Marendaz, Bill Boddy is initially castigated
for his standards of ethics and natural justice, a typical opening gambit, before launching into

a discussion on the merits of the Marendaz Special back axle, which to one's surprise includes an admission that the aluminium casting holding the torque tube to the gearbox was a mistake, although it was blamed on the eminent engineer Laurence Pomeroy Sr, who had advocated to industry the increased use of aluminium castings. In other respects, the owners who had criticised their cars were of course partially to blame as they had not bought the cars new and then had omitted to return them to the factory for maintenance, the fact that at the time of writing about their Marendaz shortcomings the factory had been shut for forty-one years seemed to have been missed by Marcus Marendaz.

A further side swipe at Bill Boddy, both with regard to what he published in *Motor Sport*, and his 'History of Brooklands Motor Course', appeared in July 1986, Marendaz being eighty-nine at this date, once again concerning hydraulic brakes. The 'mistake' in 'History of Brooklands Motor Course' was to write that the first Marendaz Special at Brooklands in 1925 was evolved from Marseal parts. It has to be said that this car does in fact defy categorisation, being unique, but almost certainly had a basis in Marseal, as the later ones certainly did. Bill Boddy's quiet assertion regarding the facts as recorded at the time caused a whole page bomb-blast from the Captain, now perceiving 'an implication [*sic.*] of my hitherto impeccable integrity'—a point that many might consider arguable. His letter continued with an item by item discussion regarding the differences between a Marseal and a Marendaz Special. Bill's statement that the records held by Marseal and Marendaz Special cars had long since been beaten, according to the RAC records, provoked Marcus Marendaz to point out that his own personal record of holding three twenty-four-hour class records, was not recorded by the RAC, but nevertheless still stood as a world record. He had a point and Bill's editorial comments, once again, were focused on stating the recorded facts.

In 1987, Captain Marendaz became aware of the existence of the Brooklands Society and its well-respected *Gazette*, another potential outlet for his opinionated and fractious comments, unfortunately requiring further responses from the hard done by Bill Boddy. Bill wrote a comment regarding ladies' only races at Brooklands, mixed races, and disputing the statement by the late Michael Sedgwick that Dorothy Summers was the first woman to win a mixed race in 1936 that recognised men and women on equal terms. His position was backed by Margaret Jennings (*née* Allan) writing to say she had won races before 1936. Marcus Marendaz weighed in correcting them wrapped around a personal attack on Bill Boddy, whose comments were in Marendaz's eyes bordering on arrogance. At the time of winning the race in 1936, Dorothy Summers was subject to publicity by the *Daily Sketch* and others, which essentially said she was the first woman to win a race at Brooklands—an inaccurate statement as they missed the important 'equal terms' qualification.

The following year, D. M. K. Marendaz from Asterby in Lincolnshire was again penning vitriol to the editor of the *Brooklands Society Gazette*. Referring to an earlier article, he makes some polite(ish) comments on events at Brooklands in 1926, but then moves on to Bill Boddy's 'fraudulent and libellous' 'History of Brooklands' regarding Marendaz's record breaking in 1927. Once again, Bill's measured responses set the record straight. Captain Marendaz's last letter to *Motor Sport* appeared in May 1988, when he was ninety-one, recalling the reason why one of his Marendaz Specials had smoked during a test: the choke had been left out.

The *Automobile* magazine has not been mentioned here as a rather more pointed reaction by Marcus Marendaz to an article that appeared in their columns is involved and also involves the author and has been covered in the Introduction.

Marcus Marendaz (centre) seen in later life with two of his cars, a 15/80 with H. D. Brown Kelly on the left and a 13/70 with John Shaw on the right. (*John Shaw*)

At the time of his death, the world at large was well aware of Captain Marendaz, his cars, his writings, and his foibles, but more than that was rather buried in folklore. It is rather hoped that these pages have clarified some of the anomalies, but almost certainly will have added to the known unknowns and possibly found a few new unknown unknowns.

EPILOGUE

It is not possible to pigeonhole Captain Marendaz, but there again why would you want to? His life took him through two world wars allied to the great expansion and adoption of all things to do with motor cars and aeroplanes. It certainly did not always look like a good time to be alive, but history will mark it down as being of vast importance for very many reasons. Marcus Marendaz played his part and was intimately involved in all of this. The fine line between failure and success was never very far away from him, but by weathering the depression in the early 1930s, he succeeded, not by much and, it has to be said, that because of his attitude to his fellow man, it could easily have resulted in failure. His approach to his superiors, his colleagues, possibly sometimes his friends, and certainly to those who worked for him was unflinchingly robust. He did, eventually, offer unacknowledged acceptance and respect to those who stood up to him, but no doubt, his superiors might not always have been of a similar disposition towards him in return. Behind all of these relationships was the bogey of money. He was grossly under-financed in most of his ventures and a lot of his waking hours must have been spent trying to raise capital. With the knowledge that he was verging on broke most of the time, his successes particularly with regard to racing and record-breaking shine through. He was lumbered with a foreign-sounding name, that he undoubtedly saw as a hindrance, but I am sure he never imagined that this would be his downfall in 1940, and the events of that year were something that I do not think he ever really recovered from. Still a relatively young man in 1945, he failed to regain any level of confidence thereafter, and the good days were over. Of course, it was difficult for everyone at that time to get back on their feet, but Marcus Marendaz frittered his undoubted abilities in a number of ill-starred projects culminating in being shopped by the South African government, the final blow. Looking back at anyone's life, one sees ups and downs and one should always reflect on the good days. Some of his good-looking cars survive today and we take pleasure from that.

I think it would be a mistake for the author to offer a valedictory statement on Donald Marcus Kelway Marendaz. There is no all-enveloping phrase that covers the man and, to put it mildly, opinions are divided. So I would encourage the reader to extract what they can from this text and form their own conclusions, hopefully in the knowledge that he had a life well lived and that he made his mark on history.

As Marcus Marendaz would probably wish to be remembered—at the head of the pack, at speed in one of his cars. He is second from the right, seen in the 1926 J. C. C. 200-mile race. (*Autocar*)

Appendix I

SUNDAY EXPRESS, 17 NOVEMBER 1940

ALL THIS MIGHT EASILY HAPPEN TO YOU

CAPT. MARENDAZ

Mine is the story of what is happening to many who are innocent

In this war, which we are supposed to be fighting for freedom, liberty and democracy, astonishing things are happening to British men and women who fall foul of the bureaucratic steam roller.

Take the case of Captain Marendaz, the famous racing motorist, owner of a flying school, clever engineer, trainer of 100 civil air guards and a pilot who served in the last war.

On his own airfield he thoughtlessly took a photograph of a seven-year-old training machine, a photograph which one can buy as a picture postcard.

He was fined £20. But, worse than that, some unknown bureaucrat decided that he should be interned under the notorious Regulation 18B, which gives the Minister of State power to plant a British subject in prison without trial.

'I am now a broken man.'

That happened last May. Captain Marendaz has just been released as a result of a vigorous appeal. This is his story of what happened to him. It is what is happening to many innocent, helpless men and women in the name of democracy—as run by bureaucracy.

'I am now a man broken in health. All I seem to have done these last four months is to face brick walls, armed guards and barbed wire.

Had it not been for the fact that I could prove that I was no enemy of Britain, the home of my family for 200 years and the country I fought for, my spirit would have been broken as well as my health.

I feel a great debt of gratitude to the *Sunday Express* for first raising my case. It gave new hope. I felt that I was not entirely a forgotten man.

Sometimes looking back I do not know how I kept sane. From the first things went badly. I was taken to Brixton, and received along with criminals from the Old Bailey. Later they put me in a bay of the prison and I was given the special privileges of a remand prisoner. All of us there were able to order our own food from restaurants outside, always providing we were ready to pay for it.

After three days we were sent by police van to a London station and entrained for Liverpool. On the journey we were given a beef sandwich each, but had nothing at all to drink.'

One tiny window in a bare wall

'Shall I ever forget that first night at Liverpool? I was marched to a cell. It was furnished plainly with a small wooden table and chair, an enamel water jug, basin, a straw 'biscuit' on wood planking and three tousled, dusty blankets. My guess that those blankets had been left as they were by the last inmate of the cell. For ventilation—certainly not for light—there was a tiny window set high in the bare wall. Once locked up for the night, I was in the dark. Exhausted I fell into a troubled sleep.

None of us were given our baggage for about a week. That meant we were without pyjamas and had to sleep in our underwear. We looked a strange crew without shaves. We could not write letters home at first, nor were we allowed to receive parcels from outside. After a fortnight, however, correspondence with our friends went pretty smoothly and we could receive visitors for fifteen minutes a week—always in the presence of a warder, of course.

A victim of neurasthenia, I applied for a better bed and a cell reasonably lighted. All I got was some physic! All 18B men were given an hour's exercise a day, split into half-hour periods mornings and afternoons. We were locked in our cells at four o'clock and not allowed out until 6.30 next morning. Food? Porridge, a round of bread and margarine, and cocoa. That was breakfast. For dinner we usually got soup, meat, potatoes, cabbage. We could, of course, supplement this diet with the things sent in parcels by friends.

After a few days a warder told us that if we wished we could be instructed in mailbag sewing. It meant a privilege of being allowed on the prison landings for a couple of hours. Those who refused to do the work—they were not many—were locked up. Candidly, I only made a pretence at doing the work. When I was sent to a southern camp the prison authorities paid me 4s 2d and told me to sign for it. 'Why this money?' I asked. I was told it was for work done on mailbags.

In Liverpool we could smoke all day long in our cells and there was no real ban on talking when we were out on the landings. Not so bad, maybe. Remember, however, that this was summertime, the glorious summer just gone. Many thought life in camp would be better. They were mistaken. Six hundred of us—Italians, Germans, members of the British Union of Fascists and the rest—found a dusty, wind-blown place. Sand everywhere, it got in the mouth, into clothes, into the mouth, the eyes. After weeks of it, the sand practically destroyed my sense of taste.

Barbed wire and bayonets

We were put in a compound surrounded by three rings of barbed wire and bristling with bayonets. We were told to strip to the buff and parade in the open for medical examination. Then we inspected our quarters—long oblong huts. Everywhere we noticed stout iron rings and bolts. They had been used to tether circus animals. We had to dump our baggage in a big pile and rummage around for our belongings as best we could.

Maybe the worst feature of this life was that one had to listen to interminable arguments on politics. All were pitched in the pro-Fascist key. The British Fascists outnumbered the rest.

They bossed the internal, if not the disciplinary, life of the camp. What they said always went. A camp council was formed, but the Fascists dictated all the proposals put forward. Once I suggested that we should put a member of the Savoy staff, detained along with us, in charge of catering. I was howled down. If the B.U. boys disagreed with anything they leapt on the platform and simply howled it down with shouts of 'Hail Mosley'.

Demonstration by the Fascists

Tom Moran, former Navy boxer who stood as a Mosley candidate for Silvertown, became virtual camp leader 'till he was sent back to Brixton. When he was moved, there was a Fascist demonstration, men squatting on the ground and refusing to budge when the guards arrived. I met the brothers of Lord Haw-Haw, who seemed to go about pretty quietly. And I met many men who, I think, would have been better outside helping Britain win the war. About 100 of the men could have been well employed in aviation work.

Suffering mentally as I did, I feel for the men who wait on month after month for their appeals, knowing they can prove their innocence. Appeals must be speeded up. In my opinion, 40 per cent of those in the camp were no more enemies of their country than I am.'

PAUL IRWIN

Appendix II

MARSEALS REGISTERED IN COVENTRY

Chassis	Engine	Hp.	Registration	Registered	Model	First	Last
821*	5603	10.5	HP3059	29/7/21	4-seater	H. Hallas, Cov.	Anfield 6/29
835*	6461Alvis	10.5	HP3337	2/12/21	4-seater	Marseal Eng'g	Coventry 12/27
1922 Production							
4003	4006	9	HP3774	1/4/22	2-seater	Marseal Motors	Marseal 6/22
4042	A146	9.8	HP4412	27/2/22	2-seater	Riley Ltd, Cov.	Surrey 9/29
4043	A147	9.8	HP4456	29/7/22	2-seater	DMK Marendaz	Eltham 9/30
4058	A174	9.5	HP6284	1/7/23	2-seater	WC Brooks, Cov.	Romford 9/27
4068	5101 Anz	11.8	HP4551	1/9/22	Sports	DMK Marendaz	Marendaz 9/23
4081	A219	9.5	HP4982	27/1/23	Coupe	Marseal Motors	DMKM, London,9/25
4091	254	10	HP4674	12/10/22		Marseal Motors	Barnstaple 12/30
4094	A180	9.8	HP4695	25/10/22	2-seater	Marseal Motors	Surrey 9/29
1923 Production							
5009	A234	9.8	HP4723	10/11/22		Marseal Motors	Antrim 6/27
5016	A251	9.26	HP4746	24/11/22		Marseal Motors	Hants. 6/34
5021	A302	9.12	HP4764	9/12/22		DO Summers, Cov	Kings Lynn 6/32
5028	308		HP4790	14/12/22		DO Summers, Cov	Balham 9/30
5029	A311	9.6	HP4789	15/12/22		Marseal Motors	Woking 12/30
5037	336	9.26	HP5463	6/4/23	2-seater	Marseal Motors	Doncaster 12/29
5046	A366	9.26	HP4929	13/1/23	2-seater	Marseal Motors	Herts 12/26
5049	S790	9.26	HP5729	4/5/23	Sports	Marseal Motors	Herts 6/23
5055	A400		HP4984	29/1/23	2-seater	Marseal Motors	Salford 6/28
5062	429	9.8	HP5071	14/2/23	2-seater	DO Summers, Cov.	AC Kelway, Cov. 6/23
5076	282	9.8	HP5072	17/2/23	2-seater	DO Summers, Cov.	Tooting 9/28
5140	644	9.8	HP5709	5/5/23	2-seater	Marseal Motors	Swansea 12/23
5155	659 Anz	11.8	HP5984	26/3/23	2-seater	Marseal Motors	Leytonstone 3/27
1924 Production							
6004	815	9.8	HP7125	27/11/23	2-seater	Marseal Motors	Wisbech 12/31
6007	A452	10.8	HP7079	17/11/23	Sports	Marseal Motors	Blackpool 12/28
6031	A449	10.8	HP7162	6/12/23	Sports	Marseal Motors	Huddersfield 12/30
6061	1042	9.8	HP7486	7/2/24	2-seater	Marseal Motors	Sutton 9/31
6087	1315	9.8	HP7533	13/2/24	4-seater	Marseal Motors	Richmond 12/30

Chassis	Engine	Hp.	Registration	Registered	Model	First	Last
6125	1772	11.27	HP9923	7/10/24	2-seater	H. Ralph, Cov.	H. Ralph, Cov. 12/25
6134	1778	9.9	HP8125	2/4/24	4-seater	Marseal Motors	Truro 9/28
6143	A809	11.27	HP8140	3/4/24	Sports	Marseal Motors	Nottingham 9/31
6170	2053	9.8	HP9077	7/6/24	4-seater	Marseal Motors	Henstridge 12/30
6204	A2222	10.8	HP8733	17/5/24	4-seater	Marseal Motors	Rossendale 9/29
6215	2399	9.8	HP9078	7/6/24	4-seater	Marseal Motors	London 9/34
6227	4177 Anz	11.9	HP9232	15/9/24	Sports	G. Banks, Cov.	Suffolk 9/29
6236	2753	9.8	HP9929	23/9/24	2-seater	Marseal Motors	Bishops Aukland 6/31
7001	7001	9.8	HP8609	10/5/24	2-seater	Marseal Motors	Marseal Motors 6/24
8001	8001 Anz	11.8	HP7570	13/2/24	2-seater	Marseal Motors	Belford 6/28
Cycle Scooter							
84*	84	1.25	HP4137	3/6/22	Cycle Scooter	A. Langley, Coventry	A. Langley, Coventry

* Registered as Marseels.

Anz: Identified as probably Anzani engines; there may be others.

Appendix III

MARENDAZ SPECIAL: KNOWN CARS

Registration	Date of Registration	Model	History
Not known	1925?	Uncertain	Raced at Brooklands, 1925
UC3933	8/2/28	11/55 works	Built 1926, First seen at Brooklands 4/26. Raced extensively 1926–9. Six Class G records at Brooklands (10.11.27) and Montlhéry (14–15/2/28). Rebodied 1930s–40s with Wolseley Hornet (Swallow) body. Owned by B&G Motors, Camden Town (1949), G. R. S. McKay, Canterbury (1949–51), G. M. Acton, York (before 1952), farmer at Middleton, Teasdale (1952 on), E. N. Robinson, Darlington (1960–1), F. Winter, Darlington (1965 on), Sothebys 15/5/69, A. E. Brown, Connaught Cars (1970), S. J. Moorwood, Shamley Green (1971–75), F. Majzub, Redditch (1975–82), M. J. Carter (1982), Graham Skillen (1983–present). Rebodied again with replica of original body 1985. Running.
YH6538	7/27	11/55	Works car until 1930 at least, blue/mottled aluminium.
YT1378	6/27	11/55	Guy Griffiths, 1933 and 1935. *Light Car and Cyclecar* 20/7/28. *Autocar* 26/10/45.
EC8193	14/4/28	11/55	*Motor Sport* 10/30. Owned W. B. Wakefield. H. G. Webb in 1930. Initially dark coloured, then light.
YW6480	13/6/28	11/55	L. L. Hanks, Class G records car (Montlhéry 5–6/11/28). H.R. Maule (Reading, 7/37–4/46), *Motor Sport* 7/43, B&G Motors, Camden (4/46–8/46), J. Parker, Plymouth (8/46–8/47), M. Morgan Giles, Teignmouth (8/47–1/48), P. Ferry, Wilts (1/48–1953, VSCC Prescott 1948), S. Phillips, Aldershot (1953 on).
GC5800	2/30	11/55	Raymond Way Motors, Guy Griffiths 22/3/35, sold to Vale Engineering.
BGW770	NK, then 9/34	13/70	Prototype 13/70 built 1931 with many non-standard features and signs of multiple trials installations. See 1931 '5-car' photo: centre car. Originally yellow, then dark blue. N. E. and F. C. Annett, London (1937–8) fitted Talbot gearbox. To F. A. French, Leigh-on-Sea (1938), then P. Piper (pre-war). With Vauxhall engine in London around 1952–5 owned by D. Boucher (running). With tinkers in Windsor to R. Pollock, M. Bell, P. Ffoulks-Halbard, to Manchester. P. Mitchell, Glos. (before 1989). Refitted with ex-Erskine Continental engine and Marendaz gearbox. *Motor Sport* 6/77. Running in England.
GW2326	1/32	13/70	Camden Motors, Cricklewood, to Guy Griffiths 3/7/39. Cream and Green. Not sold, lost during the war. *Autocar* 7/7/39.
GW2328	1/32	13/70	Car taken to Africa by Sawyer, FRGS, 1932, believed returned. *Autocar* 22/1/32 and 27/5/32. No longer extant.
GW2382	1/32	13/70	Raced at Brooklands 1932, old rose, possibly works demonstrator and car used on the cover of the brochures.

Registration	Date of Registration	Model	History
JB700	4/8/32	13/70	Stockport 3/36; Salop 9/38; Birmingham 6/39; LR 24/3/42 to A. J. Godson, Sheldon, Birmingham. Broken up 29/5/46.
JB753	30/8/32	13/70	Continental engine. Essex 3/36; Middx 9/46; Surrey 9/50; Middx 11/51; Essex 4/52; Leics 11/58; Derby 9/60; LR 9/63 to J. E. Bowles, Repton, Derbys. To Motorway Sales, Friar Gate, Derby. E. J. Bowles (1961), G. Unsworth, Derby, P. Norheim, restored by Wilkinsons of Derby. Running.
JB737	13/8/32	13/70	Middlesborough 9/36; Darlington 5/38; Durham 9/38; Gateshead 8/40; Darlington 8/45; Westmoreland 10/45; and Preston 8/46.
JB1093	7/11/32	13/70	Middlesex 9/36.
JB1200	19/11/32	13/70	Continental engine. Portsmouth 10/37; Kent 8/49; IoW 4/50; Norfolk 5/50; Essex 4/51; LCC 5/57; West Sussex, 11/71, 7/76. Tyler, exported to Malaysia, then Ron Pinto, Jack Hilton, California. Stored in Europe.
YY8383	29/11/32	17/90	A. A. Rayner, Sheffield, 1/47. Barn find, January 2005. Running in England.
JB1094	20/12/32	13/70	Continental engine. Essex 9/35; Berks; LCC 9/63; Berks 6/67. Wartime photos. J. V. Bowles, ?, J. May (1965–67), Foussier, Afchain. *Motor Sport* 2/48. Believed in Germany.
JB1476	14/1/33	13/70	Continental engine. New to P. Haslam, Belfast 14/1/33; Surrey 2/40; Worcs 5/41; Devon 9/46; Dorset 2/48; Surrey 1/55; Beds 5/58; Herts 3/59; Birmingham 9/59; Glos CC 5/68. Davico, Leonard, Barnard, Fellows, J. Shaw 1960–2001. Stored in England.
JB1477	1/2/33	13/70	Continental engine. A. and A. Moss. Black concours car with swivelling headlights and secondary gearbox. Many hill-climb, trials successes. Great Yarmouth 4/37; Essex 10/39; LR 12/61 to James N. Smith, Mill Bank, Oakley, Dovercourt, Essex. Burnt out around 1978. *Motor Sport*, 3/78, rebodied with non-standard body by M. Morton. R. Tolhurst (Kent), *Sporting Cars* 12/81. In England.
JB1582	21/2/33	17/80	Continental engine. Cambs 2/38; Middx 5/39; Wilts 7/39; Essex 11/39; LCC 5/63; Berks 6/63; Greater London (NW) 5/66; Devon CC 12/68 and 2/73. Eaton Motors, Romford (1941); Henry Smith, Aldershot; C. H. Allen, Aldershot (1950); *Motor Sport* 1/51; Rodney Bird, Sonning; John Le Sage, London; Geoff Harding, Maidenhead 6/63. Stuart Bennett, Middlesex (1964–67). Stored in England.
JB1583	25/3/33	13/70	Kent 4/35; LR 9/55 to W. Isler, Kent.
JB1937	28/4/33	13/70	Berks 7/35; Reading 11/38; Berks 6/39; Dumbarton 5/40; and Glos 10/40.
AGU559	5/33	13/70	Believed originally registered JB1938; G.B. Dartnell, Somerset (1957–9); J. W. Wilson, Essex (1959–60); J. M. King, Essex (1960–64); R. L. Pollock, Berkhampstead (1964–7), W. St Davies, Hamworthy, Dorset, (1967–83); museum in Ireland; J. A. Rosenblatt, London; Chamberlaine, London; Dodds (1985). Engine now Triumph/Coventry Climax. In Germany.
JB2070	7/7/33	17/97	Leics 10/36; Cambs 5/42; Middx 8/42; Herts 2/43; Cambs 12/45; WR Yorks 7/46; Kent 9/46. *Autocar* 12/3/43 Marendaz block.
JB3702	10/3/34	13/90	1933 works car, Zoller supercharger. No recorded movements by Berks CC. NMM photos, A. Hess.
JB2536	28/7/33	13/70	Marendaz block. Surrey 6/35; LCC 5/39; LR Essex 3/44. Wartime photos by J. V. Bowles. Monica Whincop; R. French.
JB2537	12/8/33	17/90	Kent 4/38; Coventry 12/42. *The Vintage Alvis*, p. 531. Car No. 23 at the 1935 J.C.C. Donington meeting, Race No.1. Open car, vertical rad slats, VdP long wings. Possible 17/97 model.
JB2602	18/11/33	13/70	Supplied to J. E. Farrell, Widnes. Bucks 5/37; LCC 5/38; Middx 7/38; LCC 5/39. *Autocar* 15/12/33.
AMB631	2/12/33	13/70	*Motor* 9/1/34. Supplied to J. A. Welch. Continental engine. Pilling; John Shaw; P. Landgrebe (2004). Running in Holland
JB2601	19/10/33	17/90	Black. A. E. Moss; P. Mercer (1935–6). Leics 7/36; Warks 7/41; Wolverhampton 10/43; Warks 8/45; Sheffield 6/47; WR Yorks 9/52; Sheffield 8/54; LR 12/59. K. W. Morrell, Sheffield.

Registration	Date of Registration	Model	History
JB3814	26/3/34	13/70	Fixed-head coupé, but top removed later. Derby 6/37; Coventry 6/38; LCC 7/39; Surrey 7/41; Plymouth 11/45; Devon 10/47; Glos. 8/48; WR Yorks 11/48 and 10/51; Northumberland 6/53. Harvey; R. Morgan-Giles (1947–49); Ireland (Huddersfield).
TJ3498	8/1/34	17 hp	Long Chassis Saloon. Last licensed 1/2/52 Streatham.
JB4300	29/5/34	16/80	Long Chassis, Supercharged Tourer. *Autocar* 8/3/35. Adverts *Autocar* 18/10/35. No recorded movements by Berks CC.
JB4697	2/8/34	17/80	Croydon 11/36 and LCC 3/39.
JB8519	22/4/36	17/80	Sunderland 7/37 and Northumberland 3/39. Scrapped 9/43.
?	4/34	17/80	Long Chassis Saloon. *Autocar* 27/4/34. Car sold to A. W. Sanders, Liverpool. Front doors hinged at the front. Car green with grey brake drums.
?	?	17/80	Long Chassis Saloon. Delivered by Stan Duddington to Lincs (?). Front door hinged at rear and has trafficators at rear.
JB4690	11/9/34	17/90	No recorded movements by Berks CC. No longer extant.
AFJ956	25/7/35	13/70	Fixed head Coupe. Black/silver. F. R. Oliver (Exeter, 1935). *Motor* 17/7/38. Mike Hughes, 1954. Last registered owner D. C. Barker, scrapped in Edinburgh 1961.
JB5288	16/5/35		LCC 7/37.
A A B 1 6 5 , RV9940	30/10/35	17 hp	Originally registered AAB165 in Worcs. Last licensed 24/3/39. Transferred to RV9940 (Portsmouth 11/36) on 25/11/47 by Warwick CC.
JB5289	20/7/35	17/80	Devon 10/35 and Notts 11/40.
TL3857	5/1.35	17/90	*Motor Sport* 2/52. Heap; Stacey; Taylor, Berks (1961).
BNE984	6/35	17.90	John Ireland; E. Hart; Smith; Linton; A. K. Wilson; Gilmore; Schieffelin. In Canada or USA.
TL4546	22/7/35	17/97	Convertible Coupe. P. H. Geldart, Bristol (1956), Alvis 12/50 engine. Bird, Reading (1956 on).
JB8249	13/1/36		Southport 11/38; LCC 5/39; Worcs 7/41; Birmingham 10/46; Worcs 4/51; Oxon 5/52; LCC 5/54; and Surrey 12/55. LR 3/58 to R. T. Barker, Guildford.
JB4846, DAS694	30/11/34	13/70	Marendaz block. Southampton 12/34; LCC 10/38; Middx 7/39; Kent 3/41; Surrey 4/46; Croydon 5/46; Glos 12/48; Oxford 5/52; Oxon 8/52; Northants 8/55 and 7/58; Beds 7/68; and LR Northants 8/68. Phil Kingston; S. Drage; L. D. Partlett, Oxon (9/54); WG Tyrrell, Northants (6/55); BW Burbidge, Northants (7/56); P.B. Kingston, Northants (1/58); Camden Motors; Ian Redmayne, Beds. (8/69); J. Evans, Abergavenny; D. Baldock; Haynes International Motor Museum.
BJB629	23/8/38	15/90	Works car. 1935 T.T. French GP 1936. Alfred Moss 23/8/38; Kircudbright CC 3/39; Lanark 8/45; Ayr 3/46; Berwick 1/57; LCC 4/57; E. Sussex 8/57; Kent 2/60; E. Sx 8/61; T. A. Langridge; G. de Jongh; Vintage Autos, London; F. Adler; D. Court, Aukland, NZ (1966). Len Southward, Southward Motor Museum, NZ.
DPG7	1/36	15/90	Short Chassis Tourer with steel tube/fabric body. A. Moss trials car; Pilling. Not running, England.
JB7140	12/8/35	15/90	*Autocar* 11/35. Worcs 9/38; Birmingham 4/41; Dudley 4/46; Birmingham 3/47; Warks 6/48; Staffs 3/49; Surrey 2/53; Hants 9/53; Surrey 8/54; LR 12/56 to I&M Read, Farnham, Surrey; R. J. Bird. Chassis stolen, car dispersed, 1960s–70s.
TL5172	24/3/36	15/90	J.C. Brown, Ashworth (1952-3); A. Miles, Phoenix Motors, Exeter. In England, not running.
CXM849	4/7/36	15/90	New to G. D. Pheasey. Homer, Waterfield, W. Banfield. Triumph engine. Stored, in England.
AUP155	11/4/36	15/90	Flocks, Downing, Tregenza. Riley engine. W. Urry. Trim. In Germany, running.
JB7776	16/11/35	15/90	Leeds 9/36; WR Yorks 11/40; LCC 8/44; Middx 7/50; Somerset 8/51; Glos 9/56; Nichols, Andrews, exported about 1960 to Capt. Marendaz in South Africa. Car returned to UK 2003. Running.

Registration	Date of Registration	Model	History
CLE305	11/35	15/90	Boul, *Penny Wise* 21/3/74, Brown Kelly. Modified rear end with open propshaft and radius arms. A. Van Den Eynde, Belgium. Roger Wyuts, Belgium. J. Stolze, Holland. In Germany.
JB8877	16/4/36	13/70	Built as 15/90. Beds 1/38; Essex 10/46; East Ham 2/59; West Ham 9/59; Essex 5/61. *Motor Sport* photographic files. Turner, 1961 still as 15/90, J. May, D. Mortimer, 1967. J. Shaw 1971, rebuilt with Marendaz block as 13/70, with an original 13/70 Marendaz body. Stored in England.
CVO36	11/36	17/80	Continental engine. Jackson, 1961. Tregenza, Bangham, C. Jones. In England, running.
FOF395	6/39	13/70	Colliers of Birmingham, Stirling, *Old Motor* 7-8/74. M. Fisher, Harrogate, Continental engine ex-Erskine fitted 1980s. In England, running.

LR: last registered; NK: not known

Appendix IV

EMPLOYEES: CARS AND AIRCRAFT

MARSEEL ENGINEERING /MARSEEL MOTORS (COVENTRY)

Charles B. Seelhoff, partner; Harold Irving, works manager; Bill Hucker; Arthur Sharman; and W. H. Fowdrey.

MARENDAZ SPECIAL CARS (LONDON)

J. Vennings; P. F. L. Leeson, engine builder. Also Coventry; Bailey, London Showroom; Fred Atkinson, fitter.

MARENDAZ SPECIAL CARS (MAIDENHEAD)

Nobby Clarke, foreman body shop; Freddie Plank, storeman; Eddie Long, foreman, machine shop. Also, International Aircraft; (Jim) Les Light, turner, machine shop. Also International Aircraft; Hagan, foreman, service department; Chapman, foreman, assembly and fitting shop; Claude Hodginson, fitting shop (engine building); Stan Duddington, apprentice, later fitting shop and driver; Jim Reeves, bodyshop; Johnny Macleod, panel beater and welder; Dorothy Summers, secretary, all companies; Mary Jackson, office girl and driver; John Midford-Millership, apprentice and driver; Shenk, works manager; Ken Base, driver; S. R. Mitchell, competition driver; Mac, painter; Murray, trimmer; Bailey, salesman; R. E. Meeks, fitter.

INTERNATIONAL AIRCRAFT

Geoffrey N. Wickner, aircraft designer (Maidenhead); Bill Evans (Maidenhead); C. F. Allen, chief draughtsman (Maidenhead); Ted Hillier, aircraft designer (Barton in the Clay); Oldwright or Holroyd, fitter (Barton in the Clay).

BEDFORD SCHOOL OF FLYING AND GENERAL AIRPORTS

Leslie C. Hilditch, flying instructor; A. E. Hill, flying instructor; Jack Willmot, flying instructor; T. A. Evans Freke, flying instructor; E. H. Peet, flying instructor; G. D. Garnett, flying instructor; E. Knight Bruce, flying instructor; A. R. Sarup, chief engineer; J. L. Stanton, chief engineer, S. Shaw, accountant.

INDEX

ABC Motors 129-130
Abingdon 155
A. C. 49, 61
Adamson, Lt 18
Advisory Committee 146-158
Aero Klub, Berlin 152
Aeronca C-3 135,138,142
A.I.D. 129
Airspeed Oxford 151, 154-155
Air Ministry 149,153
Airspeed Oxford 151, 155-156
Air Training Corps, Halton 142
Air Transport Auxiliary 161
Allen C. F. 130
Alvis 24-25, 28, 30, 33-34,
    173-174
Alvis Register 14, 174
Amal Carburettor 105
A. M. V. Trust 169
Annett, Frank 175
Anderson, Sir John 143, 145,
    147, 156
Anglo-American Sports Car 74
Anzani engine 30-31, 35, 38, 41,
    48-49, 51-52, 172
Armstrong Whitworth
    Company 24
F.K.3 16
F.K.8 17-22
Asterby Hall 8, 168-169, 175
Aston Hill Climb 42
Atalanta Motors 47
Atkinson, Fred 55
Atlantic Works, Harefield Road
    29, 45
Austen/Perry/Marendaz,
    Dorothy Marie 164

Automotive Manufacturing
    Industry apprenticeship 14
Avro Avian 133-135, 142

Baker, G. L. 70
Bapaume 19
B.A.R.C. 115
Barlow, Francis 162, 170
Barnstaple Trial 111, 118
Barton in the Clay 131-142, 144,
    150, 154, 158, 160-1
    airfield deficiencies 133, 139
Bass, Bob 46
Bath and West of England hill
    climb 41
Battle of Britain 143
Beaulieu 7-8
Beaverbrook, Lord 156
Bedfordshire Constabulary 145,
    148, 150, 158
Bedford School of Flying 133-
    134, 141, 144, 150, 160-1
Bentley 8, 49, 55, 174
Bergh Apton 135, 161-163, 173
Berkhampsted Police 147
Birdlip 125
Birkett, Norman 216
Blackpool Rally 118
Boddy, W.B. (Bill) 5, 61, 64,
    175-6
Boughton, Terence 135
Bowman, Hugh 160-161, 163
Bray 124, 132
Brighton-Beer Trial 118
Brinkwoods 102
Bristol F.2b Fighter 16
British Consul General,

    Johannesburg 166
British Grand Prix 62
Brixton Estate Limited 46
Brixton Prison 145-146
Brixton Road works 46-47,
    70-72
Brontë, Charlotte 7
Brooklands 8, 10, 39-41, 44,
    48-57, 61-70, 97, 109-112,
    115-118, 144, 154, 172, 175-
    176, 178
Clerk of the Course 109, 144
Society 10, 176
Brookes, W. C. 32, 38
Brown-Kelly, H. D. 175, 177
BRM 77
Bruay 18
Buckingham, Chief Constable
    149, 158
Buckingham Cyclecar 173-174
Bugatti 46, 111
Burlington Gardens 151
Burton-on-Trent 5

Cambrai, Battle of 19-20
Cape Town 164, 166
Carter Paterson 77
Castle Gresley 6
Castrol Oil 7
Chapman, Lt RGA 18
Chapman, works manager 89,
    91-92
Chepstow 12
Christies 164
Churchill, G. P. 152, 158
Churchill, W. S. 143
Cirrus Minor 137

Civil Air Guard 140-141, 144, 146, 150
Clarke, Nobby 86
Clerk, G.R., Sir 152
Cochrane, Intelligence Department 146
Collier R. H. 103
Colwyn Bay sand racing 62
Continental 8F, 9F engine 72-78, 173
Constable 162,170
Cordwallis works 74, 96,127
Corregio 162
Coventry 22-29, 144
Coventry Club Goblet Trial 42-43
Coventry Simplex engine 35-38
Coventry Technical College 13

David Brown 166
Davis, S. C. H., Sammy 154, 172
Davis, H. G. 53
Defence Regulation 18A 143
Defence Regulation 18B 143, 148
De Havilland DH.4 16, 22
De Havilland DH.9 21
De Havilland DH.60 Moth 58-59, 134-137, 142
De Havilland D.H. 82 Tiger Moth 134,142
De Havilland School of Flying 160
De Heem, Cornelis 162,170
de Wet, Carel 166-167
Delaney, Tom 49
Detention Order 146, 148-149,153,159
Dixon, F. W. 114
Don, Kaye 42, 55-56, 64-65, 81, 85, 121-122
    Mannin Beg accident 121
Don, Ralph 42
Don, Rita 100, 111, 121-123
Dou, Gerard 162
Douro 11
Duddington, Stan 73, 76-94, 98-102, 111-127
Dymock, Eric 10

Eaton Bray 139-141, 144, 151-158
Eldridge, E. A. D. 52, 56
Ebblewhite A. V. 39, 63-64
Edinburgh and District Motor Club 32, 39

Emscote car 26-28, 30-31, 49
Erskine 107, 173
Essex Motor Club 42
Essex Terraplane 92
Estrées-en-Chaussée 18
Evans, Bill 129
Evans, Dorothy Robinette 20, 159
Evans-Freke, T. A. 141, 150
Eyston George 92

Faireys 130
Fairey Seafox 133
Fairford 7
Farman Shorthorn 16
Ferrari, Enzo 10
Fifth Columnist 143, 146, 157, 159
Flying Flea 129
Foreign and Commonwealth Office 166
Forrest J. N. 66
Foster-Wickner Wicko 127-128
French Grand Prix 63, 118-120
Fuel Consumption Race 63
Fuller, George 150-151

Gainsborough 162
Gallay Radiator Company 108
General Airports Corporation 140
George III, King, 162
George VI, King, 162
German Grand Prix 66
Germany 137, 146, 150-152, 156-158, 166
Gerrard's Cross 131
Gipsy Major 128, 134-135, 142
Gipsy Six 135
Giron, Louis 119
Gliding 163
Gloucester trial 41, 125
Göring 137, 152
Gordon's Bay 164
Graham-Paige 57-58, 60, 67-71
Grand Prix regulations 50
Grice, Arthur 127
Griffiths, Guy 7, 119, 126, 172
G. W. K. 74, 127, 130

Haddenham 149
Halford, F. B. Major 59, 133
Hague, naval attaché 156
Hals, Frans 163
Hall, E. R. 42

Hamilton, Lady 162, 170
Handley Page 0/400 21
Hanks L. L. 53, 66-67
Harrison, Kenneth 156
Harvey-Noble G. P., George 70
Hawkes, Douglas 64
Hawkes , Gwenda 64-65

Harvey C. M. 39-40
Heathrow 132, 135
Helmy Aerogypt 7
Hermes engine 142
Heseltine, Alice May 170
Hilditch, L. C. 134
Hill, A. E. 134
Hill, Lionel 59
Hillier, Ted 130, 137
Hitler, A. 137, 150, 152
Hives, Lord 166
Hodgkinson, Claude 92
Holley Brothers 24, 27
Holly Lodge 161, 163-164
Home Civil Aviation, Director of 140
Home Department 143
Howe, Earl 119-120
Hudson Terraplane 125
Hull, P. M. A., Peter 13, 23
Hurst, Ken 88, 165-166

International Aircraft 127, 130, 132-133, 160
    Fire in the works 130
Isle of Man 121-122, 145, 151
Irving, Harold 24, 27, 29, 40, 174

Jackson, A. J. 7
Jackson, Mary 94-96
Jaguar 169
Jennings (Allan), Margaret 176
John, T. G. 13, 23-29, 174
Jones, Air Mechanic Second Class 18
Junior Car Club 39-42, 44, 48, 61-63, 66, 111-112, 178

Katon, F. C. H. Captain 41-42, 44
Kelway, Altair 109, 134, 157
Kelway, George S. 24-25
Keynes, Thomas, Sir 156
King's Cup Air Race 59

Lace, A. C., Mrs 116-118
Land's End Trial 39, 42

Lanstadt, Isobel, Mrs 9
Latimer-Needham, C. F. 131
Latour Fantin 162, 170
Lausanne 11
Laycock 88, 92, 114, 172
Lea Francis 56, 121
Leighton Buzzard 139, 145, 152-153
Le Mans 66
Light, Leslie (Jim) 76-94, 99-100, 103, 111, 114-119, 123-124, 127-132
Lincolnshire 159, 162, 165, 168-169
Liverpool 145-147
Lockheed brakes 50-52, 56
London, Brixton Road 46-48, 55-57, 59
London General Cab Company 46
London Stock Exchange 45
Long, Eddie 77-79, 127, 130
Louvre 162
Loveluck, Thomas 11
Lowenstein 150
Lucas 92-93, 108
Luton 131, 161
Luton aircraft 131

Maidenhead 52-53, 56, 59, 121, 123-4, 126
Maidenhead works 71, 74-98, 103, 121, 124, 130
March, Earl of (also see Richmond and Gordon, Duke of) 154
Marendaz (Kelway), Ada Frances Mrs 12
Marendaz, Brenda Cynthia 28, 45
Marendaz, David Emmanuel 11
Marendaz, Diana M. K. 45
Marendaz, Donald Marcus Kelway
35 Squadron service in France 17-22
Alvis service 24-26, 173-174
Antecedants 11-12
Auction 142, 160
Book 161-162, 164, 172
Camouflaging hangars 154
Captain title 171
Car in South Africa 167-168
Court appearances 60, 85, 121-122, 147

Crash 117-118
Death 170, 177
Detention 145, 172, Appendix I
Driving style 83-85
Fatal car accident 60
First aircraft 127-130
First Marendaz Special car 48-49
Formation of International Aircraft 127
Fractured leg 59
Glider auxiliary engine 163
Industrial accident 59
Marriage 20
Marseal Motors formation 29, 32
Marseel Engineering, formation 26
Motor shows 93
Move back to England 168
Move to South Africa 164
Patented Flap system 131, 135-136
Photographing an aircraft 147, 155-156
Portuguese origins 11,82
Record breaking 63-70, 173
Return to flying 58-59
Robbed 169
Royal Flying Corps, service 15-22
Second Aircraft 135-137
Siddeley Deasy, service13-15, 23-24
Trainer 137-139, 161
Marendaz, D. M. K. Limited 46-47
Marendaz, Dorothy Marie, Mrs 164
Marendaz, Dorothy Robinette Mrs 20, 45, 159
Marendaz, Mifanwy 26, 45
Marendaz, Richard Emmanuel 12
Marendaz, siblings 12
Marendaz Diesel Engines Pty. 165
Marendaz Engineering Corporation 164
Marendaz Special Cars
9-90 and 11-55 Models 51-52
13/70 Model introduction 71
13/70 Model 75, 84, 99, 101
15/90 Model 76, 81, 83, 112-116, 118-120
15/90 short chassis 126

17/80 and 17/90 Models 76, 80, 82, 95, 101
Cars to Spain 55
Competition 61-67, 109-120
Gearbox 52, 88
Production 86
Production numbers 103
Straight Eight engine 52-53
Winding up 103, 127
Marendaz town 164, 174
Marendaz-Bowman Transmissions 160, 163
Margam 11
Marlow Edwin S. 27-28
Marseel/Marseal
Car models 27, 35-38
Car production 33
Cycle Scooter 32-33
Demise 45
In competition 39-44, 176
Oil-cooled engine 32, 39
Technical Description 30-32
Marseel Engineering 26-29
Maurice Farman Shorthorn 15-16
Maxwell, Alexander, Sir 158
Mayerton 164-165
M. C. C. Sporting Trial 109
McCalla, W. T. 112-114
Mercedes-Benz 169
Metsu 162, 170
M. G. 99, 121-122
MI5 149-150, 158
Midford-Millership, John 96-98
Midland Flying Club 133
Miles Brothers 59, 127-128,130, 134
Miller, A. G. 67-68
Miller, Harry 52, 55-56, 70, 121-122, 126
Mitchell, Paul 9-10
Mitchell, S. R. 100, 111
Monmouth School 12, 144
Montagu, Lord 173
Montlhéry 56, 64-69, 119-120
Morgan Three-wheeler 5
Morris 9
Morrison, Herbert 156, 159
Mosley, O 144
Moss, Aileen Mrs 5-6, 81, 99-100, 109-113, 116-120, 124-125, 157, 172
Moss, Alfred 81, 108, 110-111, 113, 118-120, 124-126, 157-158
Moss, Stirling, Sir 81, 118, 124, 157

Motor Agents Association 55
Murillo 162
Murray, George 168

Nantgarw Pottery 163
Napier 132-133
National Council of Civil
  Liberties 156
National Motor Museum 8
Netscher, Caspar 162, 170
Nkruma, President of Ghana 167

Orange Free State 167

Padfield, Adrian Dr. 174
Parliament, South African
  166-167
Pembroke Dock 13
Pilcher, G. 150, 158
Pobjoy engine 127,129, 135
Pomeroy, Laurence 176
Prices Oils 94, 99
Purdy, Harold 56

Quisling 143, 159

Ramsgate Concours 109
Reubens 162
Richmond and Gordon, Duke of
  149-151, 154, 158-159
Riley 114
Rolls, Hon. C. S. 12-13
Rolls-Royce 57, 157, 166
Roura F. B. 67
Royal Aero Club 152
Royal Aeronautical Society 135
Royal Aircraft Factory
  B.E.2c 16, 21
  R.E.8 13, 16, 21-22
Royal Air Force 22, 155, 146, 171
  Royal Air Force College,
    Cranwell 155
  No.1 E. F. T. S. 160
  No. 14 S.F.T.S. 151
Royal Automobile Club Small
  Car Trial 44
Royal Automobile Club Rally
  100, 109-112, 116, 172
Royal Flying Corps 42, 45, 144,
  171
  No. 1 Aircraft Acceptance Park
    21
  No. 8 Aircraft Acceptance Park
    21

No. 9 Aircraft Acceptance Park
  18
No. 14 Aircraft Acceptance
  Park 21
35 Squadron 17, 22, 144
37 Training Squadron 16
39 Reserve Squadron 15
69 Training Squadron 16
No. 1 Depot, Pilot's Pool, St
  Omer 17
Wireless and Observers'
  School 16
Rudge-Whitworth 50

Saorstat Cup 67
Sarup, A. R. 141
Scarborough Trial 109
Scorpion engine 129, 130
Secretary of State 143, 146, 156,
  158-159
Sedgwick, Michael 8-9, 46, 55,
  173, 176
Seelhoff, Charles B. 26-27, 29
Serjeantson, Dick 10
Shaw Bernard, *Man and
  Superman* 100
Shaw, John 9, 13, 76, 79, 98,
  174-5
Shaw, S. 139, 150
Short-Mayo composite 132
Shelsley Walsh 42, 62-63, 67, 8,
  109, 111, 115, 122-123
Shuttleworth 133
Siddeley-Deasy Motor Company
  13-15, 21, 23-24, 27, 30, 144,
  174
Siddeley, John Davenport 13
Siddeley Puma 13, 24
Siddeley Tiger 13
Skegness, sand racing 61
Sophian, John, Dr. 158
Sorel W. L. 46
South Africa 159, 163-168, 173,
  178
Southport sand racing 41-42, 44
Spiers, Peter 167-168
Stanbridge 152
Stewart, Gwenda (Hawkes)
  64-65
Sterling Metals 173
Strauss Michael 164
Studebaker 172-173
S.U. carburettor 105
Summers, Ann 148

Summers, Donald 148
Summers, Dorothy Olive (Mrs
  Marendaz) 27, 38, 45, 74,
  94-95, 117, 121, 123-124, 127,
  134-135, 139-141, 146-159
  Birth 45, 150
  Children 148
  Competition 41-42, 55, 67, 97,
    115-116, 123, 176
  Secretary 75, 90, 97
  Separation 159
Sunbeam 87
Sutcliffe, W. H. 59
Swansea china, pottery 148, 163
Swaffield and Sons 142
Swallow Doretti 5

Talbot, Thomas Mansel 11
Tee, Wesley 47
Thames Ditton 124
Thomas, Edward 12
Titian 162, 170
Tourist Trophy race 67, 113-114,
  118
Tring 145-147

Vaal Triangle 164
Veendam, E. L. B. 69-70
Veteran and Vintage 173-175
Vorster, B.J. 166
Vortex Silencers Limited 59

Wallage, Peter 10
Welch, J. A. 102
Westlands 130
Wheatley-Smith, T. R. N. 155
Wickner, Geoffrey N. 127-128
Wilkinson John 175
Willis, W. J. A. 149-150, 156, 158
Willmot Jack 135
Wiltshire, G. H. 174
Wisdom, Tommy 119-120
Wolseley Hornet 8, 10
Woodley airfield 59, 127
Worcestershire porcelain 159,
  163
Worthington-Williams, Mike
  9-10, 165
Wyndham R. A. 137-138

Zoffany 162
Zoller 99, 111-112